Again

KT-511-196

101 485 760 0

23 FEB 1999

9 JAN 1999

Against Nature

Essays on history, sexuality and identity

Jeffrey Weeks

Rivers Oram Press

London

WL
306.7
WÉ

First published in 1991 by
Rivers Oram Press
144 Hemingford Road, London N1 1DE

Published in the USA by
Paul and Company
Post Office Box 442, Concord MA 01742

Set in Plantin
and printed in Great Britain
by T.J. Press (Padstow) Ltd.

Reprinted 1992, 1995

Designed by Lesley Stewart

This edition copyright © Jeffrey Weeks

No part of this book may be reproduced in any form without
permission from the publishers except for the quotation of brief
passages in criticism

British Library Cataloguing in Publication Data
Weeks, Jeffrey
  Against nature : essays on history, sexuality and
  identity
  1. Sexuality
  I. Title
  306.7

ISBN 1–85489–028–X
ISBN 1–85489–004–2 pbk

Contents

Preface   vii
Acknowledgements   ix

1. Introduction:On writing about sex   1
2. Discourse, desire and sexual deviance: some
   problems in a history of homosexuality   10
3. Inverts, perverts and mary-annes: male
   prostitution and the regulation of homosexuality in England in the nineteenth and
   twentieth centuries   46
4. Questions of identity   68
5. Against nature   86
6. Male homosexuality in the age of AIDS   100
7. AIDS: the intellectual agenda   114
8. Pretended family relationships   134
9. Uses and abuses of Michel Foucault   157
10. The Fabians and Utopia   170
11. The value of difference   184

Reference notes   197
Select bibliography   218
Index   221

Preface

This volume brings together a selection of my essays on history, sexuality and identity published over the past ten years. It records a particular personal, intellectual and political journey, but one which will, I hope, find echoes in a range of other contexts.

My major preoccupation is with the ways in which sexuality in general, and homosexuality in particular, has been shaped in a complex, and ever changing history over the past hundred years. At the centre of that history has been the making of sexual identities — identities we so readily take for granted now as rooted in nature, but which in fact have a variety of determinable sources and points of origin. I am concerned, in brief, with the invention and re-invention of identities in the modern world.

The first group of essays explores the making of (largely male) homosexual identities from the 19th century to the present. The second group is particularly concerned with the impact of the AIDS crisis: personal and cultural. The third group widens the debate, to think about the question of politics and values in the period we now increasingly think of as "post-modernity".

The aim is to show that sexual identities are both historical in nature, and essential in day-to-day life. They are constructed in a traceable history, but are the crucial means through which we negotiate the hazards of our contemporary lives. They are necessary fictions.

With the exception of the introductory chapter, all the essays have been published before. Inevitably, there is some overlap of material and argument in what has been a sustained enquiry over a number of years. Wherever possible, without distorting the argument, I have tried to eliminate unnecessary duplication. Otherwise, I have not tried to update the material, which would only distort the lines of the debate as it has developed. A brief bibliography does, however, provide some update of the references.

I am grateful to the original publishers for permission to reproduce these articles. My specific intellectual and personal debts accumulated in their writing are too numerous to record here. I hope some record of my intellectual indebtedness can be found in the arguments themselves — though it goes without saying that none of the named people are responsible for the fast and loose way in which I play with their ideas. I must particularly thank the University of Manchester for electing me to a Simon Senior Fellowship during the academic year 1989-90, and the Sociology Department for providing me with a congenial and supportive intellectual base. Without this space I would not have been able to complete this book, or other projects I have been involved with.

My personal debts are known to those who count. I dedicate the book to them, my "pretended family".

Acknowledgements

I wish to thank the following for permission to republish these essays:

Unwin Hyman for "Discourse, desire and sexual deviance: some problems in a history of homosexuality", first published in Kenneth Plummer (ed.), *The Making of the Modern Homosexual*, Hutchinson, 1981;

Haworth Press and the *Journal of Homosexuality* for "Inverts, perverts and mary-annes: male prostitution and the regulation of homosexuality in England in the nineteenth and twentieth centuries", *Journal of Homosexuality*, Vol.6, Nos 1/2, Fall/Winter 1980/1;

Routledge for "Questions of identity", published in Pat Caplan (ed.), *The Cultural Construction of Sexuality*, Tavistock 1987; and for "Pretended family relationships", published in David Clark (ed.), *Marriage, domestic life and social change: essays in honour of Jacqueline Burgoyne*, Routledge 1991;

Jhr. Mr J.A. Schorerstichting for "Against nature", published in *Homosexuality, which homosexuality?*, An Dekker, Amsterdam and GMP, London 1989;

Springer-Verlag for "Male Homosexuality in the age of AIDS", published as "Male homosexuality: cultural perspectives" in Michael Adler (ed.), *Diseases in the Homosexual Male*, Springer-Verlag, 1988;

Falmer Press for "AIDS: the intellectual agenda", published in P. Aggleton, G. Hart and P. Davies (eds), *AIDS: Social Representations, Social Practices*, Falmer Press, 1989;

Free Associations Press for "Uses and Abuses of Michel Foucault", first published in Lisa Appignanesi (ed.), *Ideas from France. The Legacy of French Theory*, Institute of Contemporary Arts, 1985, Free Associations Press, 1990;

The Fabian Society and the publishers for "The fabians and utopia", published in Ben Pimlott (ed.), *Fabian Essays in Socialist Theory*, Gower, 1984;

Lawrence and Wishart for "The value of difference", published in Jonathan Rutherford (ed.), *Identity: Community, Culture, Difference*, Lawrence and Wishart, 1989.

1 Introduction:

writing about sex

It is impossible to write without labelling yourself.[1]

The essays in this volume represent an attempt to write about sex; or more precisely, to write about the complex relationship between history, sexuality and identity. They trace an intellectual, personal and political journey over a number of years, with the aim of throwing new light on each of these themes.

"Writing" and "sex": these are two quite disparate activities, but they are strangely and intimately related. Writing, like sex, always balances precariously on the shifting frontier between the "personal" and the "public". It is apparently one of the most private and lonely of activities, demanding organisation, will-power, autonomy – and a "room of one's own", in Virginia Woolf's famous phrase. It inflicts its own very special mixture of pleasure and punishment. For those of us who try to do it, whether for work, duty or vanity, George Orwell's reflections on writing a book carry the sharp pain of experience: "a horrible, exhausting struggle, like a long bout of some painful illness".[2]

Yet to write is also among the most exhibitionistic and public of acts: the author by necessity writes for an audience, or more precisely attempts to evoke a constituency. Writers, with supreme arrogance, assume they are speaking not only for themselves but for others as well. But we write because we want to say something, and if we are lucky we have something worthwhile to say.

1

What we want to say, however, is often trapped in the coils of the language and meanings we inherit. Writing, said Roland Barthes, "is in no way an instrument for communication, it is not an open route through which there passes only the intention to speak".[3] However personal the tone, or confessional the ambition, writing represents much more than the individual essence. We are both actors and agents, originators and ventriloquists, caught by, even as we struggle against, our limited vocabularies. Behind the act of writing is the density of collective experiences and histories, and a host of motivations, some personal, some political.

Orwell asked what the political purpose of writing was, and answered: "desire to push the world in a certain direction, to alter other people's idea of the kind of society they should strive after".[4] Most writers are probably less explicit in their purpose, but they have, nevertheless, the same objective. Writing is a hard personal discipline, designed to produce desired, if not always desirable, public results.

These general reflections are prompted by some fifteen years of battling with the problems of writing about the historical and social organisation of sex, at once the most private and the most publicly discussed of phenomena. Most writing about sexuality until recently presented itself as the embodiment of some version of the truth: the truth of revealed religion or moral tradition; the truth of the science of sex, sexology, that emerged at the end of the nineteenth century; the truth of political dogmatists who purported to know what was right for us, and who wanted to make sure that legal and other forms of social regulation stuck closely to their version of the truth; or the truth of our individual selves. There have been powerful oppositional currents throughout this history, but writing about sexuality outside the acceptable discourses has carried with it the touch of scandal that inhibits the conventional career; though today you are not so much regarded as subversive as eccentric and obsessive.

At the same time, the very fact that writing about sex makes you a little suspect tells us something very interesting about the significance we do actually attribute to such writings. Nor should this be surprising to anyone. "Sexuality" as we know it has been constructed and shaped as a set of organised meanings and activities in and through language: the preaching and practices of religions, the codifications of experts such as doctors and psychologists, the prescriptions of planners, educationalists, architects, social workers. . . .Writing about sex has been one of the critical ways in which sexuality has emerged as a field of exploration, a terrain of battle, a continent of knowledge, a configuration of fear and desire – as well as a sphere of resistance and identity.

Even when we feel we are most overwhelmed by our instinctual urgings, what we are usually doing is reworking the scripts which tell us about our "needs" and "desires", about what is "right" and "wrong". It is only possible to express the feelings of the body through the lacework of meanings that envelop it. Sexuality is as much about language as it is about the sexual organs. That, at any rate, is the argument of this book.

I began writing about sex without any of these thoughts, or their attendant anxieties, in my head. The immediate stimulus was my interest in the then-new gay movement in London from 1970 onwards (I was working at the London School of Economics when the gay liberation movement had its first meetings there in 1970), and my desire to do my bit for the cause. Intellectual bent and professional training suggested that history might be my most productive sphere of intervention, and the history and social organisation of sexuality my special field.

In Britain, especially, the spirit of the left has been sustained by a profoundly historical consciousness, and I immediately found an intellectual and political affinity with the radical history that was associated with the History Workshop movement. As one of my first steps into sexual history I organised a small workshop on the history of homosexuality in London in 1974. My first essay on the topic was published in the first issue of *History Workshop Journal* in 1976. Subsequently, I became an editor of the *Journal* itself. So, alongside my emergent personal-political identity and my (rather more chequered) career as an academic, a new hybrid personality sprang up, that of the radical sexual historian and sociologist. Such has been my burden, and challenge, ever since.

Hence, history, sexuality, identity: these have been the central foci of my research and writing for the past fifteen years. The essays in this book provide a record of an attempt to develop a more relevant way of understanding their relationship.

I fairly rapidly came to the hypothesis that has dominated much of my subsequent writings on sex. Briefly, it goes something like this. The sexual categories that we take so readily for granted, that sketch the horizons of the possible, and which seem so "natural", secure and inevitable, are actually historical labels, more or less arbitrary and contingent divisions of human desire. Each of them has a history, they all have effects on the organisation of individual needs and wishes, and they structure, forcefully, the social evaluation of erotic behaviours. The prime task for a historian of sexuality, then, is to understand the evolution, and effects, of these historical inventions.

My first preoccupation was to understand the problematic nature of homosexual identities, with their variability and maleability, as well as the deep commitment to them that many of us feel. This was the task I set myself in my first solo book, *Coming Out: Homosexual Politics in Britain from the Nineteenth Century to the Present*, first published in 1977.[5] This book attempted to cast light on the emergence of a modern homosexual consciousness by exploring closely the reform movements that developed from the latter part of the last century, and culminated in the emergence of gay liberation in the 1970s. The first two essays re-published here, "Discourse, desire and sexual deviance", and "Inverts, perverts and maryannes" were written as a result of a follow-up project to that, conducted at the University of Essex with Mary McIntosh, who, more than anyone, had inspired the approach I was now adopting.

The first of these is a theoretical account of what has become known as the "social constructionist" perspective. The essay is densely argued, and some readers may wish to come back to it after reading the less theoretical accounts. I include it here because it attempts to work through key problems which have been central to my work. It argues forcefully that the history of homosexuality only makes sense if same-sex behaviour, beliefs and identities are put firmly in their proper historical context. Sexual activities, in other words, are always contextual and relational. They do not have a fixed or absolute meaning beyond time or place; which does not, of course, make them any the less important. On the contrary, it is central to the "social constructionist" case that only by considering the real forces at play, the complex interaction of power and domination on the one hand, and resistance on the other, that we can make sense of the role of sexuality in the historic present in which we live.

"Discourse, desire and sexual deviance" was originally published as part of a collection, edited by Kenneth Plummer, entitled *The Making of the Modern Homosexual*, which offered a rich body of research and argument to underpin this position. The book as a whole proved enormously influential and controversial, and remains one of the central texts about the history and sociology of homosexuality.

The second essay, "Inverts, perverts and mary-annes", was an attempt to illustrate the wider argument with a concrete and situated example. It concentrates on the prevalence of, but difficulty of defining, male prostitution in a period, the late nineteenth and early twentieth century, when the meanings of homosexuality were in unprecedented flux, and were highly contested. The evidence I was able to put forward confirmed my belief that this period was a critical one in the emergence of still familiar sexual meanings. Again it is worth mentioning the context in which it appeared: first drafted for a conference at Essex University on "History, deviance and social control", it was published in a pioneering special issue of that admirable academic publication, the *Journal of Homosexuality*, devoted to "Historical perspectives on homosexuality".

The fascinating paradox of sexual identities is that they are both artificial and essential, arbitrary but forceful, invented categories which nevertheless provide the basic directions by which we navigate the shoals of personal need and social relationships. The next two essays, "Questions of identity" and "Against nature" explore this paradox. The first of these explores the range of sexual identities that now exist, but suggests that even so they are still constraining of the full range of sexual desires. In our culture, I conclude, identity is not a destiny but a choice, and in the last resort a political choice.

"Against nature", which gives its title to the whole collection, was written for a conference held at the Free

University of Amsterdam in December 1987, entitled "Homosexuality, which homosexuality?". The conference was explicitly convened to discuss the growing polarisation in lesbian and gay studies between what have become known as the "essentialist" and "constructionist" positions. Though on the surface somewhat arcane, this debate has in fact proved enormously creative in pushing forward our understanding of sexuality in general, as well as homosexuality in particular. My paper, whilst endorsing the historical constructionist approach, was an attempt to suggest that a certain degree of false polarisation had taken place, and that the question of identity was one that demanded political clarity and a more engaged value debate as much as historical analysis and interpretation. Moreover, the whole question of sexual identity was part of a wider agenda. Increasingly we can see that changes in concepts of sexuality and gender are part of a much wider cultural shift (loosely summed up in the phrase "post-modernity") which poses major social and political challenges.

Some of these challenges were manifest as I was finalising this paper itself. "Against nature" was delivered at the Amsterdam conference the same week as the notorious "Section 28", banning the promotion of homosexuality as a "pretended family relationship" was endorsed by the British government (it had been introduced by a backbench Conservative MP as an amendment to the Local Government Bill then proceeding through Parliament). This perhaps more than any other piece of legislation in the 1980s symbolised an attempt at a moral reaction, in which the gains of the lesbian and gay movement of the previous two decades would be forced back. Behind an increasingly less hopeful political and moral climate was the growing impact of HIV disease and AIDS, and the devastating impact they were having on many individual lives, and on the wider cultural climate.

The next group of essays explores various aspects of this dual crisis for sexual liberalisation. The essays on "Male homosexuality in the age of AIDS" and "Pretended family relationships" analyse the patterns of life and forms of community developed by those who perforce live outside the norms of our culture. The essay on "AIDS: the intellectual agenda" explores the cultural meanings and the personal and symbolic impact HIV disease has had on individuals and communities.

Many intellectual influences have shaped the perspectives revealed in these essays, from the writings of feminists and lesbian and gay activists to the new social history (the categories, of course, are often interchangeable), from radical sociology to psychoanalysis. One name, however, stands out, not just because of what he wrote but because of what he came to represent, that of Michel Foucault. The first volume of *The History of Sexuality*, published in French in 1976, was by no means a bolt from the blue for those of us – especially feminist and lesbian and gay historians – who had already tilled the ground.[6] The little book itself had many inadequacies, for example in its treatment of gender difference and in its polemical rejection of psychoanalysis. But what the book did do supremely well was to dissolve certainties: the certainty that the history of sexuality was a history of repression; the certainty that liberalisation of sexual codes was a step towards sexual freedom; the certainty that "liberation" was a useful concept for thinking about meaningful political change; the certainty that power was a measurable and manageable negative force. Many of these assumptions had been challenged elsewhere. By synthesising the deconstructionist attack Foucault was able to shift the debate on to new ground. The essay republished here, "Uses and abuses of Michel Foucault", first delivered as a paper at the Institute of Contemporary Arts in London, is a brief overview of his main contribution to rethinking both sexuality and politics, at least as one worker in the same field sees it.

The final essays of the book try some rethinking of their own. The essay on "The Fabians and Utopia" was written for a volume celebrating the centenary of the first volume of *Fabian Essays On Socialism*. The aim of the new volume was explicitly to re-think some of the founding assumptions. I am not sure what the early Fabians would have thought of my particular contribution; writing it for me, however, was an important part of the ground clearing necessary for advancing into the "new times" of the 1990s. The last essay, "The value of difference" is an attempt at rethinking values, at reconstructing what the 1970s and 1980s (quite rightly) sought to problematise so radically. These two essays point to a new project I am currently involved in. Their publication may be seen as the first tentative forays into new territory, but one whose general shape and looming presence I became increasingly familiar with in the previous decade or so.

"The author", Umberto Eco has said, "should die once he has finished writing. So as not to trouble the path of the text".[7] Writers soon lose control of their works. Books develop a life of their own, laden with multiple meanings and possible interpretations. Even the magisterial writings of a Freud are now burdened with so much interpretation that the true Freud, if he ever existed, is lost in a million words. The scientists of sex who preceeded and followed him, like him, sought to lay down their prescriptions, to issue their anathemas, but they were read in many different ways. "Perverts" might hear of their pathology in the pages of Krafft-Ebing or Havelock Ellis, but found at the same time a start of recognition, the basis for asserting a new sense of self. Inchoate feelings and desires were given a name, individuals began to find a voice. Writings on sex which claim a special telephone line to the truth should be treated with a great deal of suspicion. Writing is a resource, to be played with, chewed over, debated, and above all used; but never trusted.

The best of the writings on sex over the past decade or so have started from this premise. Contemporary sexual politics have given birth to a host of writers, some excellent, some good, some bad, but most proving that writing is less a gift of the few than a craft that can be deployed by and for the many: polemicists, theorists, poets, historians, sociologists, critics, novelists, journalists, letter writers (not that these are exclusive categories). Some of the new writers have disappeared into the empyrean, trailing around the television studios and book-signing sessions. Most have addressed more specialised audiences, of feminists, lesbians, gay men, Christians, Jews, humanists, atheists, Americans, Europeans, black, white, young people, older people, disabled people.

The very profusion of often confusing and conflicting voices, lyrical and anguished, biting and caring, romantic and cynical, repelling and appealing, contentious and collective, has marked the world of sexual politics as uniquely cacophonous and disturbing. But the voices represent the diversity which to my mind is the only truth about modern sexuality. They are creating an alternative public sphere of discussion, debate and values, in which the certainties of the old are challenged by the dangers and pleasures of the new.

In writing about sex we are not decoding an elusive secret. We are sketching a map of meanings that may be glanced at and discarded, or elaborated and achieved. We are engaged in a constant process of inventing and re-inventing sexualities.

The essays collected together in this book should be read in that spirit. They attempt their own forms of deconstruction, and reconstruction. But they are intended to open debate not foreclose it. They are part of a project to clarify our understanding of the interplay between history, sexuality and identity. If in doing that I am also labelling myself once and for all, so be it.

2 Discourse, desire and sexual deviance:

some problems in a history of homosexuality

The publication by the Kinsey Institute of the book *Homosexualities* in 1978 underlined what has become a truism in recent years: that we can no longer speak of a single homosexual category as if it embraced the wide range of same-sex experiences in our society.[1] But recognition of this, tardy as it has been, calls into question a much wider project: that of providing a universal theory and consequently a "history" of homosexuality. The distinction originally made by sociologists (and slowly being taken up by historians) between homosexual behaviour, roles and identities, or between homosexual desire and "homosexuality" as a social and psychological category,[2] is one that fundamentally challenges the coherence of the theme and poses major questions for the historian. This paper addresses some of these problems, first, by examining approaches that have helped construct our concepts of homosexuality, second, by tracing the actual evolution of the category of homosexuality, third, by exploring some of the theoretical approaches which have attempted to explain its emergence and, finally, by charting some of the problems that confront the modern researcher studying "homosexuality".

■ Approaches

It has been widely recognised for almost a century that attitudes towards homosexual behaviour are culturally specific, and have varied enormously across different cultures and through various historical periods. Two closely related, and virtually reinforcing, sources for this awareness can be pinpointed: first, the pioneering work of sexologists such as Magnus Hirschfeld, Iwan Bloch, Havelock Ellis and others, whose labelling, categorising and taxonomic zeal led them, partially at least, outside their own culture, and, second, the work of anthropologists and ethnographers who attempted to chart the varieties of sexual behaviour and who supplied the data on which the sexologists relied. The actual interest and zeal in the pursuit of sex was, of course, a product of their own culture's preoccupations, and the resulting findings often displayed an acute "ethnocentric bias",[3] particularly with regard to homosexuality; but this early work has had a long resonance. The three most influential English-language cross-cultural studies – that of the traveller Sir Richard Burton in the 1880s, the work of Edward Westermarck in the 1900s, and the Human Area Files of Ford and Beach in the 1950s[4] – have deeply affected perceptions of homosexuality in their respective generations. Unfortunately, awareness of different cultural patterns have been used to reinforce rather than confront our own culture-bound conceptions.

Three phases in the construction of a history of homosexuality can be discerned. The first, manifested in the works of early sexologists as well as propagandists like Edward Carpenter,[5] attempted above all to demonstrate the trans-historical existence, and indeed value, of homosexuality as a distinct sexual experience. All the major works of writers such as Havelock Ellis had clear-cut historical sections; some, like Iwan Bloch's, were substantive historical works.[6] Writers during this phase were above all anxious to establish the parameters of homosexuality, what distinguished it from other forms of sexuality, what history suggested for its aetiology and social worth, the changing cultural values accorded to it, and the great figures – in politics, art, literature – one could associate with the experience. These efforts, taking the form of naturalistic recordings of what was seen as a relatively minor but significant social experience, were actually profoundly constructing of modern concepts of homosexuality. They provided a good deal of the data on which later writers

depended even as they reworked them, and a hagiographical
sub-school produced a multitude of texts on the great
homosexuals of the past, "great queens of history"; its most
recent manifestation is found in the egregious essay of A.L.
Rowse, *Homosexuals in History*.[7]

The second phase, most usefully associated with the
reformist endeavours of the 1950s and 1960s, took as
unproblematic the framework established by the pioneers.
Homosexuality was a distinct social experience; the task was to
detail it. The result was a new series of texts, some of which,
such as H. Montgomery Hyde's various essays, synthesised in
The Other Love in 1970,[8] brought together a good deal of
empirical material even as they failed to theorise its contradictions adequately.

As a major stimulant to the revival of historical interest
were the various campaigns to change the law and public
attitudes, both in Europe and America, the historical studies
inevitably concentrated on issues relevant to these. The
assumed distinction, derived from nineteenth century sexological literature, between "perversion" (a product of moral
weakness) and "inversion" (consitutional and hence unavoidable), which D.S. Bailey adumbrates in *Homosexuality
and the Western Christian Tradition*,[9] was highly significant for
debates in the churches. The influential essay on English legal
attitudes by Francois Lafitte, "Homosexuality and the law", was
designed to indicate that laws which were so arbitrarily, indeed
accidentally, imposed could as easily be removed.[10] Donald
Webster Cory's various works of the 1950s, such as *The
Homosexual Outlook*,[11] sought to underline the values of the
homosexual experience. Employing the statistical information
provided by Kinsey, the cross-cultural evidence of Ford and
Beach, and the ethnographic studies of social investigators, like
Evelyn Hooker, historians were directed towards the common-
ness of the homosexual experience in history, and began to
trace some of the forces that shaped public attitudes.

A third phase, overlapping with the second but more vocal
in tone, can be seen as the direct product of the emergence of
more radical gay movements in the late 1960s and 1970s in
Europe and North America. Here the emphasis was on
reasserting the values of a lost experience, stressing the positive

value of homosexuality and locating the sources of its social oppression. A major early emphasis was on recovering the pre-history of the gay movement itself, particularly in Germany, the USA and Britain.[12] Stretching beyond this was a search for what one might term "ethnicity", the lineaments and validation of a minority experience which history had denied. But the actual work of research posed new problems, which threatened to burst out of the bounds established within the previous half century. This is admirably demonstrated in Jonathan Katz's splendid documentary *Gay American History*. This was a major contribution to our knowledge, and was justly influential. But rather than exploring its virtues, I want to pick out two points which seem to me to pose fresh problems. The first concerns the title. It seems to me that to use a modern self-labelling term, "gay", itself a product of contemporary political struggles, to define an ever-changing concept over a period of four hundred years suggests a constant homosexual essence which the evidence presented in the book itself suggests is just not there. Katz in fact recognises this very clearly. He makes the vital point that the "concept of homosexuality must be historicised", and hopes that the book will revolutionise the traditional concept of homosexuality.

> The problem of the historical researcher is thus to study and establish the character and meaning of each manifestation of same sex relations within a specific time and society. . . .All homosexuality is situational.[13]

This is absolutely correct and is the measure of the break between this type of history and say, A.L. Rowse's extravaganza. But to talk at the same time of our history as if homosexuals were a distinct, fixed minority suggests a slightly contradictory attitude.

A second problem arises from this, concerning attitudes to lesbianism. Katz very commendably has, unlike most of his predecessors, attempted to give equal space to both male and female homosexuality, and although this is impossible in some sections, overall he succeeds. But this again suggests a problematic of a constant racial-sexual identity which Katz explicitly rejects theoretically. Lesbianism and male homosexuality in fact have quite different, if inevitably interconnected, social histories, related to the social evolution of distinct gender identities; there is a danger that this fundamental, if difficult, point will be obscured by discussing them as if they were part of the same experience. These points will be taken up later.

Certainly there has been a considerable extension of interest in the history of homosexuality over the past decade, and as well as the general works, a number of essays and monographs have appeared, most of which accept readily the cultural specificity of attitudes and concepts. Nevertheless considerable contradictions recur. A.D. Harvey in a study of buggery prosecutions at the beginning of the nineteenth century has noted that:

> It is too commonly forgotten how far the incidence of homosexual
> behaviour varies from age to age and from culture to
> culture. . . .In fact it is only very crudely true that there are
> homosexuals in every period and in every society. Societies
> which accept homosexual behaviour as normal almost certainly
> have a higher proportion of men who have experimented with
> homosexual activity than societies which regard homosexuality as
> abnormal but tolerate it, and societies which grudgingly tolerate
> homosexuality *probably* have a higher incidence of homosexual
> activity than societies where it is viciously persecuted.[14]

But Harvey, despite making this highly significant point, goes on to speak of "homosexuals" as if they realised a transhistorical nature. He writes of the Home Secretary complaining in 1808 that Hyde Park and St James's Park were "being used as a resort for homosexuals", apparently oblivious of the absence of such a term until the later part of the century. The actual term the Home Secretary used is extremely important in assessing his perception of the situation and the type of people involved, and the evidence suggests a problematic of public nuisance rather than a modern concept of the homosexual person.[15]

Similarly Randolph Trumbach, in his valuable study of London "sodomites" in the eighteenth century, and despite a long and carefully argued discussion of different cross-cultural patterns, writes as if the homosexual sub-culture had a natural existence serving the eternal social needs (or at least eternal in the West) of a fixed minority of people. But there is plentiful evidence that the sub-culture changed considerably over time, partly at least dependent on factors such as urbanisation, and can one really speak of the courtly or theatrical sub-cultures of the early seventeenth century as if they were the same as the modern sub-cultures of New York or San Francisco?

Implicit in Trumbach's essay is an alternative view which profoundly challenges such assumptions. He notes "only one significant change" in attitudes during the Christian millenia: "Beginning in the late nineteenth century it was no longer the act that was stigmatised, but the state of mind".[16] But this, I would argue, is the crucial change, indicating a massive shift in attitudes, giving rise to what is distinctively new in our culture: the categorisation of homosexuality as a separate condition and the correlative emergence of a homosexual identity.

We should employ cross-cultural and historical evidence not only to chart changing *attitudes* but to challenge the very concept of a single trans-historical notion of homosexuality. In different cultures (and at different historical moments or conjunctures within the same culture) very different meanings are given to the same-sex activity both by society at large and by the individual participants. The physical acts might be similar, but the social construction of meanings around them are profoundly different. The social integration of forms of pedagogic homosexual relations in ancient Greece have no continuity with contemporary notions of a homosexual iden-tity.[17] To put it another way, the various possibilities of what Hocquenghem calls homosexual desire, or what more neutrally might be termed homosexual behaviours, which seem from historical evidence to be a permanent and ineradicable aspect of human sexual possibilities, are variously constucted in different cultures as an aspect of wider gender and sexual regulation. If this is the case, it is pointless discussing questions such as, what are the origins of homosexual oppression, or what is the nature of the homosexual taboo, as if there was a single, causative factor. The crucial question must be: what are the conditions for the emergence of this particular form of regulation of sexual behaviour in this particular society? Transferred to our own history, this must involve an exploration of what Mary McIntosh pin-pointed as the significant problem: the emergence of the notion that homosexuality is a condition peculiar to some people and not others.[18]

An historical study of homosexuality over the past two centuries or so must therefore have as its focus three closely related questions: the social conditions for the emergence of the category of homosexuality and its construction as the unification of disparate experiences; the relation of this categorisation to other socio-sexual categorisations; and the relationship of this categorisation to those defined, not simply "described" or labelled but "invented" by it, in particular historical circumstances.

◼ Evolution

The historical evidence points to the latter part of the nineteenth century as the crucial period in the conceptualisation of homosexuality as the distinguishing characteristic of a particular type of person, the "invert" or "homosexual", and the corresponding development of a new awareness of self amongst some "homosexuals".[19] From the mid-nineteenth century there is a bubbling of debate, notation and classification, associated with names like Casper, Tardieu, Ulrichs, Westphal, Krafft-Ebing, Ellis, Hirschfeld, Moll, Freud, all of whom sought to define, and hence psychologically or medically to construct, new categorisations. Westphal's description of the "contrary sexual instinct" in the 1870s may be taken as the crucial formative moment, for out of it grew the notion of "sexual inversion", the dominant formulation until the 1950s.

The word "homosexuality" itself was not invented until 1869 (by the Hungarian, Benkert von Kertbeny) and did not enter English usage until the 1880s and 1890s, and then largely as a result of the work of Havelock Ellis. I suggest that the widespread adoption of neologisms such as "homosexuality" and "inversion" during this period marks as crucial a turning point in attitudes to homosexuality as the adoption of "gay" as a self-description in the 1970s. It indicated not just a changing usage but the emergence of a whole new set of assumptions. And in Britain (as also in Germany and elsewhere) the reconceptualisation and categorisation (at first medical and later social) coincided with the development of new legal and ideological sanctions, particularly against male homosexuality.

Until 1885 the only law dealing *directly* with homosexual behaviours in England was that relating to buggery, and legally, at least, little distinction was made between buggery between man and woman, man and beast and man and man, though the majority of prosecutions were directed at men for homosexual offences. This had been a capital crime from the 1530s, when the incorporation of traditional ecclesiastical sanctions into law had been part of the decisive assumption by the state of many of the powers of the medieval church. Prosecutions under this law had fluctuated, partly because of changing rules on evidence, partly through other social pressures. There seems, for instance, to have been a higher incidence of prosecutions (and executions) in times of war; penalties were particularly harsh in cases affecting the discipline of the armed services, particularly the navy.[20] "Sodomite" (denoting contact between men) became the typical epithet of abuse for the sexual deviant.

The legal classification and the epithet had, however, an uncertain status and was often used loosely to describe various forms of non-reproductive sex. There was therefore a crucial distinction between traditional concepts of buggery and modern concepts of homosexuality. The former was seen as a potentiality in all sinful nature, unless severely execrated and judicially punished; homosexuality, however, is seen as the characteristic of a particular type of person, a type whose specific characteristics (inability to whistle, penchant for the colour green, adoration of mother or father, age of sexual maturation, "promiscuity", etc.) have been exhaustively and inconclusively detailed in many twentieth-century textbooks. It became a major task of psychology in the present century to attempt to explain the aetiology of this homosexual "condition". The early articles on homosexuality in the 1880s and 1890s treated the subject as if they were entering a strange continent. An eminent doctor, Sir George Savage, described in the *Journal of Mental Science*[21] the homosexual case histories of a young man and woman and wondered if "this perversion is as rare as it appears", while Havelock Ellis was to claim that he was the first to record any homosexual cases unconnected with prison or asylums. The sodomite, as Michel Foucault has put it,[22] was a temporary aberration; the homosexual belongs to a species, and social science during this century has made various – if, by and large, unsuccessful – efforts to explore this phenomenon.

These changing concepts do not mean, of course, that those who engaged in a predominantly homosexual life style did not regard themselves as somehow different until the late-nineteenth century, and there is evidence for sub-cultural formation around certain monarchs and in the theatre for centuries. But there is much stronger evidence for the emergence of a distinctive male homosexual sub-culture in London and one or two other cities from the late-seventeenth century, often characterised by transvestism and gender-role inversion; and by the early nineteenth century there was a recognition in the courts that homosexuality represented a condition different from the norm.[23] By the mid-nineteenth century, it seems the male homosexual sub-culture at least had characteristics not dissimilar to the modern, with recognised cruising places and homosexual haunts, ritualised sexual contact and a distinctive argot and "style". But there is also abundant evidence until late into the nineteenth century of practices which by modern standards would be regarded as highly sexually compromising. Lawrence Stone describes how Oxbridge male students often slept with male students with no sexual connotations until comparatively late in the eighteenth century, while Smith-Rosenberg has described the intimate – and seemingly non-sexualised – relations between women in the nineteenth century.[24]

The latter part of the nineteenth century, however, saw a variety of concerns which helped to focus awareness: the controversy about "immorality" in public schools, various sexual scandals, a new legal situation, the beginnings of a "scientific" discussion of homosexuality and the emergence of the "medical model". The subject, as Edward Carpenter put it at the time, "has great actuality and is pressing upon us from all sides".[25] It appears likely that it was in this developing context

New legislation ✓

that some of those with homosexual inclinations began to perceive themselves as "inverts", "homosexuals", "Uranians", a crucial stage in the prolonged and uneven process whereby homosexuality began to take on a recognisably modern configuration. And although the evidence cited here has been largely British, this development was widespread also throughout Western Europe and America.

The changing legal and ideological situations were crucial markers in this development. The 1861 Offences Against the Person Act removed the death penalty for buggery (which had not been used since the 1830s), replacing it by sentences of between ten years and life. But in 1885 the famous Labouchère Amendment to the Criminal Law Amendment Act made all male homosexual activities (acts of "gross indencency") illegal, punishable by up to two years hard labour. And in 1898 the laws on importuning for "immoral purposes" were tightened up and effectively applied to male homosexuals (this was clarified by the Criminal Law Amendment Act of 1912 with respect to England and Wales – Scotland has different provisions). Both were significant extensions of the legal controls on male homosexuality, whatever their origins or intentions.[26] Though formally less severe than capital punishments for sodomy, the new legal situation is likely to have ground harder on a much wider circle of people, particularly as it was dramatised in a series of sensational scandals, culminating in the trials of Oscar Wilde, which had the function of drawing a sharp dividing line between permissible and tabooed forms of behaviour. The Wilde scandal in particular was a vital moment in the creation of a male homosexual identity.[27] It must be noted however, that the new legal situation did not apply to women, and the attempt in 1921 to extend the 1885 provisions to women failed, in part at least, on the grounds that publicity would only serve to make more women aware of homosexuality.[28] But the different legal situation alone does not explain the different social resonances of male and female homosexuality. Much more likely, this must be related to the complexly developing social structuring of male and female sexualities.

The emergence of a psychological and medical model of homosexuality was intimately connected with the legal situation. The most commonly quoted European writers on homosexuality in the mid-nineteenth century were Casper and Tardieu, the leading medico-legal experts of Germany and France respectively. Both, as Arno Karlen has put it, were "chiefly concerned with whether the disgusting breed of perverts could be physically identified for courts, and whether they should be held legally responsible for their acts".[29] The same problem was apparent in Britain. According to Magnus Hirschfeld, most of the one-thousand or so works on homosexuality that appeared between 1898 and 1908 were directed, in part at least, at the legal profession. Even J.A. Symond's privately printed pamphlet, *A Problem in Modern Ethics*,[30] declared itself to be addressed "especially to Medical psychologists and jurists", while Havelock Ellis's *Sexual Inversion* was attacked for not being published by a medical press and for being too popular in tone. The medicalisation of homosexuality – a transition from notions of sin to concepts of sickness or mental illness – was a vitally significant move, even though its application was uneven. Around it the poles of scientific discourse ranged for decades: was homosexuality congenital or acquired, ineradicable or susceptible to cure, to be quietly if unenthusiastically accepted as unavoidable (even the liberal Havelock Ellis felt it necessary to warn his invert reader not to "set himself in violent opposition" to his society) or to be resisted with all the force of one's Christian will? In the discussions of the 1950s and 1960s these were crucial issues: was it right, it was sometimes wondered, to lock an alcoholic up in a brewery; should those who suffered from an incurable (or at best unfortunate) condition be punished? Old notions of the immorality or sinfulness of homosexuality did not die in the nineteenth century; they still survive, unfortunately, in many dark corners. But from the nineteenth century they were inextricably entangled with "scientific" theories which formed the boundaries within which homosexuals had to begin to define themselves.

■ The challenge to essentialism

Clearly the emergence of the homosexual category was not arbitrary or accidental. The scientific and medical speculation can be seen in one sense as a product of the characteristic nineteenth-century process whereby the traditionally execrated (and monolithic) crimes against nature – linking up, for instance, homosexuality with masturbation and mechanical birth control – are differentiated into discrete deviations whose aetiologies are mapped out in late-nineteenth and early-twentieth century works.[31] In another series of relationships the emergence of the concept of the homosexual can be seen as corresponding to, and complexly linked with, the classification and articulation of a variety of social categories: the redefinitions of childhood and adolescence, the hysterical woman, the congenitally inclined prostitute (or indeed, in the work of Ellis and others, the congenital criminal as well) and linked to the contemporaneous debate and ideological definition of the role of housewife and mother.[32] On the other hand, the categorisation was never simply an imposition of a new definition; it was the result of various pressures and forces, in which new concepts merged into older definitions.

It is striking that the social purity campaigners of the 1880s saw both prostitution and male homosexuality as products of undifferentiated male lust,[33] and equally significant, if generally unremarked, that the major enactments affecting male homosexuality from the 1880s (the Labouchère Amendment, the 1898 Vagrancy Act) were primarily concerned with female prostitution. Indeed as late as the 1950s it was still seen as logical to set up a single government committee – the Wolfenden Committee – to study both prostitution and male homosexuality. It is clear, however, that the emergence of the homosexual category and the changing focus of the definition of homosexual behaviour are intimately related to wider changes. The problem is to find means of explaining and theorising these changes without falling into the twin traps of a naive empiricism or a reductive materialism. The former would assume that what was happening was simply a discovery of pre-existing phenomena, a problematic which, as we have suggested, has little historical validity; the latter poses the danger of seeing the restrictive definitions of homosexual behaviours as a necessary effect of a pre-existing causative complex (usually "capitalism").

Most attempts to explain this more closely have relied on

variations of role theory. Male homosexuality has been seen as a threat to the ensemble of assumptions about male sexuality and a perceived challenge to the male heterosexual role within capitalism.

> In Britain sexual intercourse has been contained within marriage which has been presented as the ultimate form of sexual maturity. . .the heterosexual nuclear family assists a system like capitalism because it produces and socialises the young in certain values. . .the maintenance of the nuclear family with its role-specific behaviour creates an apparent consensus concerning sexual normalcy.[34]

So that:

> Any ambiguity such as transvestism, hermaphrodism, transsexuality, or homosexuality is moulded into "normal" appropriate gender behaviour or is relegated to the categories of sick, dangerous, or pathological. The actor is forced to slot into patterns of behaviour appropriate to heterosexual gender roles.[35]

The result is the emergence of a specific male "homosexual role", a specialised, despised and punished role which "keeps the bulk of society pure in rather the same way that the similar treatment of some kinds of criminal helps keep the rest of society law abiding".[36] Such a role has two effects: first, it helps to provide a clear-cut threshold between permissible and impermissible behaviour and, second, it helps to segregate those labelled as deviant from others, and thus contains and limits their behaviour patterns. In the same way, a homosexual sub-culture, which is the correlative of the development of a specialised role, provides both access to the socially outlawed need (sex) and contains the deviant. Male homosexuals can thus be conceptualised as those excluded from the sexual family, and as potential scapegoats whose oppression can keep the family members in line.

The notion of a homosexual role in this posing of it has certain difficulties. It is, for example, a negative role, not one that is socially sustained. It also assumes a unilinear fit between the socially created role and the identity that it delineates, whereas all the evidence indicates that this is problematical. It also suggests an intentionality in the creation of the role that again is historically dubious. But beyond this are other related problems in the functionalist model. It apparently assumes that the family acts as a one-way funnel for the channelling of socially necessary sexual identities, and responds automatically to the needs of society (or in the Marxist functionalist model, capitalism). It assumes, in other words, that the family can be simply defined as a unitary form (the "nuclear family") which acts in a determined way on society's members, and at the same time it takes for granted a sexual essence which can be organised through this institution. Neither is true.

Mark Poster has suggested that "historians and social scientists in general have gone astray by viewing the family as a unitary phenomenon which has undergone some type of linear transformation".[37] He argues instead that the history of the family is discontinuous, evolving several distinct family structures, each with its own emotional pattern. What this points to is the *construction* of different family forms in different historical periods and with different class effects. A functionalist model which sees the family as an essential and necessary agent of social control, and with the role of ensuring efficient reproduction, ignores both the constant ineffectiveness of the family in doing so and the immense class variations in family forms.

But even more problematic are the assumptions classically made about the nature of sexuality, assumptions current both in traditionalist and in Left thought (and particularly evident in the writings of the Freudian Left: Reich, Fromm, Marcuse). They also have the undoubted strength of the appearance of common sense: in this view sex is conceived as an overpowering, instinctive force, whose characteristics are built into the biology of the human animal, which shapes human institutions and whose will must express itself, either in the form of direct sexual expression or, if blocked, in the form of perversion or neurosis. Krafft-Ebing expressed an orthodox view in the late-nineteenth century when he described sex as a "natural instinct" which "with all conquering force and might demands fulfilment".[38] The clear presupposition here is that the sex drive is basically male in character, with the female conceived of as a passive receptacle. More sophisticated versions of what

Gagnon and Simon have termed the "drive reduction" model[39] recur in twentieth-century thought. It is ambiguously there in parts of Freud's work, though the careful distinction he draws between "instinct" and "drive" has often been lost, both by commentators and translators. But it is unambiguously present in the writings of his epigones. Thus Rattray Taylor in his neo-Freudian interpretation of *Sex in History*:

> The history of civilisation is the history of a long warfare between the dangerous and powerful forces of the id, and the various systems of taboos and inhibitions which man has erected to control them.[40]

Here we have a clear notion of a "basic biological mandate" that presses on, and so must be firmly controlled by the cultural and social matrix.[41] What is peculiar about this model is that it has been adopted both by Marxists, who in other regards have firmly rejected the notion of "natural man", and by taxonomists, such as Kinsey, whose findings have revealed a wide variety of sexual experiences. With regard to homosexuality, the instinctual model has seen it either as a more-or-less pathological deviation, a failure of social necessary repression, as the effect of the morally restrictive organisation of sexual morality or, more romantically but no less ahistorically, as the "great refusal" of sexual normality in the capitalist organisation of sexuality.[42]

Against this, Gagnon and Simon have argued that sexuality is subject to "socio-cultural moulding to a degree surpassed by few other forms of human behaviour",[43] and in so arguing they are building both on a century of sex research and on a century of "decentring" natural man. Marx's formulation of historical materialism and Freud's discovery of the unconscious have been the major contributions to what, over the past few decades, in structuralism, anthropology, psychoanalysis and Marxism, has been a major theoretical effort to challenge the unitary subject (the idea that "the individual" is a fixed, stable natural entity) in social theory. "Sexuality" has in many ways been most resistant to this challenge, precisely because its power seems to derive from our natural being, but there have recently been three sustained challenges to sexual essentialism from three quite different theoretical approaches: the interactionist (associated with the work of Gagnon and Simon), the psychoanalytic (associated with the re-interpretation of Freud initiated by Jacques Lacan) and the historical, taking as its starting point the work of Michel Foucault. They have quite different theoretical starting points and different objects of study – the social sources of human conduct, the unconscious, and power and subjectivity – but between them they have posed formidable challenges to our received notions of sexuality, challenges which have already been reflected in the presentation of this paper.

Despite their different approaches and in the end different aims, their work converges on several important issues. First, they all reject sex as an autonomous realm, a natural force with specific effects, a rebellious energy which the "social" controls. In the work of Gagnon and Simon, it seems to be suggested that nothing is intrinsically sexual, or rather that anything can be sexualised (though what creates the notion of "sexuality" is itself never answered). In Jacques Lacan's "recovery" of Freud, it is the law of the father, the castration fear and the pained entry into the symbolic order – the order of language – at the Oedipal moment which instigates desire. In Foucault's work "sexuality" is seen as an historical apparatus, and "sex" is a "complex idea that was formed within the deployment of sexuality".

> *Sexuality* must not be thought of as a kind of natural given which power tries to hold in check, or as an obscure domain which knowledge gradually tries to uncover. It is the name that can be given to a historical construct: not a furtive reality that is difficult to grasp, but a great surface network in which the stimulation of bodies, the intensification of pleasures, the incitement to discourse, the formation of special knowledges, the strengthening of controls and resistances, are linked to one another, in accordance with a few major strategies of knowledge and power.[44]

It is not fully clear what are the elements on which these social constructs of sexuality play. In the neo-psychoanalytic school there is certainly rejection of the concept of a pool of natural instincts which are distorted by society, but nevertheless there seems to be an acceptance of permanent drives; and the situation is complicated by what must be termed an essentialist and trans-historical reading of Oedipus, which seems to be essential for any culture, or in Juliet Mitchell's version, "patriarchal" culture.[45] Gagnon and Simon and Ken Plummer seem to accept the existence of a pool of possibilities on which "sexuality" draws, and in this they do not seem far removed from Foucault's version that "sexuality" plays upon "bodies, organs, somatic localisations, functions, anatamo-physiological systems, sensations, and pleasures", which have no intrinsic unity or "laws" of their own.[46]

Second, then, what links the anti-essentialist critique is a recognition of the social sources of sexual definitions. In the feminist appropriation of Lacan this can be seen as a result of patriarchal structures and the differential entry into the symbolic order of the human male and female. But this poses massive theoretical problems, particularly in the attempt at a historicised position. Both the interactionists and Foucault make this clear. Gagnon and Simon suggest that:

> It is possible that, given the historical nature of human societies we are victim to the needs of earlier social orders. To earlier societies it may not have been a need to constrain severely the powerful sexual impulse in order to maintain social stability or limit inherently anti-social force, *but rather a matter of having to invent an importance for sexuality*. This would not only assure a high level of reproductive activity but also provide socially available rewards unlimited by natural resources, rewards that promote conforming behaviour in sectors of social life far more important than the sexual. (my italics)[47]

Foucault makes much clearer a historical specification and locates the rise of the sexuality apparatus in the eighteenth century, linked with specific historical processes. As a consequence of this, a third point of contact lies in the rejection, both by the interactionists and Foucault, of the notion that the history of sexuality can fruitfully be seen in terms of "repression". Foucault offers four major arguments against the repression hypothesis. (1) it is based on an outmoded model of power; (2) it leads to a narrow construction of the family's function; (3) it is class specific and applies historically to bourgeois sexuality; and (4) it often results in a one-sided conception of how authority interacts with sexuality – a negative rather than a positive conception.

Again Gagnon and Simon have been less historically specific, but both interactionists and Foucault tend to the view that sexuality is organised not by repression but through definition and regulation. More specifically, regulation is organised through the creation of sexual categories – homosexual, paedophile, transvestite and so on. In the case of Gagnon and Simon and those influenced by them (for example, Plummer) the theoretical framework derives both from Meadean social psychology, which sees the individual as having a developing personality which is created in an interaction with others, and from labelling theories of deviance. In the case of Foucault it derives from his belief that it is through discourse that our relation to reality is organised – or rather, language structures the real.

Fourth, however, in all these tendencies there is a curious relationship to history. Symbolic interactionism, by stressing the subjective and the impact of particular labelling events, has almost invariably displayed an ahistorical bias. The psycho-analytical school, almost by definition, has based itself on supra-historical assumptions which have been almost valueless in conjunctural analyses. Foucault stresses that his work is basically aimed at constructing a "genealogy", the locating of the "traces" of the present; it is basically a "history of the present".

It is this ambiguous relationship of the critique of essentialism to traditional historical work which has made it seem difficult to absorb unproblematically any one of the particular approaches. Nevertheless, each in quite different ways ultimately poses problems which any historical approach to homosexuality must confront, particularly in the difficult relationship of historical structuration to individualised meanings. A close examination of the historical implications of the various approaches will illustrate this.

■ Constructing the homosexual

The dominant theoretical framework in Britain and the USA has derived from "symbolic interactionism". Here ideas are not treated in terms of their historical roots or practical effectiveness, but are seen as forming the background to every social process, so that social processes are treated essentially in terms of ideas, and it is through ideas that we construct social reality itself. Most of the important work that has informed the theoretical study of homosexuality in Britain has derived from symbolic interactionism (for example, Kenneth Plummer's *Sexual Stigma* which is the major British study of how homosexual meanings are acquired[48]). In this theory sexual meanings are constructed in social interaction: a homosexual identity is not inherent, but is socially created. This has had a vitally important clarifying influence, and has, as we have seen, broken with lay ideas of sex as a goal-directed instinct. Linked to labelling theories of deviance, it has been a valuable tool for exploring the effects of public stigmatisations and their impact on sub-cultural formation.

But interactionism has been unable fully to theorise the sexual variations that it can so ably describe; nor has it conceptualised the relations between possible sexual patterns and other social variables. Although it recognises the disparities of power between various groups and the importance of the power to label, it has often had difficulties in theorising questions of structural power and authority. Nor has it been willing, in the field of sexuality, to investigate the question of determination. It is unable to theorise why, despite the endless possibilities of sexualisation it suggests, the genitals continue to be the focus of sexual imagination, nor why there are, at various times, shifts in the location of the sexual taboos. And there is a political consequence too, for if meanings are entirely developed in social interaction, an act of collective will can transform them; this leads, as Mary McIntosh has suggested, to a politics of "collective voluntarism". Both in theory and practice it has ignored the historical location of sexual taboos. Interactionism therefore stops precisely at the point where theorisation seems essential: at the point of historical determination and ideological structuring in the creation of subjectivity.

It is for this reason that recently, particularly amongst feminists, interest has begun to switch to a reassessment of Freud and psychoanalysis with a view to employing it as a tool for developing a theoretical understanding of "patriarchy". It is becoming apparent that if the emergence of a distinct homosexual identity is linked to the evolution of the family, then within this it is the role of the male – theorised by feminist psychoanalysis in terms of the symbolic role of the phallus and the law of the father – that is of central significance. This, it is suggested, will create the space to begin to understand the relationship between gender and sex (for it is in the family that the anatomical differences between the sexes acquire their social significance) and also to begin to uncover the specific history of female sexuality, within which the social history of lesbianism must ultimately be located. The focal point for most of the preliminary discussion has been Juliet Mitchell's *Psychoanalysis and Feminism*,[49] which takes as its starting point the work of Lacan, Althusser and Levi-Strauss. But though the question of sexuality (and its role in the creation of sexed and gendered subjects) has now been strategically linked to the whole problematic of patriarchy, there has been no effort to theorise the question of sexual variation.

The tendency of thought that Juliet Mitchell represents can be critised on a number of grounds. Historically she appears to accept the universality of the Oedipal experience. A historical materialist when analyzing capitalist social relations, she readily accepts idealist notions of the primal father when discussing the origins of patriarchy. Theoretically in her universalising of the Oedipal processes she comes close to accepting drives as autonomous, pre-individual and again trans-historical and trans-cultural. It is a peculiar feature of recent radical thought that while stressing the conjunctural forces which partly at least shape the political, social and ideological, and while stressing the historical construction of subjectivity, it has nevertheless at the same time implicitly fallen back on a form of psychic determinism which it nominally rejects.

It is this which gives a particular interest to Guy Hocquenghem's *Homosexual Desire* (first published in France as *Le Desir Homosexual* in 1972).[50] The essay is located in the area generated by the Lacanian reinterpretation of Freud, linguistic theory and the question of ideology, but its specific debt is to Gilles Deleuze and Felix Guattari, their work *Anti-Oedipus*, their critique of Freudian (and Lacanian) categories and their subsequent theory of "desire" and their espousal of schizoanalysis.[51] As in our argument, Hocquenghem recognises the culturally specific function of the concept of "the homosexual"; Hocquenghem makes references to Foucault and he points to what he calls the "growing imperialism" of society, which seeks to attribute a social status to everything, even the unclassified. The result has been that homosexuality has been ever more closely defined.

Hocquenghem argues that "homosexual desire", like heterosexual desire, is an arbitrary division of the flux of desire, which in itself is polyvocal and undifferentiated, so that the notion of exclusive homosexuality is a "fallacy of the imaginary", a misrecognition and ideological misperception. But despite this, homosexuality has a vivid social presence, and this is because it expresses an aspect of desire which appears nowhere else. For the direct manifestation of homosexual desire opposes the relations of roles and identities necessarily imposed by the Oedipus complex in order to ensure the reproduction of society. Capitalism, in its necessary employment of the Oedipalisation to control the tendency to decoding, manufactures "homosexuals" just as it produces proletarians, and what is manufactured is a psychologically repressive category. He argues that the principal ideological means of thinking about homosexuality are ultimately, though not mechanically, connected with the advance of Western capitalism. They amount to a perverse "re-territorialisation", a massive effort to regain social control, in a world tending toward disorder and decoding.

As a result the establishment of homosexuality as a separate category goes hand in hand with its repression. On the one hand, we have the creation of a minority of "homosexuals", on the other, the transformation in the majority of the repressed homosexual elements of desire into the desire to repress. Hence sublimated homosexuality is the basis of the paranoia about homosexuality which pervades social behaviour, which in turn is a guarantee of the survival of the Oedipal relations, the victory of the law of the father. Hocquenghem argues that only one organ is allowed in the Oedipal triangle, what Deleuze and Guattari called the "despotic signifier", the phallus. And as money is the true universal reference point for capitalism, so the phallus is the reference point for heterosexism. The phallus determines, whether by absence or presence, the girl's penis envy, the boy's castration anxiety; it draws on libidinal energy in the same way as money draws on labour. And as this comment underlines, this Oedipalisation is itself a product of capitalism and not, as the Lacanian school might argue, a law of culture or of all patriarchal societies.

Without going into further details several difficulties emerge. The first relates to the whole question of homosexual paranoia – reminiscent in many ways of the recent discussion of "homophobia" in Britain and the USA.[52] The idea that repression of homosexuality in modern society is a product of suppressed homosexuality comes at times very close to a hydraulic theory of sexuality, which both symbolic interactionism and Lacanian interpretations of Freud have ostensibly rejected. It is not a sufficient explanatory principle simply to reverse the idea that homosexuality is a paranoia, peddled by the medical profession in the present century, into the idea that hostile attitudes to homosexuality are themselves paranoid. Nor does the theory help explain the real, if limited, liberalisation of attitudes that has taken place in some Western countries or the range of attitudes that are empirically known to exist in different countries and even in different families.

Second, following from this, there is the still unanswered problem of why some individuals become "homosexual" and others do not. The use of the concept of Oedipalisation restores some notion of social determinancy that symbolic interactionism lacks, but, by corollary, its use loses any sense of the relevance of the specific family pressures, the educational and labelling processes, the media images that reinforce the identity and the individual shaping of meaning.

Finally, there is Hocquenghem's failure to explore the different modalities of lesbianism. It is important to note that what Hocquenghem is discussing is essentially male homosexuality, for in Hocquenghem's view, although the law of the father dominates both the male and the female, it is to the authority of the father in reproduction (both of the species and of Oedipalisation itself) that homosexuality poses the major challenge; as Deleuze and Guattari note, male homosexuality, far from being a product of the Oedipus complex, as some Freudians imply, itself constitutes a totally different mode of social relationships, no longer vertical, but horizontal. Lesbianism, by implication, assumes its significance as a challenge to the secondary position accorded to female sexuality in capitalist society. It is not so much lesbianism as female sexuality which society denies. But Hocquenghem quite fails to pursue the point, which is central if we are to grasp the formation of sexual meanings. Despite these objections, however, Hocquenghem's essay raises important questions, some of which will be taken up below.

Whereas Hocquenghem, following Deleuze and Guattari, is intent on developing a philosophy of desire, Foucault, though much influenced by and having influence on this tendency, is more concerned in his later works with delineating a theory of power and the complex interplay between power and discourses. Foucault's work marks a break with conventional views of power. Power is not unitary, it does not reside in the state, it is not a thing to hold.

By power, I do not mean "Power" as a group of institutions and mechanisms that ensure the subservience of the citizens of a given state. By power, I do not mean either, a mode of subjugation which, in contrast to violence, has the form of the rule. Finally, I do not have in mind a general system of domination exerted by one group over another. . .these are only the terminal forms power takes. It seems to me that power must be understood in the first instance as the multiplicity of force relations, immanent in the sphere in which they operate and which constitute their own organisation; as the process which, through ceaseless struggles and confrontations transforms, strengthens, or reverses them; as the support which these force relations find in one another, thus forming a chain or a system, or on the contrary, the disfunctions and contradictions which isolate them from one another; and lastly, as the strategies in which they take effect, whose general design or institutional crystallisation is embodied in the state apparatus, in the formulation of the law, in the various social hegemonies.[53]

The problem with this theory of power is that by breaking with a reductive or negative view, power "remains almost as a process, without specification within different instances".[54] And although he is unwilling to specify in advance any privileged source of power, a conception of a will to power nevertheless underlies his work (and hence his complex linkage with Nietzsche) forever expanding and bursting forth in the form of the will to know. It is the complexes of power/ knowledge that Foucault explores in his essay on *The History of Sexuality*.

It is through discourse that the complex of power/ knowledge is realised. Foucault is not interested in the history of mind but in the history of discourse:

> The question which I ask is not of codes but of events: the law of existence of the statements, that which has rendered them possible – these and none other in their place: the conditions of their singular emergence; their correlations with other previous or simultaneous events, discursive or not. The question, however, I try to answer without referring to the consciousness, obscure or explicit, of speaking subjects; without relating the facts of discourse to the will – perhaps involuntary – or their authors.[55]

What he is suggesting is that the relationship between symbol and symbolised is not only referential but productive. The order of language produces its own material forms and desires as much as the physical possibilities. But there is no single hidden hand of history, no complex causative complex, no pre-ordained goal, no final truth of human history. Discourses produce their own truths as the possibilities of seeing the world in fresh ways emerge.

The history of sexuality therefore becomes a history of our discourses about sexuality. And the Western experience of sex, he argues, is not the inhibition of discourse but a constant, and historically changing, deployment of discourses on sex, and this ever-expanding discursive explosion is part of a complex growth of control over individuals, partly through the apparatus of sexuality.

But behind the vast explosion of discourses on sexuality

since the eighteenth century, there is no single unifying strategy valid for the whole of society. And in particular, breaking with an orthodox Marxist problematic, he denies that it can be simply interpreted in terms of problems of "reproduction". In the "Introduction" to *The History of Sexuality* (which is a methodological excursus, rather than a complete "history") Foucault suggests four strategic unities, linking together a host of practices and techniques, which formed specific mechanics of knowledge and power centering on sex: a hysterisation of women's bodies, a pedagogisation of children's sex, a socialisation of procreative behaviour, a psychiatrisation of perverse pleasures. And four figures emerged from these preoccupation, four objects of knowledge, four subjects subjected, targets of and anchorages for the categories which were being simultaneously investigated and regulated: the hysterical woman, the masturbating child, the Malthusian couple and the perverse adult. The thrust of these discursive creations is control, control not through denial or prohibition, but through production, through imposing a grid of definition on the possibilities of the body.

> The deployment of sexuality has its reasons for being, not in reproducing itself, but in proliferating, innovating, annexing, creating, and penetrating bodies in an increasingly detailed way, and in controlling populations in an increasingly comprehensive way.[56]

This is obviously related to Foucault's analysis of the genealogy of the disciplinary society, a society of surveillance and control, in *Discipline and Punish*[57] and to his argument that power proceeds not in the traditional model of sovereignty but through administering and fostering life.

> The old power of death that symbolised sovereign power was now carefully supplanted by the administration of bodies and the calculated management of life.[58]

The obvious question is why? Foucault's "radical nominalism" rejects the question of causation, but he quite clearly perceives the significance of extra-discursive references. In *I*,

Pierre Riviere, the French revolution is perceived as having deep resonances.[59] In *The History of Sexuality*, as in *Discipline and Punish* he refers to the profound changes of the eighteenth century:

> What occurred in the eighteenth century in some western
> countries, an event bound up with the development of capitalism,
> was. . .nothing less than the entry of life into history.[60]

And in the emergence of "bio-power", Foucault's characteristic term for "modern" social forms, sexuality becomes a key element. For sex, argues Foucault, is the pivot of two axes along which the whole technology of life developed; it was the point of entry to the body, to the harnessing, identification and distribution of forces over the body, and it was the entry to control and regulation of populations. "Sex was a means of access both to the life of the body and the life of the species".[61] As a result, sex becomes a crucial target of power organised around the management of life, rather than the sovereign threat of death which organises "pre-modern" societies.

Foucault stresses not the historical cause of events but the conditions for the emergence of discourses and practices. Nevertheless there appears to be a strong functionalist tendency in his work. "Social control" is no longer a product of a materially motivated ruling class but the concept of subjection within discourse seems as ultimately enveloping a concept. "Where there is power, there is resistance", he argues, but nevertheless, and *because* of this, resistance is never in a position of exteriority in relation to power.[62] Indeed the very existence of power relies on a multiplicity of points of resistance, which play the role of "adversary, target, support, or handle in power relations". Foucault apparently envisages the power of social explosions in forcing new ways of seeing: the great social changes of the eighteenth and nineteenth centuries, the French Revolution, the possibilities opened up by the "evenements" of 1968. But one reading of his work would suggest that without such explosions, techniques of discipline and surveillance, strategies of power/knowledge leave us always, already, trapped.

But an alternative reading is possible. First of all there is the possibility of struggles over definition. This can be seen both in struggles over definitions of female sexuality and over the various and subtle forms of control of homosexuality.

> There is no question that the appearance in nineteenth-century psychiatry, jurisprudence, and literature of a whole series of discourses on the species and sub-species of homosexuality, inversion, pederasty, and "psychic hermaphrodism" made possible a strong advance of social controls into this area of "perversity"; but it also made possible the formation of a "reverse" discourse: homosexuality began to speak on its own behalf, to demand that its legitimacy or "naturality" be acknowledged, often in the same vocabulary, using the same categories by which it was radically disqualified.[63]

This reverse affirmation is the sub-text of the history of the homosexual rights movement; it points to the significance of the definitional struggle *and* to its limitations. Hence Foucault's comment:

> I believe that the movements labelled "sexual liberation" ought to be understood as movements of affirmation starting with sexuality. Which means two things: they are movements that start with sexuality, with the apparatus of sexuality in the midst of which we're caught, and which make it function to the limit; but, at the same time, they are in motion relative to it, disengaging themselves and surmounting it.[64]

The ramifications of this "surmounting" are not clear, but it is apparent that both the evolution of homosexual meanings and identities is not complete or "scientifically" established and that homosexuals are, possibly for the first time, self-consciously participating as a group in that evolution.

The other point of high importance in Foucault's work is the emphasis on the genesis of particular institutions: of prisons, the clinic, medical and psychiatric practices which both produce and regulate the objects of knowledge. Appreciation of this emphasis will draw us away from such questions as: what is the relationship between the mode of production and this form of sexuality? Instead we can concentrate on the practices which actually constitute social and sexual categories and ensure their controlling impact. But, in turn, to do this we need to recognise that discourses do not arbitrarily emerge from the flux of possiblities, nor are discourses our only contact with the real: they have their conditions of existence and their effects in concrete, historical, social, economic, and ideological situations.

■ Perspectives and projects

We are now in a sounder position to indicate more effective lines of historical research, or rather to pose the questions to which the historians of sexuality need to address themselves. They are effectively in two parts. First, what were the conditions for the emergence of the homosexual category (or indeed other sexual categories), the complex of factors which fixed the possibilities of homosexual behaviours into a system of defining concepts? Second, what were and are the factors which define the individual acceptance or rejection of categorisations? This is a question that many might regard as invalid but which seems to us of critical importance in determining the impact of control and regulation.

□ Conditions

Foucault and others have stressed the growing importance of the "norm" since the eighteenth century.

> Another consequence of this development of bio-power was the growing importance assumed by the action of the norm at the expense of the juridical system of the law.[65]

A power whose task is to take charge of life needs continuous regulatory and corrective mechanisms. It has to qualify, measure, appraise and reorder: "it affects distributions around the norms". This is not far removed from a more commonplace observation that the development of liberal ("individualistic") society in the nineteenth century led to an increase of conventionality, or to discussions of ideological "interpellations" in the construction of hegemonic forms.[66] But the examination of the "norm" does point effectively to the centrality since the nineteenth century of the norm of the monogamous, heterosexual family. The uncertain status of sodomy points to the fact that before the nineteenth century, the codes governing sexual practices – canonical, pastoral, civil – all centred on non-reproductive relations. Sodomy was part of a continuum of non-procreative practices, often regarded as more serious than rape precisely because it was barren. But these regulations were not extra-marital; they entered the marriage bed, were directly about non-reproductive sex in conjugality, whatever the effectiveness of enforcement. From the nineteenth century the regulations are increasingly of non-conjugal relations: from incest and childhood sex to homo-sexuality. As sexuality is increasingly privatised, seen as the characteristic of the personal sphere, as its public manifesta-tions are challenged (in terms that speak all the time of sex while denying it), so deviant forms of sex become subject to more closely defined public regulation. The family norm is strengthened by a series of extra-marital regulations, which refer back all the time to its normality and morality. This is, of course, underlined by a whole series of other developments, from the enforcement of the Poor Laws and the Factory Acts to the Welfare State support of particular household models in the twentieth century. To repeat a point made earlier, the specification, and hence greater regulation, of homosexual behaviour is closely interconnected with the revaluation and construction of the bourgeois family. This is not necessarily as a conscious effort to support or sustain the family but because, as Plummer has put it:

> The family as a social institution does not of itself condemn
> homosexuality, but through its mere existence it implicitly
> provides a model that renders the homosexual experience
> invalid.[67]

But if we accept this outline as a fruitful guideline for research we need to stress its class specificities. For if "sexuality" and its derivative sexual categorisations are social constructs, then they are constructions within specific class milieux, whatever the impact of their "diffusion" or re-appropriation. We need to explore, in much greater depth than before, the class application of the homosexual categorisations. The common interest among many early twentieth-century middle-class, self-defined homosexuals with the male working class, conceived of as relatively indifferent to homosexual behaviour, is a highly significant element in the homosexual sub-culture.

There was in fact a notable predominance of upper middle-class values. Perhaps on one level only middle-class men had a sufficient sense of a "personal life" through which to develop a homosexual identity. The stress that is evident among male homosexual writers on cross-class liaisons and on youth (typically the representative idealised relationship is between an upper middle-class man and a working-class youth) is striking, and not dissimilar, it may be noted in passing, to certain middle-class heterosexual patterns of the nineteenth century and earlier.[68] The impossibility of same-class liaisons is a constant theme of homosexual literature, demonstrating the strong elements of guilt (class and sexual) that pervade the male identity. But it also illustrates a pattern of what can be called "sexual colonialism", which saw the working-class youth or soldier as a source of "trade", often coinciding uneasily with an idealisation of the reconciling effect of cross-class liaisons.

But if the idealisation of working-class youth was one major theme, the attitude of these working-class men themselves is less easy to trace. They appear in all the major scandals (for example, the Wilde trial, the Cleveland Street scandal) but their self-conceptions are almost impossible to disinter. We may hypothesise that the spread of homosexual consciousness was much less strong among working-class men than middle-class – for obvious family and social factors – even though the law in Britain (on, for example, importuning) probably affected more working-class than middle-class men. We can also note the evidence regarding the patterns of male prostitution as, for example, in the Brigade of Guards, a European-wide phenomenon. Most of the so far sparse evidence on male prostitution suggests a reluctance on the part of the "prostitute" to define himself as homosexual.

A third point relates to this, concerning the gender specificity of homosexual behaviour. The lesbian sense of self has been much less pronounced than that of the male homosexual and the sub-cultural development exiguous. If the Wilde trial was a major labelling event for men, the comparable event for lesbianism, the trial of Radclyffe Hall's lesbian novel, *The Well of Loneliness*, was much less devastating in its impact, and a generation later. Even science, so anxious to detail the characteristics of male homosexuals, largely ignored lesbianism.

These factors underline the fact that what is needed is not so much a single explanation for the emergence of a "homosexual identity" as a differential social history of male homosexuality and lesbianism. But this in turn demands an awareness of the construction of specific gender definitions, and their relationship to sexual identities. Gagnon and Simon have noted that:

> the patterns of overt sexual behaviour on the part of homosexual
> females tend to resemble those of heterosexual females and to
> differ radically from the sexual patterns of both heterosexual and
> homosexual males.[69]

The impact on lesbianism of, for example, the discourses on (basically male) homosexuality must therefore also become an object of study.

Fourth, this underscores again the need to explore the various practices which create the terrain or space in which behaviour is constructed. There is a long historical tradition, as we have seen, of exploring legal regulation, but its impact in constructing categories has never been considered. The role of the medicalisation of sexual deviance has also been tentatively explored, but it is only now that its complexly differentiated impact is being traced. Equally important are the various forms of ideological representations of homosexual behaviour, whether through the press or through the dramatising effects of major rituals of public condemnation, such as the Oscar Wilde trial in the 1890s.

Fifth, there is an absence of any study of the political appropriation of concepts of sexual perversity, although there is a great deal of empirical evidence from the nineteenth century to the present that sexual deviance had a significant place in sexual-political discourse. This indicates the need for a close attention to specific conjunctures of sexual politics and to the social forces at work in constructing political alliances around crimes of morality. The role of sexual respectability in helping to cement the dominant power bloc in the nineteenth century and the relevance of sexual liberalism in constructing the social democratic hegemony of the 1960s in Britain and elsewhere are examples in point.[70]

What this schematic sketch suggests is the importance of locating sexual categorisation within a complex of discourses and practices, but also at the same time it is important not to reject descriptions which ignore the importance of external referents. The agitation for legal regulation, the impact of medicalisation and the stereotyping of media representation all have sources in perceptions of the world and in complex power situations. One may mention, for example, the network of fears over moral decay, imperial decline and public vice behind the 1885 Criminal Law Amendment Act, or the Cold War fears that form the background to the establishment of the Wolfenden Committee in 1954. Or, with regard to the growth of a medical model, we cannot disregard the significance of the growing professionalisation of medicine in the nineteenth century, its ideological and material links with upper middle-class male society and its consequent role in defining sexuality as well as "sexual perversions". So although it would be wrong to see the regulation of homosexual behaviour as a simple effect of capitalist development, it is intricately linked to wider changes within the growth of a highly industrialised, bourgeois society.

☐ Identities

All ideologies work by addressing and evoking ("interpellating") particular subjectivities. The ideological discourses that establish the categories of sexual perversity speak to individuals as if their personal desires defined them absolutely. Yet they also, as Foucault suggest, create the possibility of reversals within the discourses: where there is power, there is resistance.

Foucault is here delineating a space for the self-creation of a homosexual identity, but what is absent is any interest in why some are able to respond or recognise themselves in the interpellation and others are not. There are major problems in this area for which our guidelines are tentative. There is abundant evidence that individual, self-defined homosexuals see their sexuality as deeply rooted, and often manifest at a very early age. This would, on the surface at least, seem to deny that interaction with significant others creates the desire (as opposed to the identity), hence undermining a purely voluntarist position. On the other hand, the notion of a deeply structured homosexual component is equally questionable, if for no other reason than that all the evidence of historical variations contradicts it. Labelling theory has been quite able to accept the distinctions we are making, for example, by making a conceptual separation between primary and secondary deviation:

> Primary deviation, as contrasted with secondary, is polygenetic, arising out of a variety of social, cultural, psychological, and adventitious or recurring combinations . . . secondary deviance refers to a special class of socially defined responses which people make to problems created by the societal reaction to their deviance. . . .The secondary deviant, as opposed to his actions, is a person whose life and identity are organised around the fact of deviance.[71]

This is a valuable distinction stressing the real importance of social labelling and definition, but it ignores precisely those historical (and hence variable) factors which structure the differences. To put it another way, if the homosexual component is not a factor present only in a fixed minority of people, but on the contrary an aspect of the body's sexual possibilities, what social and cultural forces are at work which ensure its dominance in some people, whereas in others the heterosexual element is apparently as strong and determined? Social labelling is obviously central in making the divide between "normal" and "deviant", but what shapes the components at the level of the human animal?

This must lead us again to ask whether we can rescue any lessons from psychoanalytic speculations. A recent attempt to reinterpret Freud's analysis of Little Hans throws some light on this question. Mia Campioni and Liz Gross appear to accept the arguments of Deleuze and Guattari (and Foucault) that Freud's work was simultaneously a recognition of, and another form of control over, the organisation of desire under capitalism.[72] The function of Oedipus is thus to organise sexuality into properly different gender roles to accord both with patriarchal norms *and* a society which privileges sexuality.

> The purpose of concentrating on the case of Little Hans is to reveal the precise mechanisms whereby a system of representation (ideology), correlative with existing social structures, is inscribed upon the child within the constraints of relations specified by the family. . .the process by which Hans is inserted into his patriarchal heritage gives us an indication of this process's mechanisms – at least in the case of male socialisation. . . . .Moreover, the case allows us to clarify the strategies by which the child is inscribed into the power relations that stratify society, and to discover that this occurs by means of the sexualisation of privileged erogeneous zones. It is by the privileging of sexual zones, desires and objects, and by their social control through psychical defence mechanisms, in particular repression, that class and patriarchal social values are instilled in the child which are constructive of his or her very identity. Sexualisation is the means both of the production and the limitation of desire, and therefore is also the locus of the control of desire. Sexual desire provides the socio-political structure with a specific site for power relations (relations of domination and subordination in general) to be exercised.[73]

At the beginning of Hans's case what is most apparent are the overwhelming number of objects and aims of his eroticism. Over the two years of the analysis this sexuality is channelled into the forms of masculine sexuality demanded by familial ideology, and in this we can see, dramatically at work in Freud's analysis and the father's work as agent, the actual imposition of the Oedipal network by the psychoanalytical institution, a paradigm of its controlling role in the twentieth century.

Several points come out of this which are worth underlining. First, this re-analysis does not assume the family is a natural, biological entity with single effects. On the contrary, it is seen as historically constituted and a consequent intersection of various developments, including the development of childhood and the social differentiation of women and men. Second, the analysis does not assume the naturalness of heterosexuality. Instead it relates its privileging precisely to the construction of masculinity and femininity within the monogamous (and socially constituted) family. Third, it does not see the Oedipus complex as in any way universal. Not only is it historically specific, but it is also class specific. Fourth, the analysis suggests that the child's development is neither natural nor internal to the family unit. The young human animal, with all his or her potentialities, is structured within a family, which all the time is a combination of social processes, and by constant reference to the social other.

It is within this context that psychological masculinity and femininity are structured at the level of the emotions. It seems likely that the possibilities of heterosexuality and homosexuality as socially structured limitations on the flux of potentialities are developed in this nexus in the process of emotional socialisation. The emotion thus draws on sexuality rather than being created by it.

But what is created, this would suggest, in not an identity but a propensity. It is the whole series of social interactions, encounters with peers, educational processes, rituals of exclusion, labelling events, chance encounters, political identifications, and so on, which structure the sexual identities. They are not pre-given in nature; probably like the propensities themselves they are social creations, though at different levels in the formation of psychological individuality. This again suggests a rich field for historical explorations: the conditions for the growth of sub-cultural formations (urbanisation, response to social pressure, etc.), the degree of sub-cultural participation, the role of sub-cultural involvement in the fixing of sexual identities, the impact of legal and ideological regulation, the political responses to the sub-culture, both from within the homosexual community and without, and the possibilities for transformations.

■ Conclusion

What has been offered here is neither a prescription for correct research procedures nor a collection of dogmatic answers, but a posing of important and fundamentally *historical* questions which the historians of sexuality have generally ignored. Earlier in the paper, the problem was posed on two levels: the level of the *social* categorisation and the level of the *individual*, subjective construction of meaning. Until very recently, as Mary McIntosh pointed out, the latter level was exclusively concentrated on, to the extent that the question of aetiology dominated. Since then, particularly with the rise of sociological studies, the social has rightly been emphasised. What I am now tentatively suggesting is that we must see both as aspects of the same process, which is above all an historical process. Social processes construct subjectivities not just as "categories" but at the level of individual desires. This perception, rather than the search for epistemological purity, should be the starting point for future social and historical studies of "homosexuality" and indeed of "sexuality" in general.

3 Inverts, perverts and mary-annes:

male prostitution and the regulation of homosexuality in England in the nineteenth and early twentieth centuries

■ The problem

Writings on male prostitution began to emerge simultaneously with the notion that "homosexuals" were an identifiable breed of persons, with special needs, passions, and lusts. The early studies of male prostitution by F. Carlier, head of the morals police in Paris in the 1860s, were also the first major quantitative studies of homosexuality.[1] Havelock Ellis, Iwan Bloch, Magnus Hirschfeld, and Sigmund Freud also commented on the prevalence of homosexual prostitution, while "Xavier Mayne", who wrote on the homosexual sub-culture in the early part of this century, suggested that male was no less frequent than female prostitution in major European cities. In 1948, Alfred Kinsey noted that male prostitutes were not far inferior in number to females, while in the 1960s, D.J. West suggested that homosexual males' "inclination to such an outlet with prostitutes" was greater than that of heterosexual males. The latter, it was suggested, were usually married, and consequently had less pressing sexual urges as well as less time or opportunity to consort with prostitutes.[2]

But although the existence of male prostitution is mentioned frequently, it has been studied less often as a worthy topic of historical or sociological research. Most of our information is anecdotal and impressionistic.[3] As late as the mid-1960s, a writer on the subject could complain that the literature on boy prostitutes was scant when compared with studies of female prostitution.[4] This neglect is unfortunate. The subject should not be regarded as marginal. A study of homosexual prostitution could illuminate the changing images of homosexuality and its legal and social regulation, as well as the variability of sexual identities in our social history and their relationship to wider social structures.

Iwan Bloch, writing in 1909, suggested that a discussion of male prostitution in E.A. Duchèsne's *De la Prostitution dans la Ville d'Alger depuis la Conquete*, published in Paris in 1853, was:

> . . . an expansion of the idea of prostitution which is, as far as my knowledge goes, found here for the first time. Naturally, in earlier works we find allusions to men who practice pederasty for money, but the idea of "prostitution" had hitherto been strictly limited to the class of purchasable women.[5]

Bloch pinpoints the need to locate studies of prostitution within their specific social conditions, and discriminates between promiscuity in earlier cultures and modern forms of prostitution, for the social meanings ascribed to the two behaviors are usually quite different.

Much recent work has stressed the vital importance of distinguishing among behaviour, role, and identity in any sociological or historical approach to the subject of homosexuality. Cross-cultural studies, as well as studies of schoolboy sex play, prison homosexuality, and sex in public places, show that homosexual behavior does not give rise automatically, or even necessarily, to a homosexual identity. Homosexual roles and identities are historically constructed. Even if the homosexual "orientation" were given in a fixed minority of the population, as some recent writers suggest, the social definitions and the subjective meaning given to the orientation can vary enormously. The mass of typologies and categorisations in the works of Krafft-Ebing, Albert Moll, Havelock Ellis, Magnus Hirschfeld, and others at the beginning of the century was an early attempt to grapple with this fact.[6]

Historians and social scientists alike have, not surprisingly, failed to fit everyone who behaves in a homosexual manner within a definition of "the homosexual" as a unitary type. Even those categorised as "homosexuals" often have had great difficulty in accepting the label. If this is the case for the clients of male prostitutes (the "steamers" or "punters", "swells" or "swanks"), how much more true is it for the prostitute himself who must confront two stigmatised identities – that of the homosexual and that of the prostitute? There is no legitimising ideology for homosexual prostitution similar to that which condones heterosexual prostitution even as it condemns the female prostitute. A number of studies have suggested that many males who prostitute themselves regard themselves as heterosexual and devise complex strategies to neutralise the significance of their behaviour.[7] Our knowledge of this phenomenon is speculative, however, limited to particular classes of people, such as delinquents, and we do not know how attitudes change historically or in a particular lifetime. More generally, there is the problem of what constitutes an act of prostitution. One of Oscar Wilde's pickups in the 1890s, Charlie Parker, who eventually gave evidence against him, commented: "I don't suppose boys are different to girls in taking presents from them who are fond of them."[8] On a superficial level this is true, but the association with a stigmatised sexual activity has shaped profoundly the contours of male prostitution and made it different from female prostitution.

This essay does not pretend to be an exhaustive study of the patterns of male prostitution. The necessary detailed empirical research still has to be done.[9] Rather, the intention is to examine some of the practical and theoretical problems attendant upon this research and to make specific reference to evidence from the late-nineteenth and early-twentieth centuries. There are three broad areas of concern. First, we must pay closer attention than hitherto to the specific social circumstances that shaped concepts of, and attitudes toward, homosexuality. Second, the close, indeed symbiotic, relationship between forms of prostitution and the homosexual subcultures has to be recognised and analysed. Third, the nature of the prostitution itself, the self-concepts it led to, the "way of life" it projected, and its differences from female prostitution must be articulated and theorised.

■ The social and legal context

Certain types of subcultural formations associated with homosexual activity have existed in Britain for centuries, at the courts
of certain monarchs (where the royal "favourite" can be seen as
analogous to the "courtesan"), in the theatrical profession from
the sixteenth century, or in developing urban centres, such as
London and Bristol, from the late-seventeenth century. Forms of
prostitution undoubtedly existed within these subcultures and
became more complex as the subculture expanded in the
nineteenth century. Well into the present century however, the
lineaments of the subcultures were much less well defined in
Britain, even in London, than in such places as Paris and Berlin,
and as a result the evidence of prostitution is less concrete.[10]
Different legal practices and moral traditions have had highly
significant effects. In Britain, in contrast to France, homosexual
behaviour *per se* (not just prostitution) was regarded as a
problem. Contemporary foreign observers had no doubt that
male prostitution was as rife in England as elsewhere,[11] but its
visibility was minimal. Much of our evidence for British
prostitution is consequently sporadic, often the result of zealous
public morality drives or of spectacular scandals.

Police, legal, and medical attitudes were manifestly
confused. When the two "men in women's clothes", Ernest
Boulton and Frederick Park, were arrested in 1870 for indecent
behaviour (for cross-dressing in public), they were immediately
and without authorisation examined for evidence of sodomy
and eventually charged with conspiracy to commit such acts.[12]
The police, who had been observing the two men for over a
year, often in notorious haunts of female prostitution, were of
the opinion that Boulton and Park were male prostitutes.
Indeed, some of the letters exchanged between Boulton, Park,
and other defendants mentioned money. It is obvious,
however, from the transcripts of the trial (before the Lord Chief
Justice, in Westminster Hall) that neither the police nor the
court were familiar either with male homosexuality or prostitution. It is not even clear whether the men were charged with
male prostitution.

The opening remarks by the Attorney General hinted that it

was their transvestism and their soliciting men as women that were the core of the crime.[13] A Dr Paul, who examined them for sodomy upon their arrest, had never encountered a similar case in his whole career. His only knowledge came from a half-remembered case history in Dr Alfred Swaine Taylor's *Medical Jurisprudence*.[14] The unclaimed body of one Eliza Edwards in 1833 had turned out on inspection to be the body of a twenty-four-year-old male: "The state of the rectum left no doubt of the abominable practices to which this individual had been addicted."[15] The implication was that sodomy might itself be an indication of prostitution, but even Dr Taylor, who also gave evidence in the case, had had no other previous experience, and the other doctors called in could not agree on what the signs of sodomitical activity were. The Attorney General observed that "it must be a matter of rare occurrence in this country at least for any person to be discovered who has any propensity for the practices which are imputed to them."[16]

The only "scientific" literature to which the court had recourse was French. Dr Paul had not heard of the work of Tardieu, who had investigated over two hundred cases of sodomy for purposes of legal proof, until an anonymous letter informed him of its existence.[17] The Attorney General suggested with relief that it was fortunate that there was "very little learning or knowledge upon this subject in this country."[18] One of the defence counsel was more bitter, attacking Dr Paul for relying on "the newfound treasures of French literature upon the subject which thank God is still foreign to the libraries of British surgeons."[19]

It is striking that as late as 1871 concepts both of homosexuality and of male prostitution were extremely undeveloped in the Metropolitan Police and in high medical and legal circles. Neither was there any comprehensive law relating to male homosexuality before 1885. Prior to that date, the only relevant law was that concerning buggery, dating from the 1530s, and notionally carrying the maximum of a death sentence until 1861. Other male homosexual acts generally were subsumed under the heading of conspiracy to commit the major offense. Proof was notoriously difficult to obtain, however, and it was ostensibly to make proof, and therefore conviction, easier that Henry Labouchère introduced his famous amendment to the Criminal Law Amendment Act of 1885. He claimed, though the substantiating evidence for this appears no longer to exist, that it was a communication from W.T. Stead about homosexual prostitution in London that prompted Labouchère to act.[20] The amendment defined "acts of gross indecency" between two men whether in public or private as "misdemeanors", punishable by up to two years of hard labour. This in effect made all male homosexual acts and all homosexual "procuring" illegal.

The 1898 Vagrancy Act further affected homosexual activities by enacting that any male person who knowingly lived wholly or in part on the earnings of female prostitutes, or who solicited or importuned for immoral purposes, was to be deemed a rogue and a vagabond under the terms of the Vagrancy Acts. The latter clauses were applied almost invariably to homosexual offenses. By a further Criminal Law Amendment Act ("The White Slave Trade Act") in 1912, the sentence was set at six months' imprisonment, with flogging for a second offense, on summary jurisdiction (that is, without a jury trial), a clause which, as G.B. Shaw put it, "is the final triumph of the vice it pretends to repress.[21] It is not entirely clear why the soliciting clauses were in practice confined exclusively to men meeting each other for homosexual purposes. The Royal Commission on the Duties of the Metropolitan Police noted in 1908 that there was nothing in the Act to prevent the clauses being applied to men soliciting women for immoral purposes, but in fact they never were. The 1928 Street Offences Committee recommended that no change take place in these provisions.[22]

Although obviously less severe than a death sentence or life imprisonment for buggery, the new clauses were all-embracing and more effectively applied. They had specific effects on the relationship between male prostitution and homosexuality. All male homosexual activities were illegal between 1885 and 1967, and this fact largely shaped the nature of the homosexual underworld in the period "between the Acts." In particular it shaped the relationship between those who defined themselves as "homosexual" and those who prostituted themselves; for instance, it increased the likelihood of blackmail and violence. It also affected the nature of the prostitution itself, certainly making it less public and less sharply defined. As observers noted at the time, the male prostitute had the professional disadvantage of being obliged to avoid the open publicity of solicitation available to female prostitutes. This had important consequences.

In terms of social obloquy, all homosexual males as a class were equated with female prostitutes. It is striking that all the major enactments concerning male homosexuality were drawn from Acts designed to control female prostitution (1885, 1898, 1912). The juncture of the two concerns was maintained as late as the 1950s, when the "Wolfenden Committee" was established to investigate both.

After the repeal of the Contagious Diseases Acts in the 1880s, female prostitution was subject to a peculiar "compromise" that sought neither outright repression nor formal state regulation.[23] Prostitution was frowned upon, and the female prostitute was an outcast increasingly defined as a member of a separate caste of women, but prostitution was "tolerated" as fulfilling a necessary social need. Beyond this was the distinction, which social purity campaigns sought to emphasise, between the sphere of public decency and that of private behavior. There were periods, particularly in the early decade of the twentieth century, when the advocates of social purity did reach toward straightforward repression, but by and large the compromise held.

On a formal level, the compromise never applied to male homosexuality. Even the sodomy provisions were applied to private as well as public behavior,[24] and after 1885 the situation was even more explicit. In practice, of course, enforcement varied between different police areas, depending on local police chiefs, the power of watch committees and, over time, on the general social climate and the effectiveness of social-purity campaigns. There were also difficulties in the legal situation. Juries often refused to convict under the 1885 Act, and police often preferred not to prosecute if "public decency" were reasonably maintained.[25] Even after 1885, the government's legal officers preferred caution. In 1889, the Director of Public Prosecutions noted "the expediency of not giving unnecessary publicity" to cases of gross indecency. At the same time, he felt that much could be said for allowing "private persons – being full grown men – to indulge their unnatural tastes in private."[26]

When the law was applied, however, it was applied with rigour, particularly against males who importuned. Figures are difficult to come by, for until 1954 statistics for prosecution of male solicitation were always published with those for men living off immoral earnings, but one observer has suggested that the law was the cause of even greater misery than the 1885 Act.[27] It was enforced through summary jurisdiction (that is without trial by jury), and, compared to the forty-shilling fine imposed on female prostitutes before 1959, the maximum sentence of six months' imprisonment and the associated stigmatisation ground hard on homosexual males.

Given the social restrictions on forms of sexual contact, the demand for special services, and, in the case of homosexuality, the continuing difficulties of leading an openly homosexual life, there is undoubtedly at all times a market for prostitution. Given the legal situation since the end of the nineteenth century and the simultaneous refinement of hostile social norms, homosexual activity was potentially very dangerous for both partners and carried with it not only public disgrace but the possibility of a prison sentence. This also fed into the market for prostitution and dictated much of the furtiveness, guilt, and anxiety that was a characteristic of the homosexual way of life.

In the diaries of Roger Casement, the Irish patriot executed in 1916, notes on his work for the colonial service lie cheek by jowl with descriptions of pickups, the price he paid for them, the size of their organs, and the occasional cry of despair. When he heard of the suicide of (the homosexual) Sir Hector Macdonald, Casement called for "saner methods of curing a terrible disease", but the surrounding entries joyfully extol his own recent adventures:

December 6, 1903
Very busy on report with typer. Did 6000 words today and revised a lot. Dined at Comedy Restaurant alone. First time there in life. Porter good excellent dinner, French chef, then walked. Dusky depradator huge, saw 7in. in all. Two beauties.

December 7, 1903

Awful mistake. Dine with Cui B and Mrs C., jolly dinner, strolled. Dick, West End biggest and cleanest, mui mua ami.

December 8, 1903
Busy all day and then to Robertson's at 30, Hemstall Road. Home by Marble Arch. D.W. 14. C.R. £1. Drizzle, home tired and to bed. Bertie walked part of way.[28]

The frequency of encounters varied from thirty-nine in the 1903 diary to several hundred in 1911.[29] These adventures were completely hidden from friends and colleagues but evidently were a central part of his life, entering into his regular financial accountancy. The 1911 ledger, for instance, contains brief accounts of all activities and financial transactions, including payments for boys. Casement was exceptional in recording such (ultimately damning) details, but his life cannot have been unique. Indeed, there are striking parallels with the anonymous author of the Victorian sexual chronicle, *My Secret Life*, who also wrote of having a secret homosexual life, hidden from respectable friends and colleagues: "Have all men had the strange letches which late in life have enraptured me?"[30] Casement might well have asked the same question, for he seems to have had no sustained contact with a subculture or with other homosexual men except through casual prostitution.

■ The homosexual subculture

A sexual subculture can fulfill a number of complementary functions: alleviating isolation and guilt, schooling members in manners and mores, teaching and affirming identities. The most basic purpose of the homosexual subculture in the nineteenth and early twentieth centuries, however, was to provide ways to meet sexual partners. Until comparatively recently, very few people found it either possible or desirable to incorporate sexual mores, social activities, and public identity into a full-time homosexual "way of life." Perhaps the only people who lived wholly in the subculture were the relatively few "professionals," the chief links between the world of aristocratic homosexuality and the metropolitan subculture of Molly houses, pubs, fields, walks, squares, and lavatories.

As early as the 1720s, these meeting places had been known as "markets", corresponding to the contemporaneous heterosexual use of the term "marriage market". This does not differ much from Evelyn Hooker's description of the 1950s American gay bar scene as free markets in which the buyer's right to enter is determined solely by having the right attributes and the ability to pay.[31] By the 1870s, any sort of homosexual transaction, whether or not money was involved, was described as "trade". One defendant in the Boulton and Park scandal wrote to the other, "I will confess that I give you reason to think that I care for nothing but trade and I think you care too little for it as far as I am concerned."[32] In this world of sexual barter, particularly given the furtiveness, the need for caution, and the great disparities of wealth and social position among the participants, the cash nexus inevitably dominated.

Despite the wide social range of the subculture, from pauper to peer, it was the ideology of the upper classes that seems to have dominated, probably because there was a much more clearly defined homosexual identity amongst men of the middle and upper-middle class, and because these men had a greater opportunity, through money and mobility, to make frequent homosexual contacts.[33] A related phenomenon was the widely recognised upper-middle-class fascination with crossing the class divide, a fascination that shows a direct continuity between male heterosexual and male homosexual mores.[34] J.A. Symonds might have disapproved of some of his friends' compulsive chasing after working-class contacts,[35] but it was undoubtedly an important component of the subculture. The Post Office messenger boys of the Cleveland Street scandal and the stable lads, newspaper sellers, and bookmakers' clerks in the Wilde trial illustrate a few of the many sections of the working class involved. The moving of class barriers, the search for "rough trade", or Wilde's "feasting with panthers" could become the defining tone. Lasting partnerships did develop, but in a world of relatively easy sex, promiscuity was a temptation, despite the dangers. Middle-class men generally had non-sexual relationships with friends, sex with casual pickups. One respondent of mine who found it difficult to have sex with friends of his own class had a fascination with the Guards and "suffered", as he put it, from "scarlet fever":

I have never cared for trading with "homosexuals". . . .I always
wanted to trade with "men". But of course, mine's always been
prostitution . . . I don't say I never went with homosexuals
because I did. But I would say that as a rule I wanted men.[36]

The desire for a relationship across class lines (the product,
perhaps, of a feeling that sex could not be spontaneous or
"natural" within the framework of one's own class), interacted
with a desire for a relationship with a "man", a real man, a
heterosexual. E.M. Forster wanted "to love a strong young man
of the lower classes and be loved by him", and finally
developed an ambiguous relationship with a policeman.
Edward Carpenter proclaimed his love for the poor and
uneducated in obviously erotic tones: "The thick-thighed, hot,
coarse-fleshed young bricklayer with the strip around his
waist." J.R. Ackerley sometimes felt that "the ideal friend . . .
should have been an animal man . . . the perfect human male
body always at one's service through the devotion of a faithful
and uncritical beast."[37]

There are very complex patterns recurring here. On the one
hand was a form of sexual colonialism, a view of the lower
classes as a source of "trade." On the other were an often
sentimental rejection of one's own class values and a belief in
reconciliation through sexual contact. As J.A. Symonds put it,
"The blending of Social Strata in masculine love seems to me
one of its most pronounced and socially hopeful features".[38]
With this went a common belief that the working class and the
Guardsmen (notorious from the eighteenth century and
throughout Europe for their easy prostitution) were indifferent
to homosexual behavior. One regular customer of the Guardsmen observed: "Young, they were normal, they were working
class, they were drilled to obedience."[39] They also were widely
available:

The sceptic has only to walk around London, around any English
garrison centre, to stroll around Portsmouth, Aldershot,
Southampton, Woolwich, large cities of North Britain or Ireland
to find the soldier prostitute in almost open self-marketing.[40]

With the guards, the money transaction was explicit. In the

rarefied atmosphere of the "Uranian" poets, money would change hands but ideology minimised its significance. The Uranians worshipped youth, spoke of the transience of boyhood, and delighted in breaking class barriers.[41]

These class and gender interactions ("working-class" equals masculine equals "closeness to nature") were to play important roles in the rituals of prostitution, affecting, for instance, the stance adopted by the "prostitute" and the behaviours he was expected to tolerate.[42]

The nature of prostitution

The exchange of money could create a host of different symbolic meanings for both parties, while the uncertainty of both could make the transaction itself very ambiguous. It was not always easy, for instance, to distinguish among extortion, blackmail, and a begging letter. The giving of gifts could have the same complex inflection. Oscar Wilde's gift to his contacts of a dinner at Kettner's and a silver cigarette box (varying in cost from £1 to £5) could be interpreted either as payment for services about to be rendered or as tokens of friendship. A working-class man like George Merrill, Edward Carpenter's long-time companion, was able to recount quite unselfconsciously his liaison in the 1880s with an Italian count who gave him presents, flowers, neckties, hand-kerchiefs, and money, which Merrill usually sent home to his mother.[43] In this sort of situation, the significance attached to the transaction could be quite complex, with the money and gifts often playing a quite secondary role.

Even when the commercial element was quite unambiguous, complex mechanisms could be adopted to mask the exchange. A client could easily adopt a self-saving attitude: "I seemed always to be pretending that the quid that usually passed between us at once (the boys were always short of cash) was not a *quid pro quo* but a gift."[44] Joe Ackerley has told of his nightly search for an ideal comrade and of his numberless pickups (Guardsmen and policemen). He writes, however:

The taint of prostitution in these proceedings nevertheless

displeased me and must, I thought, be disagreeable to the boys themselves . . . I therefore developed mutually self-saving techniques to avoid it, such as standing drinks and giving cash at once, without any suggestive conversation, leaving the boy free to return home with me if he wished out of sexual desire or gratitude, for he was pretty sure to know what I was after.[45]

Payment could also be a necessary ritual to alleviate guilt:

There's a famous place behind a pub – in Camberwell, which was very interesting. And there was an Army Captain there, who showed interest in me, and I in him. And he said, "Oh well, there are a lot of ditched houses over there, let's go round there." Which we did. And afterwards he pressed a ten shilling note into my hand. I said "I don't want this money. I don't take money, I enjoyed your company", and so on. "I said I will not have it." He said "But you've got to have it." "I said I won't have it." And he went on and on. And eventually pressed it into my hand and ran. Now I think he got a thrill out of paying people. Most extraordinary.

Fernando Henriques defined prostitution as "any sexual acts, including those which involve copulation, habitually per-formed by individuals with other individuals of their own or the opposite sex, for a consideration which is non-sexual."[46] A definition as all-embracing as this, however, is meaningless in the case of male prostitution. Terms like "habitually" and "non-sexual" are inappropriate where, as most commentators indicate, casual prostitution was the norm and casual pickups might evolve into "companions", "private secretaries", or "personal assistants". An alternative definition suggests that activities be determined along a continuum between in-strumentality and expressiveness and only those transactions in which the "instrumental" (that is, the sexual services for money) is greater than the "expressive" (the degree of affection generated) be called prostitution.[47] The crucial question becomes: would the transaction go on if goods and services were not exchanged? – a question involving self-concepts and identity as well as affection.

In an historical survey it is often very difficult to determine which actions are purely instrumental and which are affective.

It is easier to describe the motivations and fantasies of the clients than to delineate the experiences and beliefs of those who prostituted themselves. Late-nineteenth-century theorists of the aetiology of homosexuality looked to masturbation, bad parentage, congenital degeneracy, or corruption as explanations. A consensus developed among sexologists that, whatever one's moral views of homosexual behaviour, there were essentially two types to distinguish: those who were inherently, perhaps congenitally, homosexual, "the inverts"; and those who behaved in a homosexual way from lust, "the perverts". Thoinot noted that "male prostitution finds as clients, on the one hand, true Uranists, or the passionates as they are called in the language of the French police, and, on the other hand, libertines, old or young disgusted with normal relations and impotent towards women".[48] This was an important distinction because it coloured a great deal of public reaction. The Director of Public Prosecutions, reflecting on the affair of the Cleveland Street brothel in 1889, wrote that it was a duty "to enforce the law and protect the children of respectable parents taken into the service of the public . . . from being made the victims of the unnatural lusts of full-grown men".[49] The notion of the upper class corrupting the working class into vice is repeated in Labouchère's description of the boys named in the Cleveland Street affair as being "more sinned against than sinning". The Constable in charge of the boys came to the conclusion that "they were ignorant of the crimes they committed with other persons".[50] The merging of homosexuality with the class question was recurrent in the press during the Cleveland Street scandal and continued through the century into the 1950s.[51]

Alongside this view, and to some extent contradicting it, was the theory that the prostitute exhibited a characteristic predisposition toward corruption and sexual degeneracy, a characteristic sign of which was effeminacy. It is true that throughout Europe, from the eighteenth century on, those who prostituted themselves often displayed stereotyped "effeminate" characteristics and adopted female names,[52] but it is wrong to assume that male prostitutes were drawn from any particular type of person pre-disposed toward prostitution. Effeminate behaviour can be as much an adopted role as inherent and, as we have seen, the homosexual subculture stressed the desire for "manly" men.

A variety of factors drew people into prostitution. Writing of Berlin in the 1920s, Werner Picton mentions two prostitute populations: an "outer ring" that fluctuated in numbers and composition and was caused by unemployment and want; and

> the inner and more stable nucleus of this variable, arid, non-coherent body, less driven by want or unemployment than by other circumstances, such as psychopathy, hysteria, mental instability, sexual curiosity, love of adventure and longing for luxuries.[53]

Some of these categories ("psychopathy", "hysteria", "mental instability") conform to the view that prostitutes were "degenerate" or had been pushed into prostitution by emotional inadequacy or sex-role confusion. The other categories, however, suggest what appears to have been commonly the case: that the men had experienced a general and characteristic "drift" (described as a "sliding down"[54]) that had varying, and certainly not predetermined, effects on their self-concepts and identities.

"Drift" has been identified as characteristic for both female and male prostitution, with "situational and cognitive" processes tending to be the dominant influences.[55] Whereas with female prostitution frequent sexual relations with men can lead to a woman's decision that her future transactions will be for money, the pattern is significantly different for male prostitutes. Here the dominant pattern seems to be one of chance contacts, accidental learning, or association with a sub-culture (such as that of the Guards) with a tradition of casual prostitution.

Youthful sex play frequently led to casual prostitution. Thickbroom, a boy messenger for the Post Office who was involved in the Cleveland Street affair, told how mutual masturbation in a water closet with Newlove, another messenger, had been followed by Newlove asking him, in Thickbroom's words, "if I would go to be with a man. I said no. He then said: you'll get four shillings for a time and persuaded me."[56] The messenger boys did not prostitute themselves frequently and, were it not for the subsequent scandal, their involvement probably would have had minor impact on their lives. Sometimes, however, the decision could be more calculating. Charlie Parker recounted how he became involved with Alfred Taylor and Oscar Wilde. Taylor approached him:

> passed the compliments of the day, and asked us to have a drink. We got into conversation with him. He spoke about men. Taylor said, "You could get money in a certain way easily enough if you cared to." I understood to what Taylor alluded and made a coarse reply . . . I said that if any old gentleman with money took a fancy to me, I was agreeable. I was agreeable. I was terribly hard up.[57]

These initial purposeful contacts could slide easily into a transitional career of blackmail and threat, but this was not a necessary development.

A third route to prostitution was through a world symbiotic with homosexuality, such as the Guards. A working-class recruit would soon learn how extra money could be made with little effort and with no risk of stigma by his fellows. Indeed, tradition and perennial shortage of funds among the Guards sanctioned these activities.[58] Sub-cultural support from peers was likely to militate against a Guardsman becoming a "professional." Sometimes a propensity for leading an explicitly homosexual life, a particular skill for learning the ways of the subculture, support from other prostitutes or homosexual men, or the willingness to recognise himself as a prostitute would turn a man to "professionalisation," but "professionals" were very much in a minority among Guardsmen and non-military youths alike.

The records of professional prostitutes are rare, which gives a particular interest to *Sins of the Cities of the Plain* (1881),[59] the life story of Jack Saul (a historical character who later – in 1890 – gave evidence in the Euston libel case as part of the Cleveland Street brothel scandal). A choice piece of homosexual pornography, the book is purportedly Saul's autobiography and, despite its presumably fictionalised account, gives vivid insights into male prostitution. In the libel trial, Saul asserted proudly that he was still a "professional mary-anne": "I have lost my character and cannot get on otherwise. I occasionally do odd jobs for different gay people."[60] These odd jobs, as he made clear in his cross-examination, were house cleaning for women on the beat, suggesting a commitment to a career as a professional, the ghettoisation that could result from this choice of career, and its vagaries as age diminished charm. The life was by no means completely harsh, however, as this dialogue shows:

> "And were you hunted by the police?"
> "No, they have never interfered. They have always been kind to me."
> "Do you mean they have deliberately shut their eyes to your infamous practices?"
> "They have had to shut their eyes to more than me."[61]

The likes of Saul were few, however: his purported memoirs note that "We do not know of many professional male sodomites in London."[62]

■ The life

The professional organisation that has been characteristic of female prostitution never arose within homosexual prostitution. Even in the larger European cities, such as Berlin and Paris, the "boy-houses" were rare, though numerous places of rendez-vous existed under the guise of literary clubs and athletic societies. In England, the Criminal Law Amendment Act of 1885 had been directed partly against brothels but was ambiguous in its application to homosexual haunts. The Director of Public Prosecutions complained to the Home Secretary in 1889 that he was "quite aware that although it is a legal offence to keep a bawdy house – it is not a legal offence to keep or frequent a house kept for the accommodation of sodomites."[63] Labouchère claimed in 1889 to have in his possession "a short list of houses, some in fashionable parts of the city which are every inch as bad; if not worse" (than female brothels)[64] but nothing seems to have followed from his threat to reveal them.

Such establishments had dozens of clients. Soldiers, MPs,

peers, members of the National Liberal Club, a tailor, and a banker all frequented 19 Cleveland Street, for example. The boys were paid "sometimes a sovereign, sometimes half a sovereign; 4/- was kept by themselves and the rest given to Hammond or kept by Newlove."[65] Jack Saul lived with Hammond for a while, and both earned their livelihood as "sodomites": "I used to give him all the money I earned, oftentimes as much as £8 or £9 a week."[66]

Hammond lived a fully professional life as a "madam", married a French prostitute, Madame Carolino, and lived with her thereafter. He also had a "spooney-boy," one Frank Hewitt, who used to "go with him" and procure boys for the establishment.

Even within this twilight world there were subtle distinctions. Saul complained to Hammond of his allowing boys "in good position in the Post Office to be in the house while I had to walk the streets for what is in my face and what is shame."[67] Professional mary-annes with neatly printed calling cards like gentlemen's visiting cards existed,[68] but were scarcely the norm. More common contact would be the likes of Mrs Truman, who received orders for Guardsmen at her tobacconist shop near the Albany Street barracks in Regent's Park.[69] The Guards themselves also might take up an informal pimping role. One customer tells how he met one Guard several times:

> and then he said, "well do you want anybody else . . . I can bring them along". . . ."So I said . . . have you got one with ginger hair?". . . . And then of course (he) procured me – oh – dozens. Dozens of them.

There were also widespread informal coteries.[70] Oscar Wilde made many of his contacts through his friend, Alfred Taylor, who lived in exotically furnished rooms in Little College Street near Westminster Abbey. The son of a wealthy cocoa manufacturer, Taylor became notorious for introducing young men to older men and as the centre of a "sort of secret society."[71] Others, like John Watson Preston, who lived at 46 Fitzroy Street (near Cleveland Street), held openly transvestite parties, one of which was raided by the police. One such raid precipitated Taylor's first arrest.[72]

Similar arrangements continued into the 1930s:

> I was introduced to somebody called Tommy. He had a flat. And
> he used to have "friends" who used to call on him for tea, and he
> would invite his "friends" and pair them off. And presents used to
> change hands. His clients were MPs, doctors, lawyers and
> professional gentlemen. They paid him. He paid the boy.

In London, however, most contacts would be made in the
normal picking-up places and at "watering holes" (public
lavatories), the occasional "mixed" pubs, the rare, private
clubs, the public walks, and parks. Some places, such as
Piccadilly Circus, were notorious, and here the more "obvious"
or blatant young prostitutes might gather. Some of the more
obviously effeminate prostitutes wore women's clothing and
powder,[73] but most young men were more discreet. Discretion
was indeed the hallmark of homosexual prostitution.

■ Definitions of homosexuality

Picton's survey of 154 Berlin prostitutes revealed that ap-
proximately two-thirds spent between one and five years on the
game, having started between the ages of seventeen and
twenty-five. This admittedly very rough survey suggests that
most men had quit the trade by their mid-twenties.[74] The routes
out were numerous, from becoming a "kept boy" (either in a
long-term relationship or in successive relationships), to
integration into the homosexual world, or to a return to
heterosexual family life. At least two of the boys involved in the
Cleveland Street affair founded "modest but upwardly mobile
family dynasties"[75] and lost all contact with the world of
prostitution. The participants' self-concepts, as homosexual and
as prostitute, were likely to-determine how long a man
remained a "Mary-anne." Historically specific definitions are
all important here.

Most discussions of homosexuality, as we have seen, have
been dominated by an essentialism that presupposes a given,
and unproblematic, homosexual "condition" and identity. From

this have developed the confusions of typologies and categorisations: invert, pervert, bisexual, degenerate, and so on. There
are three possible ways to address the task of definition. The
first would be to suppose that all those who take part in
homosexual behavior are themselves "homosexuals", even if
the concept of "the homosexual" is not known to them or, as in
some cultures, does not exist. This is plainly unsatisfactory. The
second approach is to assume that the willingness to practice
homosexuality, whatever one's self concept, indicates an
"unconscious" or latent homosexuality, which is generally
repressed. This neo-Freudian approach is widely credited
among self-identified "homosexuals" themselves. As one respondent put it, "I don't see once you've been to bed with a
man how you can possibly say you're straight again." This may
or may not be the case, but in fact it merely displaces the
problem from the social construction of sexual ideologies to the
individual level. The third approach, and the one that I believe
offers the most satisfactory entree to historical work, would
concentrate on the social level, and would recognise the ways
in which sexual meanings and identities are historical constructs. A human identity is not a given in any particular
historical situation but is the product of different social
interactions, of the play of power, and sometimes of random
choices. The homosexual orientation may be strong, but its
significance depends on a host of factors that change over time.

An individual who could identify as "a homosexual" was
more likely to be absorbed into the homosexual subcultures, to
develop friendship networks and relationships (whether as
"kept boy" or as partner), and to use his homosexuality as a
way to rise in the world. One respondent, who took pride in
having been "passed from hand to mouth" in the 1930s, moved
from a poor working-class background in the North of England
to the centre of the metropolitan subculture as the companion
of a gregarious member of the London intelligentsia: "I was
never kept in the background, he wore me like a badge." The
respondent was fully prepared to adapt himself to his new
ambience, adopting a new accent and learning to "entertain":
"You weren't just taken out because you were pretty, you
weren't taken out the second time because you were just a
pretty face." Such a person is likely to be able to cope with a

wider range of sexual demands than one who is anxious to preserve a male and heterosexual self-image. (A Guardsman, for example, might charge extra for taking an "active" role in anal intercourse ["taking a real liberty"] but would baulk at taking a "passive" role.[76])

Reiss's classic study of delinquent youth has shown the sort of norms that may govern casual transactions. First, because the boy must make it clear to his partner and to himself that the relationship is solely a way to make money, the boy must not actively pursue his own sexual gratification. Second, the sexual transaction must be limited to specific sexual acts (for example, no buggery) or sexual roles ("active"). Third, the participants must remain emotionally neutral for fear of endangering the basis for the contract. Violence can be avoided as long as these rules are maintained but could erupt if they were threatened.[77]

Clearly, a variety of self-definitions is possible: as homosexual, as homosexual prostitute, as a prostitute but not homosexual, or as neither homosexual nor prostitute. One respondent, who admitted to having been maintained by a friend, was highly indignant at having, been described in a book as a "well-known male prostitute". Another interviewee, who as a Guardsman had had a large number of homosexual experiences and had followed these by a lifelong friendship with a homosexual man, was careful to explain that he was neither homosexual nor bisexual, but a "real" man who did it for the money.

The general impression that emerges from the nineteenth and early twentieth century is that the more casual the prostitution, the less likely was the individual to identify himself as homosexual or as a prostitute in the absence of any firm public categorisation. Conversely, the longer the person stayed in the homosexual subculture the more likely he was to accept its values and to identify himself as primarily homosexual. In each case the important factor was not an inherent propensity but the degree to which the man's activities and self-concepts were supported by the subculture. Prostitution flourished among the Guardsmen and among the messenger boys of Cleveland Street precisely because the ideology operating in both networks acted to sustain the men's existing self-images as heterosexual "trade".

■ Conclusion

It is difficult to define homosexual prostitution, dependent as it is on changing definitions of homosexuality and shifts in the homosexual subculture. Clearly, there was a vast difference between the casual act of prostitution in a public lavatory for a small amount of money and the conscious adaptation of homosexuality as a "way of life". The experiences are related, however, not so much by the fact of the sexual acts as by the experience of homosexuality as a stigmatised category. This opprobrium demanded strategies of adaptation and techniques of avoidance.

In this regard, male prostitution was strikingly different from the experience of female prostitution, for once the barrier to the initial act of prostitution has been crossed, the female prostitute could enter a world of values that served to support the choices she made and to reinforce the identity she was adopting. There was no comparable subculture of homosexual prostitution. For the young man who prostituted himself, the choices were effectively between retaining a conventional self-concept (and hence adopting neutralising techniques to explain his behaviour to himself and to others) or accepting a homosexual identity with all its attendant dangers in a hostile society. Once the choice had been made, however, full integration into the non-professional homosexual subculture could take place. In this there were advantages unavailable to the female prostitute. The asymmetry of relationship between the female prostitute and client was permanent, and the stigma of prostitution was lasting. In the homosexual world the patterns and relationships were inevitably more ambiguous; the "deviance" of prostitution was supplementary to the "deviance" of homosexuality.

4 Questions of identity

Sexual identity and sexual desire are not fixed and unchanging.
We create boundaries and identities for ourselves to contain what
might otherwise threaten to engulf or dissolve into formlessness.[1]

The very idea of a *sexual* identity is an ambiguous one. For
many in the modern world – especially the sexually marginal –
it is an absolutely fundamental concept, offering a sense of
personal unity, social location, and even at times a political
commitment. Not many, perhaps, say "I am a heterosexual"
because it is a taken-for-granted norm, the great unsaid of our
sexual culture. But to say "I am gay", "I am a lesbian", or even
"I am a paedophile. . . . or sado-masochist" is to make a
statement about belonging and about a specific stance in
relationship to the dominant sexual codes. It is also to privilege
sexual identity over other identities, to say in effect that how we
see ourselves sexually is more important than class, or racial, or
professional loyalties. As the song puts it: "I am what I am, my
own special creation", and in saying that we are ostensibly
speaking of our true essence of being, our real selves.

Yet, at the same time, we now know from a proliferating
literature that such identities are historically and culturally
specific that they are selected from a host of possible social
identities, that they are not necessary attributes of particular
sexual drives or desires, and that they are not, in fact, essential
– that is naturally pre-given – aspects of our personality.[2] So
there is a real paradox at the heart of the question of sexual

68

identity. We are increasingly aware, theoretically, historically, even politically, that "sexuality" is about flux and change, that what we so readily deem as "sexual" is as much a product of language and culture as of "nature". Yet we constantly strive to fix it, stabilize it, say who we are by telling of our sex.

It seems, as Jane Gallop has put it, that "Identity must be continually assumed and immediately called into question";[3] or alternatively, constantly questioned yet all the time assumed. For it is provisional, precarious, dependent on, and incessantly challenged by, social contingencies and psychic demands – but apparently necessary, the foundation stone of our sexual beliefs and behaviours. Over the past century, in particular, the search for identity has been a major characteristic of those whom our culture has designated as outside the norms, precisely abnormal: male homosexuals, lesbians, and a whole catalogue out of the pages of Krafft-Ebing (paedophiles, transvestites, bisexuals). The defining sexologists have provided the basis for a multiplicity of self-definitions, self-identifications; sexual identities.

So what do we mean when we use the term "sexual identity"? Does it offer us the "truth of our beings", or is it an illusion? Is it a political trap that imprisons us into the rigid and exclusive categorizations of those arbiters of desire, the sexologists? Or is it a necessary myth, the pre-condition of personal stability? Is it a snare . . . or a delusion, a cage . . . or an opportunity? The debate over sexual identity may seem arcane and specialized to some, especially when a great deal of the evidence of it comes from discussions about the execrated sexualities. It is, however, actually central to any discussion about sexuality in the modern world, illuminating its meaning and political connotations, which is probably why sexologists have been obsessed with the question, even when they did not use the term; and why modern sexual radicals find the concept so problematic, even as they deploy the term all the time.

■ Identity as destiny

Let us start by looking at the history of the concept itself. Its theoretical roots lie in the valiant efforts of the early sexologists, in the last decades of the nineteenth century and the early years of the present century, to capture the essence of that mysterious but all-powerful force of sex by categorizing its diverse manifestations, and thus attempting to make sense of its incessant flux. Tissot's awful warnings in the eighteenth century about the disastrous effects of masturbation had already marked a crucial transition; what you did was now more than an infringement of divine law; it determined what sort of person you were. Desire was a dangerous force which pre-existed the individual, wracking his (usually his) feeble body with fantasies and distractions which threatened his individuality and sanity.

This search for the primeval urge in the subject itself was the decisive step in the individualizing of sex. By the 1840s Henricus Kaan was writing about the modifications of the "nisus sexualis" (the sexual instinct) in individuals,[4] and other formative works followed: on the presence and dangers of childhood sexuality, the sexual aetiology of hysteria, and the sexual aberrations. Karl Heinrich Ulrichs, himself homosexually inclined, published twelve volumes on homosexuality between 1864 and 1879, an achievement that was greatly to influence Carl Westphal's "discovery" of the "contrary sexual impulse" by 1870, and Krafft-Ebing's wider speculations on sexual aberrations thereafter.[5]

But two moments are particularly important in this emergent discourse, imparting elements which were to inflect its course profoundly. The first was the impact of Darwinism. Charles Darwin's *Origin of Species* had already hinted at the applicability of the theory of natural selection to humans. With Darwin's *The Descent of Man, and Selection in Relation to Sex* another element was added: the claim that sexual selection (the struggle for partners) acted independently of natural selection (the struggle for existence) so that survival depended upon sexual selection, and the ultimate test of biological success lay in reproduction.[6] This led to a revival of interest in the sexual "origins" of individual behaviour, and a sustained effort to delineate the dynamics of sexual selection, the sexual impulse, and the differences between the sexes. Biology became the privileged road into the mysteries of nature, and its findings were backed up by the evidence of natural history in all its wondrous peculiarity and order.

The second decisive moment was the appearance of Richard von Krafft-Ebing's *Psychopathia Sexualis*, which went through various ever-expanding editions from 1886 to 1903. A compendium, in its last edition, of 238 case histories, it represented the eruption into print of the speaking pervert, the individual marked for ever by his or her sexual impulses.[7] His success amongst certain circles, of esteem as well as (especially in England) scandal, encouraged many others: between 1898 and 1908 there were over one-thousand publications on homosexuality alone. In his *Three Essays on the Theory of Sexuality* published in 1905, simultaneously a product of, and contribution to, the growth of sexual theory, Freud acknowledged the influence of nine writers: Krafft-Ebing, Albert Moll, P.J. Moebius, Havelock Ellis, Albert Schrenck Notzing, Leopold Lowenfeld, Albert Eulenburg, Iwan Bloch, and Magnus Hirschfeld.[8] To these could be added a host of other names out of the proliferating volumes of the time, from J. L. Casper and J.J. Moreau, to Cesare Lombroso and Auguste Forel, Valentin Magnan and Benjamin Tarnowsky, names dimly remembered today, some almost forgotten during their lifetimes, but significant influences nevertheless on the modern discourse of sexology – and of identity.

At the heart of their work was the firm belief that underlying the diversity of individual experiences and social effects was a complex natural process which needed to be understood in all its forms. This endeavour demanded in the first place a major effort at the classification and definition of sexual pathologies, giving rise to the exotic array of minute descriptions and taxonomic labelling so characteristic of the late-nineteenth century. Krafft-Ebing's *Psychopathia Sexualis* announced itself as a "medico-forensic study" of the "abnormal" and proffered a catalogue of perversities from acquired sexual inversion to zoophilia. Urolagnia and caprolagnia, fetishism and kleptomania, exhibitionism and sado-masochism, frottage, chronic satyriasis, and nymphomania made their clinical appearance via, or in the wake of, his pioneering cataloguing. Meanwhile, Iwan Bloch bravely stepped out to describe the strange sexual practices of all races in all ages. Charles Féré intrepidly explored sexual degeneration in man and animals. Albert Moll described the perversions of the sex

instinct. Magnus Hirschfeld wrote voluminously on homosexuality and later on transvestism, while Havelock Ellis's
Studies in the Psychology of Sex offered a compendious
encyclopedia on the variations of sexual behaviour and
beliefs.[9]

Second, this concentration on the "perverse", the "abnormal", cast new light on the "normal", discreetly shrouded in
respectable ideology but scientifically reaffirmed in clinical
textbooks. Ellis began his life's work on the "psychology of sex"
by writing *Man and Woman*. First published in 1894, but
subsequently reissued in much revised versions, it is a detailed
study of the secondary, tertiary, and other characteristics of and
differences between men and women. The study of the sexual
instinct in the writings of others became an exploration both of
the source of sexuality and of the relations between men and
women.[10] Just as homosexuality was defined as a sexual
condition peculiar to some people but not others in this period,
so the concept of heterosexuality was invented to describe
"normality", a normality circumscribed by a founding belief in
the sharp distinctions between the sexes and the assumption
that gender identity (to be a man or a woman) and sexual
identity were necessarily linked through the naturalness of
heterosexual object choice. All else fell into the vaguely written
but powerful catalogue of perversity.

The scientific fervour of these early sexologists is undoubted, but their efforts cannot be detached from the wider
currents of their time. Sexologists were something more than
agents of anonymous social forces or even of male imperatives
of sexual control as some recent feminists have argued. They
were also something less than neutral observers of the passing
sexual scene. One of the major roles of the sexologists was to
translate into theoretical terms what were increasingly perceived as concrete social problems. Problems concerning the
social definition of childhood are transformed into a prolonged
debate over the existence, or non-existence, of child and
adolescent sexuality. The question of female sexuality becomes
focused on discussions about the origins of hysteria, the
relation of the maternal to the sex instinct, and the social
consequences of female periodicity. A concern with the
changing relations between the genders produces a crop of

speculations about bi-sexuality, transvestism, intersexuality, and the reproductive instinct. A growing precision in the legal pursuit of sexual abnormality, with the abandonment of old ecclesiastical for new secular offences, leads to a controversy over the cause of homosexuality (hereditary taint, degeneration, seduction, or congenital) and consequently over the efficacy of legal control. As Krafft-Ebing noted, the medical barrister "finds out how sad the lack of our knowledge is in the domain of sexuality when he is called upon to express an opinion as to the responsibility of the accused whose life, liberty and honour are at stake".[11]

It was in particular through its relationship with the medical profession that sexology became respectable. A new thoroughness in the systematic exploration and understanding of the body in the nineteenth century in a very important sense made sexology possible by reshaping the questions that could be asked about the human (sexed) body and its internal processes. But the more dangerous side of this was that sexological insight could easily become subordinated to a medical norm. Many commentators on the nineteenth century, especially feminists, were noting the elevation of the medical profession into a new priestly caste, as the profession sought to consolidate itself, and as its principles and practices were utilized in social intervention, especially in relation to women. At best doctors, with few exceptions, generally acquiesced in stereotyped ideas of womanhood even if they were not militant in shaping them. At worst doctors actually intervened to shape female sexuality, through casework, organizing against women's access to higher education because of their supposed incapacity for intellectual work, supporting new forms of legal intervention and evidence, and campaigning against abortion and birth-control.[12]

The production in sexological discourse of a body of knowledge that is apparently scientifically neutral (about women, about sexual variants, delinquents, or offenders) can become a useful resource for the production of normative definitions that limit and demarcate erotic behaviour. By the 1920s the traditional social purity organizations, deeply rooted as they were in evangelical Christian traditions, were prepared to embrace a selection of insights from Ellis and Freud.[13] Today even the moral Right finds it opportune to legitimize its religious crusades by reference to sexological findings. Sexology has never been straightforwardly outside or against relations of power; it has been deeply involved in them.

Sexology, then, is not simply descriptive. It is at times profoundly prescriptive, telling us what we ought to be like, what makes us truly ourselves and "normal". It is in this sense that the sexological account of sexual identity can be seen as an imposition, a crude tactic of power designed to obscure a real sexual diversity with the myth of a sexual destiny. This seems to be the argument of Michel Foucault in at least some of his writings. His edition of the tragic memoirs of the mid-nineteenth-century hermaphrodite, Herculine Barbin, is a paean to the "happy" limbo of a "non-identity" and a warning of the dire consequences of insisting upon a true identity hidden behind the ambiguities of outward appearance:

> Biological theories of sexuality, juridical conceptions of the individual, forms of administrative control in modern nations, led little by little to rejecting the idea of a mixture of the two sexes in a single body, and consequently to limiting the free choice of indeterminate individuals.[14]

The seeking out of a "true identity" is here seen as a threat and a challenge, because it is not freely chosen. It claims to be finding what we *really* are, or should be, and as a result identity becomes an imposition.

■ Identity as resistance

Yet at the same time, as Barry Adam has put it, "identity is differentiation":[15] it is about affinities based on selection, self-actualization, and apparently choice. For the social theorists of the 1950s who first brought the question of "identity" on to the agenda of the anguished liberal west – Erik Erikson, Erving Goffman, *et al.*[16] – personal identity roughly equalled individuality, a reality to be struggled for in the hazardous process of maturation or against the awesome weight of the social, rummaged out in the interstices of society, amongst the crevices forgotten or ignored by weighty social forces. For the "sexual minorities" coming to a new sense of their separateness and individuality during the same period – male homosexuals and lesbians particularly – the finding of "identity" was like discovering a map to explore a new country.[17] As Plummer has put it, categorization and self-categorization, that is the process of identity formation, may control, restrict, and inhibit, but simultaneously they offer "comfort, security and assuredness".[18] This is the paradox of the sexological endeavour. It not only sought to regulate through naming; it also provided the springboard for self-definition and individual and collective resistance.

The theoretical seeds of this counter-discourse – what Foucault has called a "reverse affirmation"[19] – were sown within the sexological discourse itself. At the same time as he enthusiastically deployed the latest findings of the sexual science, Freud was working to undermine some of its founding assumptions. Though he never personally gave up the belief that a complex biological mechanism underlay the workings of the mind, his account of the dynamic unconscious and of the autonomy of psychic life served to challenge the fixity of all biologically given positions, the inevitability of sexual difference, and the essentiality of sexual identity.[20] Identity for Freud was clearly not an inevitable produce of inbuilt instincts; it was a struggle through which a tentative accommodation of conflicting drives and desires with the structures of language and reality was precariously achieved. If, *ab initio*, in some mythical point of origin, everyone was potentially bisexual and "polymorphously perverse", if a sense of being masculine or feminine was only attained through complex psychic struggles, never preordained, and if the line between normal and perverse development was so fine that the distinction constantly breaks down in adult life, how could the neat demarcations of the sexologists be true?

As Freud himself noted, homosexuality is a peculiarity of object-choice, not a constitutional, perverted instinct. The implication of this is that homosexuality is not absolutely separable from heterosexuality for "one must remember that normal sexuality too depends upon a reduction in the choice of object". Both are compromises from the range of possibilities rooted in the original, undifferentiated nature of the libido. It followed that:

> From the point of view of psycho-analysis the exclusive sexual interest felt by men for women is also a problem that needs elucidating and is not a self-evident fact based upon an attraction that is ultimately of a chemical nature.[21]

Looked at from the complexities of adult object-choice, achieved at the cost of sacrifice, renunciation, and pain, heterosexuality was no more naturally privileged than homosexuality.

Freud, of course, did not fully accept *that* implication. Even less so did many of his successors, who proceeded to erect on the subtleties of Freud's insights a dogmatic orthodoxy through which it became possible to argue that identity could only be satisfactorily achieved by adjustment to a pre-selected normality; all else was arrested development.[22] But the radical insights of Freud have remained as a constant reminder of an alternative way of conceiving of sexual difference and sexual identity. It is at this point that contemporary feminism and the radical sexual movements seek to reappropriate Freud as a guide to a non-essentialist theory of identity.[23]

An alternative (and sometimes complementary) route to the same point has been through the sociological and anthropological investigations of social life. At the most general they show that things had changed, that other times and other cultures lived their sexualities differently. More specifically, particular traditions of social investigation managed to normalize the peculiarities of sexual diversity and (from the contemporary Western view) moral unorthodoxy. The sociological tradition initiated by George Herbert Mead, and culminating in the proliferating modern anatomies of minority sexual subcultures, sought to understand sexual diversity in its own terms and to suggest that the hazards of social scripting and the chances of contingency and drift played as much part in sexual identification as anatomy or destiny.[24] Almost at the same time the social anthropological tradition most famously represented by Margaret Mead offered vivid descriptions of other patterns of socialization and personal identity, with the suggestion that perhaps all was not well with Western patterns of child rearing and family organization.[25]

The psychoanalytic and the sociological/anthropological discourses have their problematic elements, of course, but this is not the place to pursue them. The point that needs to be underlined here is that these two positions both sought to challenge the certainties of the "sexual tradition" by asserting the tentative nature of sexual identification. Identity could never quite be seen as destiny again.

These fractures in the theoretical certainty of sexological accounts have been paralleled, as already suggested, by other developments on the terrain of individual lives and subcultural response. It is very tempting to write as if sexology created the sexual subjects it so enthusiastically attempted to describe, and in the radical critique of sexology that has developed over the past decade this is an ever-present temptation.[26] But the actual history is far more complex and the role of sexology more subtle than this would suggest. What sexology did was indeed to set up restrictive definitions, and to be regularly complicit with the controlling ambitions of a variety of social practices. At the same time it also put into language a host of definitions and meanings which could be played with, challenged, negated, and used. Sexology, usually against its intentions, contributed through its definitions to the self-definition of those it sought to identify.

The most obvious reason for the emphasis on identity as resistance is that for countless numbers of people it was their sexuality that had been denied. Modern society is fractured by many divisions, along lines of class, race, religion, ideology, status, and age. These intersect with, and complicate, but do not cause, two other major divisions, of gender and sexual preference. It is only at certain times, in certain cultures, that these divisions become the central foci of political controversy. Though feminism has swept the West (and parts of the Third World) since the late 1960s, by and large more specific questions of sexual choice have not become major mobilizing issues. In countries like Britain and France active gay movements have successfully inspired thousands of people, but as political forces they have largely been subordinated to more traditional progressive politics. Issues of class and ideology weigh heavier than sexuality. But in the United States, where class loyalties are less fixed, politics more coalition-minded, "minority" politics (especially the struggles of blacks) better established, and social loyalties more fluid, sexuality has become a potent political issue, and sexual communities have become bases for political mobilization.[27]

This is not, however, merely another product of West Coast esotericism. A city like San Francisco has become a forcing house of sexual radicalism because, for a variety of historical reasons, it has been a refuge for those escaping the sexual ethics of moral America. San Francisco, Edmund White wittily argued, became "a sort of gay finishing school, a place where neophytes can confirm their gay identity".[28] Women and men have mobilized around their sense of sexual identity in such a place because it was in their sexuality that they felt most powerfully invalidated.

The resulting preoccupation with identity among the sexually marginal cannot be explained as an effect of a peculiar personal obsession with sex. It has to be seen, more accurately, as a powerful resistance to the organizing principle of traditional sexual attitudes. It has been the sexual radicals who have most insistently politicized the question of sexual identity. But the agenda has been largely shaped by the importance assigned by our culture to "correct" sexual behaviour.

But politicized sexual identities are not automatic responses to negative definitions. For their emergence, they need complex social and political conditions in order to produce a sense of community experience which makes for collective endeavour. Barry Adam has suggested that five conditions are necessary for this: the existence of large numbers in the same situation; geographical concentration; identifiable targets of opposition; sudden events or changes in social position; and an intellectual leadership with readily understood goals.[29] Each of these has been present in the emergence of the most spectacularly successful of politicized sexual identities, the lesbian and gay identities, over the past twenty years. The growth of urban subcultures since the Second World War especially in North America, but also in Europe, the emergence of general currents of hostility, from McCarthyism to moral panics around the impact of "permissiveness" and the sexual revolution, the growth of new social movements with radical sexual agendas, such as feminism and the lesbian and gay movements, not to mention the movements of the "sexual fringe" following in their wake – each of these has helped to make for the emergence of "the modern homosexual" now not so much a curiosity in the fading pages of sexology textbooks but the bearer of a fully blown social and human identity.[30]

■ Identity as choice

One difficulty is that not all homosexually inclined people want to identify their minority status – or even see themselves as homosexual. Sexologists, at least since Kinsey, have pointed out that there is no necessary connection between sexual be-haviour and sexual identity. According to Kinsey's best-known statistic, some 37 per cent of men had homosexual experiences to orgasm. But perhaps less than 4 per cent were exclusively homosexual – and even they did not necessarily express a homosexual identity, a concept of which, in any case, Kinsey disapproved.[31]

Sexual identification is a strange thing. There are some people who identify as gay and participate in the gay community but do not experience or wish for homosexual activity. And there are homosexually active people who do not identify as gay. Many black homosexuals, for example, prefer to identify primarily as "black" rather than "gay" and align themselves with black rather than gay political positions. Obviously, as Barry Dank has argued, "the development of a homosexual identity is dependent on the meanings that the actor attaches to the concepts of homosexual and homo-sexuality".[32] These processes in turn depend on the person's environment and wider community. Many people, it has been argued, "drift" into identity, battered by contingency rather than guided by will. Four characteristic stages have been identified by Plummer: "sensitization", when the individual becomes aware of the possibility of being different; "significa-tion", when he or she attributes a developing meaning to these differences; "subculturalization", the stage of recognizing oneself through involvement with others; and "stabilization", the stage of full acceptance of one's feelings and way of life.[33] There is no automatic progression through these stages; each transition is dependent as much on chance as on decision; and there is no necessary acceptance of a final destiny, in an explicit identity. Some choices are forced on individuals, whether through stigmatization and public obloquy or through political necessity. But the point that needs underlining is that *identity* is a choice. It is not *dictated* by internal imperatives.

The implication of this is that "desire" is one thing, while subject position, that is identification with a particular social position and organizing sense of self, is another.[34] This means that labels such as "gay" and "lesbian" increasingly become *political* choices, and in that process the sexual connotations can all but disappear. This is clearest in recent debates about a lesbian identity. Among gay men the issue has fundamentally concerned sex, validating a denied sexuality. In debates on lesbianism, on the other hand, there have been heated exchanges about the necessary connection of a lesbian identity to sexual practices. Conventional wisdom and, even more stringently, sexological expertise, have defined lesbianism as a sexual category. But increasingly it has been proposed by feminists as primarily a political definition, in which sexuality plays a problematic role. As Lillian Faderman puts it, "Women who identify themselves as lesbians generally do not view lesbianism as a sexual phenomenon first and foremost".[35] It is instead a relationship in which two women's strongest emotions and affection are directed towards one another. It becomes a synonym for sisterhood, solidarity, and affection, and as such a fundamental attribute of feminism.

Recent lesbian-feminist writers have understandably largely rejected the social-science and sexological definitions of lesbianism. Traditionally female homosexuality has been seen almost exclusively in terms derived from the experience or study of males. Male homosexuality has invariably been more closely observed and researched than lesbianism, partly because of its greater public salience, partly because it challenged the dominant definitions of male sexuality, and partly because female sexuality has usually been studied only in so far as it was responsive to male sexuality, and lesbianism was hardly understandable in those terms. More recently, ethnographies of female homosexuality have tended to adopt research techniques honed in investigation of male behaviour, concentrating, for example, on "coming out", contact patterns, sexual expression, and duration of relationships.[36] The impact of this has been to conceptualize lesbianism, like male homosexuality, as a specific minority experience little different in its implications from male patterns. This has been criticized in turn by some lesbian feminists as inevitably having the effect of establishing male homosexuality as the norm, while ignoring the implications of lesbianism for feminism.

The most powerful exponent of a "political lesbianism" position has been Adrienne Rich. In her influential essay "Compulsory Heterosexuality and Lesbian Existence" she argues that a distinction has to be made between the "lesbian continuum" and "lesbian existence".[37] The latter is equivalent to a lesbian identity but its character is not defined by sexual practice. It is the sense of self of women bonded primarily to women who are sexually and emotionally independent of men. In turn this is the expression of the "lesbian continuum" the range through women's lives of woman-identified experience. Such experiences go beyond the possibility of genital sex, to embrace many forms of primary intensity, including the sharing of inner life, the bonding against male tyranny, practical and political support, marriage resistance, female support networks and communities. Such possibilities of bonding between women are denied by "compulsory heterosexuality". Rich speaks of "the rendering invisible of the lesbian possibility, an engulfed continent which rises fragmentedly to view from time to time only to become submerged again".[38] "Compulsory heterosexuality" is the key mechanism of control of women, ensuring in its tyranny definition the perpetuation of male domination. Lesbianism is the point of resistance to this heterosexual dominance, its central antagonistic force.

Lesbianism is thus about the realization of the male-free potential of women, and in drawing on this essence, male definitions are cast aside. Rich sharply dissociates lesbianism from male homosexuality because of the latter's presumed relationship, *inter alia*, to pederasty, anonymous sex, and ageism. Lesbianism, on the other hand, she argues, is a profoundly *female* experience, like motherhood, and she looks forward to a powerful new female eroticism.

Against the passion and conviction of Rich's position three fundamental criticisms have been made.[39] In the first place it is based on a romantic naturalization of female bonds. It is not always clear whether Rich sees the "lesbian continuum" as a powerful solidarity that is there but constantly suppressed, or as a potentiality that could be realized in a mythical future, but in either case it stretches towards an essentialism about femininity which can distort the complexities of the construction of women, and obscure the necessary politics. As Cora Kaplan has noted, in Rich's scenario, "female heterosexuality is socially constructed and female homosexuality is natural. . . . Political lesbianism becomes more than a strategic position for feminism, it is a return to nature".[40] Nature is now benign, female and affectionate, sensual and creative, revolutionary and transcendent – and lesbian. But all the problems in naturalistic explanations of sex still come to the fore: its untheorized and untheorizable claims to truth, its trans-historical pretensions, and its strong moralism: this is how you must behave because nature tells us so. The result is a narrowing in political focus, and this is the second major objection. The view that attributes all women's oppression to "compulsory heterosexuality" suggests that somehow women are always socially controlled by men. Women are, in consequence, inevitably presented as perpetual sufferers and victims, beyond the possibility of resistance.

Finally, the political lesbian position tends to deny the specifics of lesbian sexuality. Lesbian activists such as Pat Califia[41] have suggested that there is a history of a specific lesbian eroticism which has been historically denied, and which has produced its own forms of struggle and in-stitutionalization. According to Ann Ferguson, Rich's view:

> undermines the important historical development of an explicit identity connected to genital sexuality. My own view is that the development of such an identity, and with it the development of a sexuality valued and accepted in a community of peers, extended women's life options and degree of independence from men.[42]

For such feminists, the elevation of female sexuality in general into a semi-mystical bonding, where bodily contact and genital pleasure are secondary or even non-existent, denies the possibilities of female eroticism, including the real potentiality of lesbianism.

This is not the place to enter a full discussion of these differing positions. The point that requires emphasizing here is that like the gay male identity, the lesbian identity has a political as well as a social and personal implication. That means that there need be no necessary relationship between sexual practice and sexual identity. On the other hand the existence of a specific identity testifies to the historic denial of a particular form of female desire – and the struggle necessary to affirm it. As with the homosexual male, the lesbian identity – whatever its "true" meaning – is historically contingent but seemingly inevitable; potentially limiting – but apparently politically essential.

▉ Identity and relationships

Identity is not a destiny but a choice. But in a culture where homosexual desires, female or male, are still execrated and denied, the adoption of lesbian or gay identities inevitably constitutes a *political* choice. These identities are not expressions of secret essences. They are self-creations, but they are creations on ground not freely chosen but laid out by history. So homosexual identities illustrate the play of constraint and opportunity, necessity and freedom, power and pleasure. Sexual identities seem necessary in the contemporary world as starting-points for a politics around sexuality. But the form they take is not pre-determined. In the end, therefore, they are not so much about who we really are, what our sex dictates. They are about what we want to be and could be. But this means they are also about the morality of acts and the quality of relations. We live in a world of proliferating "sexual identities" as specific desires (paedophile, sado-masochistic, bisexual) become the focus either for minute subdivisions of well-established notions (gayness or lesbianism) or spin off into wholly new ones. Can we therefore say that all identities are of equal value, and that minute subdivisions of desire, however apparently bizarre and esoteric, deserve social recognition on the basis of the right to erotic difference and sexual identity?[43]

Such questions have led to the development of what may be termed a "relationship paradigm" as opposed to the traditional "identity paradigm" as a way of thinking through some of the conceptual – and political – issues.[44] If, as many advocates of gay politics have suggested, identity is a constraint, a limitation on the flux of possibilities and the exploration of desires, if it is only an historical acquisition, then surely its assertion should be historically junked or at least modified.[45] The difficulty is to find a replacement that would equally satisfactorily provide a basis for personal coherence and social recognition. One possibility is to celebrate the flux, to indulge in a glorification of the "polysexualities" to which, on a radical reading of the Freudian tradition, we are all heirs[46]. The unfortunate difficulty with this is that most individuals do not feel "polymorphously perverse". On the contrary they feel their sexual desires are fairly narrowly organized, whatever use they make of those desires in real life. Moreover, a social identity is no less real for being historically formed. Sexual identities are no longer arbitrary divisions of the field of possibilities; they are encoded in a complex web of social practices – legal, pedagogic, medical, moral, and personal. They cannot be willed away.

The aim of the "relationship paradigm", in contrast, is not to ignore questions of identity but to displace them, by stressing instead the need to examine relationships. If this is done we can look again both at our sexual history and our sexual presence. Historically, we need no longer look for the controversial emergence of identities. Instead we can see the complicated net of relationships through which sexuality is always expressed, changing over time. Looked at from a contemporary point of view, we see not the culmination of a process of identity development but the formation of new types of relationships, validating hitherto execrated sexualities, in complex communities of interest around sex.

This is a very tempting position to adopt. In particular it potentially allows sexual thinking to move away from a "morality of acts", where all debate is about the merits of this form of sexuality as opposed to that, to an "ethics of choice", where the question becomes one of the quality of involvement and the freedom of relationships. This puts the whole debate on quite a new footing, allowing questions of power, diversity and sexual pluralism to be brought in.

The difficulty with the "relationship paradigm" is that it is offered as an alternative to questions of identity. This is a false antinomy. Identities are always "relational" in the general sense that they only exist in relation to other potential identities. More crucially, identities must always be about relationships: to ourselves, precarious unities of conflicting desires and social commitments, "composed of heterogeneous fragments of fossilized cultures";[47] and to others, who address us and call upon our recognition in diverse ways and through whom our sense of self is always negotiated. A sense of identity is essential for the establishment of relationships. As Foucault has argued, "sex is not a fatality, it's a possibility for creative life".[48] For a variety of historical reasons that possibility is mediated through a recognition of identity. Identity may well be a historical fiction, a controlling myth, a limiting burden. But it is at the same time a necessary means of weaving our way through a hazard-strewn world and a complex web of social relations. Without it, it seems, the possibilities of sexual choice are not increased but diminished.

5 | Against nature

I want to start with a simple statement: "The only thing that one really knows about human nature is that it changes. Change is the one quality we can predicate of it."

That's not me, Jeffrey Weeks, in the late 1980s – it's Oscar Wilde in the early 1890s.[1]

Put baldly like that, no one could dispute the words. But I am going to take this little quotation as my starting text because it seems to me that when we talk about sexuality we still do assume that whatever else changes, our sex does not. Man is a man, a woman a woman, a heterosexual is a heterosexual a homosexual is a homosexual, beyond the bounds of history, social transformation, conscious choice and political will.

The question of the nature of our sexual natures is at the heart of the debate about "essentialism" and "social construction" around which this conference has been structured. The majority of papers have attempted to show that this dichotomy is an increasingly arid and false one. I agree. It is a polemical distinction that all the time needs to be tested against the empirical evidence and re-evaluated in the light of our evolving theoretical sophistication.

At the same time I firmly believe that if we are going to be true to the protocols of an historical approach and to the methods of social science then we cannot afford to question

[This is the text of a paper given at the "Homosexuality, Which Homosexuality?" conference, Free University of Amsterdam, December 1988.]

everything else – conventional morality, oppressive social regulation, political prejudice and the like – and ignore what lies at the heart of all these things, the shaping and reshaping, in a complex and prolonged history, of the sexual categories we inhabit and the identities we bear. Before we can really understand and come to terms with who we are, and what we are to become, we need to understand how we are and why we are.

These sorts of questions, it needs to be said, are not peculiar to the growing but still relatively small world of lesbian and gay studies. They in fact pervade the whole debate about what we mean by modernity and post-modernity, how we characterise our age. It often seems to be suggested that a concern with the emergence and development of distinctive lesbian and gay identities – and with a problematisation of these identities – is somehow the product of esoteric schools of thought, or the malign influence of this or that over-hyped philosopher. The real situation is that the debate within our own ranks is a reflection of a much wider realisation that if everything else changes, why shouldn't sexuality.

What I want to try to do in this paper is show how our own local debates are shaped by, and in turn of course help reshape, a wider attempt to understand the flux and complexity of the modern world. To put it bluntly, we cannot understand homosexuality just by studying homosexuality alone. We would lack the language, concepts and basic historical understanding to do so.

I started of with a quotation from Oscar Wilde. Before going on, I should like to complete it: "The systems that fail," he writes, "are those that rely on the permanency of human nature, and not on its growth and development."[2] As I argued in my book, *Sexuality and its Discontents*,[3] appeals to nature, to the claims of the natural, are amongst the most potent we can make. They place us in a world of apparent fixity and truth. They appear to tell us what and who we are, and where we are going. They seem to tell us the truth.

And yet, as we know, there are so many truths. The textbooks used to tell us that homosexuality was unnatural. Lesbians and gay men, on the contrary, assert that homosexuality is natural. Who is to tell us which of these two "truths" is true? The fact is – I almost said the truth is – that, as Jonathan Katz has said, when we explore the histories of terms like "heterosexuality" or "homosexuality" we can only conclude that Nature had very little to do with it.[4]

This raises, to my mind, three types of questions: about the status of history; about the social and historical forces that shape subjectivity and identity; and about the implications of deconstructing the categories of nature, history and identity for contemporary politics. Each carries us beyond the confines of homosexuality in particular or sexuality in general. They pose critical questions about the character of the culture we live in.

■ History

Many of the political debates within the lesbian and gay movement, are played out in terms of historical argument. These debates have stimulated historical work. In turn, historical investigation had fed into political controversy. This is very characteristic of political movements generally, and of the new social movements – movements such as those of blacks, women, gays – particularly.

But there is a paradox in this: this resort to history comes at a time when historical studies themselves are in crisis, when the very possibility of "history" is itself being questioned. And the new social history, concerning, for example, women, blacks, and lesbians and gay men, is contributing to that crisis. Not only do the new histories pinpoint the omissions of past histories; they also challenge the fundamental categories by which the past has been understood.

Take for instance the impact of women's history. This not only provides evidence about those previously "hidden from history". It also asks difficult and challenging questions, about the sexual division of labour, about reproduction, about the categories of masculinity and femininity, and about the very dynamics of history.

In the same way histories of black people do more than provide the oppressed with an awareness of their roots or the continuity of their struggles. They also critically undermine. the conventional histories of for example, industrialisation, the material base of our modernity. Once you realise that the slave trade was a major element in the capital accumulation that led to Britain's, and later the world's, industrial revolution, then it becomes impossible to accept conventional accounts of the inevitability of "modernisation". Instead we must learn to accept that the modern world is rooted in exploitation and domination – and resistance to those forces.

Lesbian and gay history may seem, at first, less radical in its implications – especially if you are wedded to the idea that we are a "permanent minority". But not if you begin to see that our history is part of a much wider pattern of sexual regulation. Lesbian and gay history has led the way in challenging the conventional view that sex is a private, unchanging, "natural" phenomenon, outside the bounds of history. On the contrary, patterns of alliances, sexual taboos, family formation, sexual identities are at the very centre of the historic process, constitutive and not derivative.

The histories that have emerged over the past ten to fifteen years have, then, broadened the scope of historical work and challenged its conventional categories. Within the area of gay and lesbian history we may not always agree on the interpretation of events or trends. We may argue about the evidence for the existence of subcultures in this or that city during this or that century, or the continuity of identities throughout the Christian era. We may disagree on the timing of major transformations. But there can no longer be, to my mind, any dispute that these are legitimately historical questions.

Having said that, however, we are still left to decide what the purpose of this great endeavour of historical excavation is. We know it is popular, and widespread. There are many pleasures in delving in the archive, in reading old documents, in trying to find across the centuries the experience that echoes our own. But we surely do not do it for its own sake. That's the argument of the most conservative type of historian – though one, alas, currently resurging rapidly in Britain – who does not normally look very favourably on the sort of history we are interested in.

There are a variety of possible justifications. We could for instance see the past as a great romance, a story of great kings

and especially queens. This appeals to many a gay heart. Or
we could see in history a series of lessons, of opportunities lost
and of chances to be grasped, a cautionary tale to bolster
current struggles. Or there is the history that exhorts us to repay
the sacrifices of the past by battling in the present in order to
win the future.

Each of these, however, assumes a linear pattern, a grand
narrative of history in which the present is the undisputed heir
of the past.

What if however, we can no longer trust the grand
narrative? Lyotard has written: "I define postmodern as
incredulity towards meta-narratives".[5] This implies that many of
the old certainties – about the unity of history, about the
inevitability of progress, about the possibilities of scientific
understanding of the past and the present – no longer hold.

There are many reasons for this scepticism. Some are
epistemological: a questioning of the very possibility of
knowing something to be true. How do we know that what we
think we know is not "ideology"? Some are political: the
decline in the impact of progressive and Marxist views over the
past decade. Some are the result of the emergence of the social
movements themselves, which, as I have suggested, challenge
traditional notions, on Left and Right, about the dynamics of
history, the nature of subjectivity, and the configurations of
power and politics.

These currents are reflected widely in our debates. The
work of Michel Foucault has, for example, been influential on
lesbian and gay writing precisely because his work addresses
that scepticism and those problems.[6] He asks, for instance,
whether it is possible to see the history of sexuality as a history
of progress. Might it not be instead a history of invention of
categories of the sexual in order to regulate and discipline the
population?

In the same way he queries the legitimacy of the category
of science. To what extent can the claims of medicine, or
sexology, the self-proclaimed "science of desire", or of
psychoanalysis be regarded as neutral, value-free, precisely
"scientific", when you know their dubious origins in the murky
byeways of power?

It does not matter whether you agree with all his

interpretations. As it happens, I do disagree with many elements of his work. My point is that he has been influential because he encapsulates so many currents in our attempts to come to grips with the present, a present where so many of the old truths no longer seem to hold.

It is here with the present that we find a crucial justification of the new social history. Historians have always argued about the degree to which the present is the source of the questions we ask of the past, and the interpretation we impose on it. I think the really interesting thing about the new histories, of women, blacks, lesbians, and gays, is what it forces us to ask about the present. Increasingly we can see the present not as the culmination of the past but as itself historical: a complex series of interlocking histories whose interactions have to be reconstructed, not assumed.

This does not mean that we should only study the immediate past. My point is that this historical present is the product of many histories, some of which are ancient, some very recent. But what we should use history for – whether it is the history of homosexuality in Tahiti or in ancient Rome – is to problematise the taken for granted, to question our own culturally specific pre-occupations, and to try to see whether what we assume is natural is not in fact social and historical.

■ Identity

The sort of history I am advocating is one concerned with attempting to understand the conditions – intellectual, moral, material – which made possible our present. It is an approach that both reflects and contributes to a sense of the extreme diversity and complexity of the present.

At the heart of this understanding is an awareness of the range of possible identities that consequently exist – based on class, ethnicity, status, occupation, gender, sexual preference, and so on. We can all identify with many of these categories simultaneously, but which we give priority to depends on a number of historical variables. In times of heightened industrial conflict we might emphasise our class positions – as working-class or middle-class, and make fundamental political decisions on that basis. In periods of racial conflict and intensified racism our loyalties, as black or white, might well come to the fore.

Nietzsche noticed a hundred years or so ago that the "tropical tempo" of modernity was fragmenting traditional identities.[7] During the past generation the pace has speeded up dramatically. The effects can be seen throughout the West. It is no longer easy to predict in advance on what basis individuals or groups will make their fundamental social or political commitments. The decline of traditional working-class based political parties is one dramatic index of this.

What has this got to do with lesbian and gay politics? Over the past twenty years a number of conditions, products of the development of new social antagonisms and of new social movements, have made sexual identities critical battlegrounds. It is not an accident that the New Right in both the USA and Britain has targeted lesbian and gay movements and communities as sources of moral pollution and a measure of social decline. The new, openly gay identities proclaim the need for a new social space, for the primacy of sexual choice and for challenging the relations of power that fix us, like insects in a spider's web, in categories labelled "natural" or "unnatural". This is deeply threatening.

Leaving aside for the moment the question of whether sexual orientation and preferences are inborn or not, it seems self-evident that these social identities and intimacies based on sex are relatively new. They have not, could not have existed throughout the mists of time, because the conditions that gave rise to them just did not exist.

"Modern society is to be distinguished from older social formations," Niklas Luhmann has written, "by the fact that it has become more elaborate in two ways: it affords more opportunities both for impersonal and for more intensive personal relations."[8] Put another way, the growing complexity of modern society has made possible the rise of a range of possible sexual identities and of sexual communities. At the same time, these have become sites of conflict, giving rise to important social movements of the oppressed against a social order that seeks to dominate. "Community" provides the language through which the resistance to domination is expressed.

If we really want to understand and come to grips with the present, the crucial task is to unravel the tangled strands that made these things possible. Why has modern culture been so concerned with the details of individuals' sexual behaviour, seeking out in the way we look, the ways we dress, the ways we wave our hands or cross our feet, our ability or not to whistle, the true secrets of our being? Why does freedom of the individual, the cornerstone of Western values, always stop short of sexual freedom? Why do the main sufferers in the West from the effects of a particular virus get blamed for it?

We might disagree over our answers to these questions, but it is impossible to deny that these are critical questions to ask. In order to understand them we might need to explore the sustained rewriting of general sexual codes in the late nineteenth century as part of the response to urbanisation and the transformation of traditional values, as I have tried to do in various studies.[9] Or we might speculate on how and why patterns of female friendship came to be transformed into pathological categories, as Carroll Smith-Rosenberg and Lillian Faderman have done.[10] Or we might look at the gender revolution in the late eighteenth century as Randolph Trumbach is doing.[11] Or we might, like Alan Bray, explore the new language of friendship and desire, and the growth of the subculture of molly-houses in early eighteenth-century London.[12] Or we might even go back to the roots of our civilisation in ancient Greece and early Christian Rome to trace the source of our preoccupation with sex as truth, as Michel Foucault did in his last works.[13]

What we cannot do, if we want to understand why we are where we are is simply assume that nothing changes, that gays and lesbians have always existed as we exist today, that homophobia has always remained constant, and that there is a mystical continuity between our desires and their desires across the ranges of cultures and histories. We do not do it for any other aspect of our social existence. We should not do it for our sex.

My arguments so far have been in terms of the historical evidence. But behind them are a number of theoretical assumptions that I want to spell out. The starting point is the sustained challenge in Western thought during much of this century to the naturalness of "natural man", and to the constitutive centrality of the "unitary subject". The idea of the individual as a unified pre-constituted whole, the fount and origin of all things, has been at the heart of liberal ideology for centuries. The challenge to this concept has therefore been profoundly troubling. I suspect that much of the heat generated by the argument over sexual essentialism has its roots in a fear that respect for the individual will disappear in a welter of social explanations.

Nevertheless, challenged essentialism has been, in a wide variety of fields, and from a variety of sources – from radical sociology, structuralist anthropology, Marxism, and psycho-analysis, from the prophets of post-modernism, and from feminist scholars. Marx's view that the individual is a product of social forces, "an ensemble of the social relations", is ambiguous, but very troubling.[14] Even more subversive is Freud's concept of consciousness constantly undermined by unconscious forces outside rational control. Freud's work is, in its implications if not always in its application, the most radical theoretical challenge this century to the fixity of gender and sexual identities.[15] These insights have been taken up in turn by feminist writers disinterring the intricate connections between our psychic structures and the play of male power.[16]

Two conclusions flow from this work: first, that subjectivity is always fractured, contradictory, ambiguous, and disrupted; second, that identity is not inborn, pregiven, or "natural". It is striven for, contested, negotiated, and achieved, often in struggles of the subordinated against the dominant. Moreover, it is not achieved just by an individual act of will, or discovered hidden in the recesses of the soul. It is put together in circumstances bequeathed by history, in collective experiences as much as by individual destiny. As Alasdair MacIntyre has put it, "The unity of a human life is the unity of a narrative quest."[17] The elements of that narrative we find around us as much as in ourselves.

None of this must be taken to mean that I reject the importance of lesbian and gay identities. On the contrary, it is because I have a strong sense of their contingency, of the conditions of their existence in concrete historical circum-stances, and of their critical importance in challenging the imposition of arbitrary sexual norms, that I am deeply committed to their value, emotionally, socially and politically. Lesbian and gay identities, and the communities that made them possible, and which in turn they sustain, are the precondition for a realistic sexual politics in the age of AIDS.

And notice in this that I stress the importance of collective activity and of selfmaking. Modern lesbian and gay identities are not the results of sexological or medical labelling, let alone the invention of historians. They are the results of that process of definition and self definition that I described in my first solo book, *Coming Out*, and which has been the constant feature of homosexual politics over the past century.[18]

The word *community*, James Baldwin has written, "simply means our endless connection with, and responsibility for, each other."[19] This serves to remind me, at least, that the values of humanism, of collective endeavour, and of individual freedom do not depend on a supposed "natural man" or "woman", but on a politics and ethics that we shape for ourselves in this historic present.

■ Politics

Implicit in all I have said so far is a critique of an essentialist approach both to sexuality and to other social phenomena. By this I mean a method which attempts to explain the properties of a complex reality by reference to a supposed inner truth or essence, whether that essence is assumed to be the emanation of an individual, a class, a nation or "society". I believe that this is a reductionist method, in that it reduces the complexity of the world to the imagined simplicities of its constituent parts. It is also deterministic, in that it seeks to explain individuals as automatic products of inner propulsions, whether we dignify these as the products of the instincts, the genes, the hormones, or something altogether more mysterious.

Against this, I argue that the meanings we give to sexuality in general, and homosexuality in particular, are socially organised, but contradictory, sustained by a variety of languages, which seek to tell us what sex is, what it ought to be, and what it could be. Existing languages of sex, embedded in moral treatises, laws, educational practices, psychological theories, medical definitions, social rituals, pornographic or romantic fictions, popular assumptions, and sexual communities, set the limits of the possible. We, in our various ways, try to make sense of what we are offered.

The problem lies in their contradictory appeals, in the babel of voices. How can we make sense of these various languages, and translate them into a common tongue?

The pioneers of modern homosexual politics, from Ulrichs through Hirschfeld and Carpenter up to the early Mattachine leaders had no fundamental problem. They borrowed the common language of their contemporaries, especially the sexologists, and simply reversed their terms. The language of sexual science that, by and large, denied the validity of homosexuality, was turned into a language which asserted its naturalness.[20] This was supported by an optimism that the humane sciences would be able to convince people rationally of the justice of the cause. Through science to justice, Hirschfeld nobly proclaimed.[21]

The problem was, as I have suggested earlier, that science did not always see eye to eye with itself, let alone with the pioneers of reform. And today, with a clearer awareness that "science" provides no ready-made, let alone consistent, guidelines, we are more reluctant to give it too much credence. Recent liberation movements, Foucault observed in a late interview, "suffer from the fact that they cannot find any principle on which to base the elaboration of the new ethics (other than) an ethics founded on so-called scientific knowledge of what the self is, what the unconscious is, and so on."[22]

If, as I have argued, we can no longer base our values on nature; if we are no longer quite sure what the self is; and if we do not really believe in the unconscious, on what basis do we elaborate any ethics at all? "Where, after the meta-narratives", asked Lyotard, "can legitimacy reside?"[23]

This question, I believe, is at the heart of our contemporary political and moral dilemmas. We have all witnessed, over the past decade, a number of issues that have torn our communities apart. Conflicts between men and women, between black and white. Divisions over pornography, sadomasochism, butch-femme, paedophilia, about lesbian sexuality. Arguments, even, over our response to AIDS.

These are genuine divisions of commitment and conviction. I do not want to argue that they could or should have been subsumed under some cosy consensus. What I do want to pinpoint, however, is that we lacked even a common language to talk to one another with, let alone common analytical tools. What we got was a language of assertion on all sides.

The reasons for this are rooted in the very conditions which have made our identities possible. Communities are always about both identity and difference: what we have in common, and what differentiates us. Over the past few years it has often seemed that we wanted to fragment our identities and communities into even smaller splinters, each proclaiming its toe-hold on the truth.

This is, I suggest, a reflection on a smaller stage of a wider political crisis. Many of the old landmarks of progressive politics have been severely shaken during the 1980s. Liberal, radical, and socialist values have been under sustained assault, and have been further undermined by their collapse of confidence and failure of nerve. The New Right has been much more successful in capitalising on signs of social strain than the Old or New Left. A powerful wave of political and moral fundamentalism has tried to reshape the moral contours that many of us were beginning to take for granted in the 1960s and 1970s. In this context the new social movements have been thrown onto the defensive. Most tragically of all, at this very moment of political challenge, the AIDS crisis has provided the excuse and justification for a moral onslaught on the lives of lesbian and gay people.[24]

In the light of all this, how can we justify a theoretical position that problematises sexuality and sexual identity? How valid is it to propose a history that offers no easy consolations? Is it right to argue that people have a choice of social and political identifications? I can only answer that there is only hope for the future if we are able to confront the past and the present dispassionately. We must learn the contours and hidden obstacles of this historic present before we can realistically face the future.

What my attempt at a dispassionate understanding shows is

that the lesbian and gay identities are both constructed and essential, constructed in the sense that they are historically moulded and therefore subject to change, essential in the particular sense that they are necessary and in the end inescapable. Frank Kermode has made a distinction between "myth" and "fictions". Myth, he says, "operates within the diagram of ritual, which presupposes total and adequate explanations of things as they are and were: it is a sequence of radically changeable gestures. Fictions are for finding things out, and they change as the needs of sense-making change. Myths are the agents of stability, fictions the agents of change."[25]

In that sense, gay and lesbian identities are fictions, the necessary ways we mobilise our energies in order to change things. The emergence over the past few decades of large gay communities is one of the signs of a major shift in the political geography of the West. New "elective communities", or communities of interest and choice, have provided a focus for the growth of new sorts of social and political identification. As Cohen has argued, people map out their social identities and find their social orientations in the relationships which are symbolically close to them, rather than in relation to an abstract notion of society.[26] Through these relationships we are able to negotiate the complexities of the modern world, come to some understanding of it, and contribute to changing it. I don't think that's an ignoble achievement for a necessary fiction.

■ Conclusion

"A title must muddle the reader's ideas", Umberto Eco argues, "not regiment them."[27] I chose the title, "Against Nature", that was deliberately vague, and at the same time, I hope, provocative. Vague because I wanted an opportunity to range widely through a number of issues that have run through our discussions. Provocative because I wanted to challenge the idea that there is any solution to our current discontents in a search for what is truly natural.

That does not mean that I want to deny the importance of

biology, let alone deny the body. But I do want to insist that we can only fully understand our needs and desires when we grasp the social and historical forces, the unconscious motivations, and the personal and collective responses that shape our sexualities. Understanding where we came from seems to me the starting point for thinking about both the politics and ethics of sexuality, and where we want to go.

I have introduced a word we do not often use, but one we should perhaps use more: "ethics". By this I do not mean a set of prescriptions on right behaviour, but rather a set of values that can help to shape the way we live. I don't want here to offer my own thoughts on what the contents of these should be. But I'll end with two quotations which might just show the way my thoughts are going.

The first comes from the English philosopher, Bernard Williams. "No one", he writes, "should make any claims about the importance of human beings to the universe: the point is about the importance of human beings to human beings."[28]

I like that because it does not root its humanism in grand metaphysical schemes, let alone nature. Rather it stresses the ordinary, the commonplace, but the fundamental value we share, or should share: our need for one another.

The second quotation comes from Oscar Wilde again, in fact from the same essay from which the earlier quotes were taken, "The Soul of Man Under Socialism". Towards the end of it he writes: "Pain is not the ultimate mode of perfection. It is merely provisional and a protest. It has reference to wrong, unhealthy, unjust surroundings. When the wrong, and the disease, and the injustice are removed, it will have no further place."[29]

That was written nearly a hundred years ago. It has a poignant echo today. But its sentiments are no less true in the 1990s than they were in the 1890s.

That's the limit of my attempts to regiment your ideas.

6 Male homosexuality in the age of AIDS

> This much has become certain: deviancy isn't just a waste
> product of society, and nor is it intrinsic to the deviant subject. It
> is, rather, a construction, one which when analysed, says less and
> less about the individual deviant and more and more about the
> society – its structure of power, representation and repression –
> identifying or demonising him or her.[1]

■ Introduction

Anyone writing on homosexuality, especially male homosexuality, in the present does so under the shadow of HIV
infection and AIDS. This is not because it is a peculiarly "gay
plague", as the more scabrous of the popular press would have
it; nor, on a world scale, are gay men the chief experiencers of
the syndrome. As a newly recognised, and potentially devastating, phenomenon in the early 1980s AIDS would, moreover,
have made a major impact wherever it came from and
whomever were identified as its "victims". Yet, it is surely
undeniable that a major part of the symbolic power of AIDS
stems from its association with a still stigmatised sexuality and
an unpopular sexual minority in the industrialised countries of
the "advanced" West. To that extent, AIDS and homosexuality
are today intertwined in a difficult and complicated history.

"History", writer James Baldwin has said, "is the present –
we, with every breath we take, every move we make, *are*

History – and what goes around, comes around".[2] The association between AIDS and homosexuality, and its resultant effect on the way AIDS has been perceived and responded to by everyone from vocal minorities of the fundamentalist Christian Right to prison wardens, theatrical staff, restaurateurs, refuse collectors, undertakers, laboratory technicians, government officials and ministers, is shaped by a living history, by what can be best described as an unfinished revolution in attitudes to lesbian and gay life-styles.[3] Although attitudes to homosexuality have liberalised over the past two decades, the subject still trails clouds of fear, prejudice and misapprehension.

■ Changing laws: the secularisation of sex

The liberalisation of the laws affecting male homosexuality in Britain after 1967, despite their real importance in creating a new social space, have not fundamentally altered the formal, legal situation regarding homosexuality that we inherited from the nineteenth century. Certain sexual practices in certain situations amongst certain individuals ("consenting adults, over twenty-one, in private") have been decriminalised. Homosexuality itself, however, was not legalised, nor has it been given a status equal with that of heterosexuality.

In a host of examples from the age of consent (twenty-one for homosexual men, sixteen for heterosexual women) to the lack of job security, to difficulties encountered by homosexual parents in child custody cases – formal inequality and discrimination remains. AIDS has accentuated this deeply ingrained prejudice. An opinion poll conducted for London Weekend Television (24 January 1988) suggested that the proportion supporting the legalisation of homosexual relations had fallen from 61 per cent in 1985 to 48 per cent in 1988.

The formal legal changes are closely related to a second major shift, that can best be described as the "secularisation of sex". There has been a progressive detachment of sexual values from religious values, even among many of the religious. This has a long history, but a key element has been the process by which the initiative for judging sexuality passed from the churches to the agents of social and mental hygiene, primarily in the medical profession. Moral and medical matters remain, of course inextricably linked. You can still be judged simultaneously as both sick and immoral if you stray too far from the norms. Nevertheless, sexuality has become increasingly the province of non-religious experts – in sexology, psychology, welfare services and social policy as well as in medicine itself.

This can be seen in the changing ways in which homosexuality has been conceived. From being one aspect of a generalised moral state ("sin"), homosexuality increasingly came to be seen as a peculiar psychosocial condition, with its own aetiology, characteristic features and effects.

The belief that you will know the whole person by knowing his or her sexual desires and preferences has had curious results. On the one hand it lends itself to an approach where the caring professions can find a new responsiveness to particular individual needs. On the other, it can become another weapon in the process of labelling and fixing. If you know someone is "homosexual" then you can draw from the literature, and received prejudice, a host of assumptions by which that person can be placed microscopically, so a gay man can be immediately marked off as "promiscuous", "emotionally unstable", "incapable of full commitment" and so on. This has had dramatic effects in the "professional" approach to homosexuality.

Behind this is a less explicit but very widespread assumption that approval or disapproval of particular forms of behaviour is closely related to health or sickness, hygiene or disease. Disease sanctions still largely frame and organise many of our deepest sexual beliefs. It thus becomes easy for certain diseases that are connected, however tangentially in some cases, with sex, such as genital herpes, cervical cancer or more recently AIDS, to appear as punishments: nature's retribution for sexual misdemeanours. In the case of homosexuality, it has over the past couple of hundred years been seen both as a disease itself, and as a cause of disease, a contagion which, unless contained, will not only lead to the innocent young becoming homosexual but will cause even worse diseases.

Given this background, it is not surprising that in the 1980s the response to the emergence of a real disease, like AIDS, could be shaped and coloured by the lingering belief in the "disease of homosexuality". Moral entrepreneurs of the New Right in America and Europe have seized on AIDS as a justification for their moral crusade against homosexuality and the challenges to conventional family life that it is deemed to pose. As Mrs Mary Whitehouse put it in an attack on Channel 4 television for thinking of planning a programme on homosexuals: "Over recent years homosexuality has increasingly been represented as being perfectly normal. . . .But now the laughing is over. . . .Everything possible must be done to protect the public at large from this new and terrible threat [i.e. AIDS]".[4]

■ Identity and belonging

Modern lesbian and gay identities have emerged in this complex, and hostile, political moral and ideological environment. Not surprisingly, many men and women have borne the scars of social hostility and internalised self-hatred. Yet there is evidence over several hundred years, of what has been called a "reverse affirmation", of a sustained effort at self-definition in a constant resistance to the hostile norms. The modern lesbian and gay male identities have been created by this process of self-organisation and self-making, in a continuous history from at least the eighteenth century. The people that the early sexologists described were not figments of their pigeon-holing imaginations, but real people often seeking assistance or advice in an increasingly hostile world.

There was not, of course, a single homosexual identity developing. The homosexual experience then as now was varied, differing along lines of class, geography and even personal need and inclination. Sexuality is far too fluid, far too susceptible to diverse social influences to be understood through a single lens. The intricate patterns of same-sex interaction that develop in such closed societies as prisons illustrates clearly the range of potential roles and identities that emerge.

There has been no linear development of a single homosexual sense of self. Yet undoubtedly, behind the apparent and real diversity of needs, aspirations and life-styles, a strong sense of common identity embracing men and women has developed, predicated on a strong sense of common experience. Modern lesbian and gay identities are not products of any *essential* differences between homosexual and other people, whether rooted in biology, psychology or environmental shaping. Such identities are, however, ways of grappling with a legacy of social hostility, discrimination and prejudice, which have in turn produced a variety of different ways of life.

This is not a new phenomenon, as we have seen. Embryonically, at least, individuals have made claims for the priorities of their sexual natures over all other demands for several hundred years, and since the late nineteenth century there have been more or less explicit collective endeavours to affirm the value of homosexual choices. But it is only since the late 1960s that these have become open and forceful, associated with the emergence of new social movements of lesbians and gay men and the growth of gay communities.

A social movement can be seen as: "a kind of *ideological hatstand* – a single piece of furniture which, nevertheless, can accommodate a large number and wide variety of hats".[5] It would be difficult to see in these movements of "sexual minorities" a single ideological affinity, a common social, economic or even ethical location. Yet the lesbian and gay male movements, like feminism, have succeeded in all the major Western countries, and above all in the USA, in transforming the traditional debates on sex by asserting a new claim to self-definition and self-determination on all issues concerning the body and its pleasures.

At the heart of this has been an engagement with, and rejection of, the medical model of homosexuality, and of the right of experts to pin down a person's nature by defining his or her sexuality. The decision of the American Psychiatric Association in 1973 to withdraw homosexuality from its list of diseases was not a result of careful scientific reassessment. It was transparently a result of political lobbying and mobilisation, which reflected a new willingness on the part of homosexual people to break with hostile categorisation.[6]

The new social-sexual movements have created, in effect, an alternative public sphere of personal interaction, debates, publications and social and intellectual involvement that have challenged the certainties of what has been described as the "sexual tradition".[7] These movements, which start with "sexuality" and go beyond it in their impact, are by no means unified or coherent in either their means or ends. They have nevertheless introduced a powerful new element into contemporary politics, producing a new "vocabulary of values"[8] through which individuals construct their understanding of the social world, new constituencies for politicians and businesses to woo, and new "communities of interest", through which a sense of identity is affirmed and reaffirmed.

Such elective communities are not peculiar to sexual minorities. They are in fact an increasingly common feature of the social and political geography of Western industrial countries. Rapid social change has produced new social tensions and antagonisms, forms of domination and resistance, that have shaken traditional political forms and methods. This has given a new political saliency to lesbian and gay male politics in certain areas where numbers of homosexual people are concentrated and where politics are susceptible to interest group influence. Classic examples are provided by San Franscisco and New York. But even in Britain, where the political structure is still to a large degree organised around traditional party groupings and issues, lesbian and gay male activists succeeded in making some gains – for example, in the establishment of lesbian and gay units by some local authorities and by local government supported campaigns against job discrimination, biased sex education ind the like. These in turn have provoked a backlash, represented for example by Section 28 of the Local Government Act (1988), banning the intentional promotion of homosexuality by local authorities in the United Kingdom.

The precondition for this new assertion of community rights is a feeling that terms like "gay"and "lesbian" now "connote much more an entire life-style, a way of being in the world which only incidentally involves sexual activity with persons of the same sex."[9] People, as Cohen has argued, construct a sense of community "symbolically", making it a resource and repository of meaning, and a major referent of their identity.[10] The lesbian and gay male communities may in some areas have a recognisable geographical location (for example, parts of San Francisco, Greenwich Village, or West Hollywood). Specific physical sites may have a powerful influence as a forcing-house of a sense of identity and community: bars and bath houses have been identified as such. But much more important, the "community" exists as an idea, embodied in a series of activities (such as gay pride parades, festivals, candlelit vigils for people with AIDS, as well as more intimate and personal involvements) that constantly evoke, recreate and sustain a common belonging, whatever the class, racial, ethnic and gender differences that nevertheless exist and continue to flourish.

■ Sex and relationships

Homosexuality has become more than a personal predeliction, or a series of erotic practices: it is for hundreds of thousands of women and men a way of life. Yet this way of life is, inevitably, inextricably concerned with sexual needs and desires and with intimate relationships. It is the "sex" that is stigmatised (as the moral Right can unctuously put it, "we love the sinner but hate the sin"), and the relationships that are invalidated by continuing social hostility.

Not surprisingly, the emergence of a major health crisis associated with AIDS can be seen as more than a threat to individual lives and certain sexual *practices*. It is also, potentially, a threat to only recently achieved positive identities and to a whole way of life. As the full depth of the health crisis became apparent in the early 1980s, many lesbian and gay male activists resisted what they saw as the threat to their hard fought for sexual spaces. Attempts to close down gay bath houses, as in San Francisco in 1984, when it seemed likely that the spread of AIDS was closely linked with the easy promiscuity that they promoted, met fierce opposition, bitterly dividing the gay community. For some, the right to promiscuous sexual freedom was absolute: sexual promiscuity, it was argued, was the thread that bound the gay male community together. For others, the bath houses were an essential social space for the growth of a sense of identity and community.[11] But for both approaches, the closure of the baths, or their tighter regulation, were seen as new attempts to bring homosexuality once again under authoritarian social control.

For similar reasons, many in the gay community expressed deep suspicion of what was seen as the "remedicalisation" of homosexuality in the wake of the AIDS crisis. Given these attitudes, it is important to clarify what are the attitudes of the homosexual world to sexuality and relationships in order to disentangle the myths and stereotypes from the lived reality of gay life.

The first point that should need no underlining is that gay men, like other men, and women, display a huge variety of sexual needs. Kinsey made the point forcefully some forty years ago, when he observed with glee the example of two men who might live in the same town, meet at the same place of business, have common social activities, and yet experience enormously different sexual lives: if one had thirty ejaculations a week, the other one ejaculation in thirty years, the difference would be 45,000 times. "This", he wrote, "is the order of the variation which may occur".[12]

In a later study, carrying on the Kinsey tradition by looking in detail at the lives of homosexuals in the Bay area of California in the late 1960s, Bell and Weinberg concluded that:

> homosexual men and women cannot be sexually stereotyped as either hyperactive or inactive. Rather the amount of sexual activity they reported varied among individuals, with black males reporting more than white males, men reporting more than women, and (with the exception of the black males) younger people of either sex being more sexually active than their older counterparts.[13]

The frequency of sexual activity, then, varies enormously and this is hardly surprising. There is also some evidence that, other things being equal, it is not dissimilar to the male heterosexual pattern. Kinsey and some subsequent commentators noted that, on average, homosexual men had sex less often than their heterosexual brothers – partly because of the lower incidence of settled partnerships – but experienced it with a large number of partners. However, Blumstein and Schwartz in their survey of the sexual lives of different types of

American couples concluded that: "gay men have sex more often in the early years of their relationship than any other type of couple. But after 10 years they have sex together far less frequently than married couples. . . .Sex with other men balances the declining sex with partners".[14] What apparently distinguishes gay men from heterosexual is a greater number of partners or, to use the more loaded term, "promiscuity".

Even here, it is possible to exaggerate. Institutionalised promiscuity (in the form of prostitution) is largely a heterosexual rather than a homosexual phenomenon; and the most notorious form of gay promiscuity, the bath house, has had its heterosexual parallels, as in the Sandstone Sex Commune in California or Plato's Retreat in New York.[15] To balance this, many gay men do not, of course, have multiple partners.

Nevertheless, the 1970s did witness an explosion of what has been described as "public sex" amongst gay men, with the appearance in most of the major American, Australian and European cities (with the partial exception of Britain where the laws remained restrictive) of such facilities as bath houses, backroom bars and public cruising areas where casual, recreational sex with multiple partners became the norm. It was possible to see this development as a de-repressive challenge to the puritan tradition, as the forerunner of a Whitmanesque democracy,[16] or as the harbinger of sexual anarchy, which the American Moral Majority professed to see. Whatever its ultimate meaning (and by the mid-1980s the situation was changing dramatically in the wake of AIDS), it clearly represented some form of de-coupling of sex and intimacy, and a normalisation in a new way of sex as recreation and pleasure. It is too early to say whether this will survive the impact of AIDS. The increasing emphasis in the gay community on avoiding sexual practices (such as those, like anal intercourse, which involve the interchange of body fluids) which are likely to encourage the spread of HIV, and the corresponding emphasis on developing safer sexual activities, suggests that there is less likely to be a whole-scale move into celibacy or monogamy than a search for different forms of sexual pleasure.

This brings us to the second point: the link between sexual activity and emotional partnerships in the male gay community. There is no reason to think that, other things being equal, gay men find it more difficult to establish intimate emotional and sexual relationships than heterosexuals. Masters and Johnson provided evidence which suggests that in sexual partnerships gay men and lesbian couples tend to be more relaxed, more concerned with a full exchange of pleasure at all levels, less performance oriented and more sensitive to one another's needs than heterosexuals. They conclude that: "the committed heterosexual couple is handicapped sexually, first by theological covenant, and – a far more important second – by a potentially self-destructive lack of intellectual curiosity about the partner".[17]

On the other hand, gay couples tend to ask different types of questions about their relationships from heterosexuals. According to the detailed (Californian) study of gay male couples conducted by McWhirter and Mattison, heterosexual couples did not have to grapple with issues about roles, finances, ownership and social obligations in the same way as gay men do, and were less preoccupied with acceptance by family and neighbours. Heterosexual couples lived with some expectation that their relationships would last "until death do us part", while gay male couples wondered if theirs would survive.[18] On the other hand, gay male relationships were potentially as long lasting, with a patterned development through successful stages of intimacy that is unlikely to be dissimilar to the heterosexual pattern. And where gay male relationships do end, it is necessary to ask if that is any different from the development of a growing heterosexual pattern of divorce and remarriage. As one of Berger's respondents put it: "My sister has gone through three husbands and I have gone through three lovers. The difference is that I have remained good friends with all my ex-lovers".[19] Where gay male relationships do seem to differ substantially, however, is in attitudes to sexual activity outside the partnership. McWhirter and Mattison speak of "fidelity without sexual exclusivity" as a normal pattern.[20]

Expectations of fidelity are high among gay men, but they are measured in terms of commitment, not sex. This does not mean that the fact of sex outside the partnership is un-problematic. When the option is exercised, feelings of jealousy, fear of loss and abandonment, and anger can easily erupt. But there seems to be a greater willingness to accept that intimacy and long-term commitment do not necessarily go hand in hand with sexual loyalty.

This not a peculiarly homosexual preoccupation. The "desacralisation" of sex in the contemporary world, the recognition that sex in itself does not carry a moral weight or obligation, has opened up the way to seeing sex as a matter of choice; what matters is less the nature of the act than the quality of the experience and the context in which it takes place. This is an ambiguous change. On the one hand it opens the way to the full incorporation of sex into the world of commodities and consumerism so that potentially nothing retains any special meaning. Every act can be something to be purchased, consumed and thrown away. This has been one aspect of some feminist criticism of the "sexual revolution". On the other hand, the breakdown of old restraints has opened up the possibility of different forms of relationships, alternative ways of living together, and new possibilities of intimacy. Sexuality and sexual relationships are in a state of unprecedented flux. It is indicative, for example, that Blumstein and Schwartz's examination of American couples places the traditional pattern as only one amongst four viable forms: the married couple, the cohabiting heterosexual couple, the lesbian couple, and the gay couple.[21] In such a situation, gay relationships can come to be seen less as marginal than as one among many ways of living together.

This brings us to a third point that needs underlining: the central place of *relationships* in the gay community. Bruce Voellar[22] has argued that much of the work of the first decade of the gay rights movement was less concerned with questions of sexuality as such and more with the creation of "surrogate families", composed of other gay persons for mutual support. We may quibble with the "surrogate", because this implies an attempt simply to replicate a traditional family pattern; the evidence does not suggest this. On the other hand, there are clear signs of inventiveness and adaptability in the development of rich and fulfilling friendship networks. As Bell and Weinberg observed: "it would appear that homosexual men and women are apt to have more close friends than heterosexuals do".[23]

In fact relationships are often more complex and critical to many people's lives than the conventional term "friendship" would indicate. They range from the sharing of property to mutual support in ill health and misfortune, to caring in old age, to simple relationships of affection and openness. For many gay people these relationships can be more than substitutes for conventional couple relationships; they are positive ways of leading a supported and involved life.

Some recent studies of ageing among gay men support this hypothesis. Berger for example, argued that gays need to learn to master the "crises of independence" earlier than do heterosexuals, as they are forced to risk breaking with family and friends when they come out as gay.[24] This experience, in turn, helps them to negotiate the crises of middle and old age more successfully. Whereas heterosexuals may experience the first crisis of independence in old age, homosexuals have become used to coping without their family of procreation, and are less likely to have become totally dependent on a single relationship: they have in place a more secure network of friends.

This is counterbalanced, of course, by the hazards of prejudice and discrimination. The law does not readily recognise gay partners as next of kin; and in cases of medical emergency, hospitals will often refuse visiting rights to those not connected by blood. Wills, life insurance protection, transfer of property, appropriate recognition of grief and loss, all pose real difficulties for gays facing ill health or death. These problems can become acute in a situation where the illness itself carries a stigma – as HIV/AIDS does. Nevertheless, what is remarkable is that, contrary to the traditional pathologising accounts, lesbian and gay people have been able to create, in the face of difficult social circumstances, resilient and enduring relationships that provide the real bonds that knit the gay community together.

■ Conclusion

An examination of the recent history of homosexuality casts light on two particular elements. The first is the centrality of collective activity. The emergence of a distinctive sense of lesbian and gay male identity is predicated upon the existence of the strong social ties that constitute the lesbian and gay community. This now represents a dense network of loyalties, obligations, friendship ties, social involvements, institutions, meeting places, self-help groupings, newspapers, and so on. It exists symbolically, as a form of identity and belonging. It exists materially as well, in a rich series of activities.

In recent years this collective self-consciousness has been tested to the full. AIDS has had many consequences, but not least among them is its testing of the reserves of strength of the lesbian and gay community. What is surely remarkable is that the community has proved to be resilient and has met the challenge head on. The development of self-help groupings like Gay Men's Health Crisis in New York or the Terrence Higgins Trust or Body Positive in Britain, all as the result of gay initiative, testify not only to a healthy readiness to confront problems, but also to the strong common ties that have been built up over the previous decades. The second element that needs stressing follows from this. I have argued that the "modern homosexual" is in a real sense an "invention" of the past couple of hundred years. The word itself did not exist until the later 1860s. The concept barely existed even in the minds of the "experts" until the early part of the century. An awareness of common identity had a slow and uneven spread among homosexually inclined women and men during this century. Yet today we can see a strong lesbian and gay presence that is not simply a product of social change but an active participant in furthering change. This is the significant point.

It would be wrong to suggest that there has been an easy evolution; but even more wrong to believe that history has now reached an end. The AIDS crisis poses not just a tragic threat but also a challenge and an opportunity. The changes that have been observed in the male gay community in recent years, particularly with the widespread promotion and adoption of "safer sex" practices, suggest that the process of adaptation and development of personal life-styles is continuing. Many gay people have reported, moreover, that the health crisis has strengthened their sense of identity and belonging to their chosen community. There is no reason to believe that these are isolated responses. The whole history of the past hundred years or so suggests that homosexual people will respond to the opportunity and face the challenge.

7 AIDS:
the intellectual agenda

All diseases have social, ethical and political dimensions. Diseases affect individuals, not abstract entities or collectivities, and affects them in variable ways, according to their general social condition and bodily health. What makes disease culturally and historically important, however, is the way in which meanings are attached to illness and death, meanings and interpretations which are refracted through a host of differing, and often conflicting and contradictory social possibilities. These shape the ways we interpret illness, and therefore organise the ways in which we respond.

There is a long tradition of connecting disease with moral issues: "sickness" and "sin" are terms which have long been linked, and often interchangeably, especially in periods of heightened social anxiety. So there is nothing intrinsically new in the ways in which AIDS has been culturally interpreted, signified and given strong moral meaning. Some time ago, Susan Sontag famously deplored the tendency for illness to become a metaphor – a process whereby the specifics of individual suffering are lost in a welter of social fantasy.[1] More recent historical studies have shown that sex-related diseases have gained a particularly powerful grip on the social imagination: in nineteenth century England, for example, syphilis became known as the "social disease", while its supposed source of infection, prostitution, was known as the "social evil".[2]

At the same time, other diseases became the bearers of

114

sexual meanings. Frank Mort's book *Dangerous Sexualities*[3] has demonstrated very clearly that at least from the early nineteenth century responses to epidemics of various types have been shaped by a host of moral assumptions about the sexual behaviour of those they affected. These assumptions insensibly infiltrate medical theories and responses, and in turn shape and reshape popular attitudes. Illnesses such as cholera and typhoid, TB and cancer, have all carried a heavy burden of moral anxiety, and have attained a massive symbolic significance, because attempts have been consistently made to link individual failings (especially with regard to sex), social marginality, and moral inadequacy with a tendency to acquire one or other of them.

In one sense, then, the social response to AIDS has been governed by the same tendency to moral inflation that has characterised a number of other life-threatening diseases in the past. But there are also important differences, differences which reveal much about the times we are living in. In the first place we are living through this disease, and the ways in which it is affecting us, and people we know and love, and the communities we inhabit. Second, we are living in a culture which at one time seemed to promise the triumph of technology over the uncontrollable whims of nature, and yet here is a new virus that has apparently confounded science. As Neil Small put it "The impact of AIDS is essentially linked with modernity – its virulence and relative untreatability lead us to question a cornerstone of faith in science, experts and progress".[4]

Third, and perhaps most important, AIDS has become the symbolic bearer of a host of meanings about our contemporary culture: about its social composition, its racial boundaries, its attitudes to social marginality; and above all, its moral configurations and its sexual mores. A number of different histories intersect in and are condensed by AIDS discourse. What gives AIDS a particular power is its ability to represent a host of fears, anxieties and problems in our current, post-permissive society.

My aim in this chapter is not so much to provide an exhaustive explanation of why this is the case as to offer an intellectual framework within which we can identify the main forces at work. I shall begin by identifying the main phases of the social reaction to AIDS thus far in its history. Through this it will be possible to characterise the present. Put briefly, my argument will be that AIDS already has a complex history which irrevocably shadows the way we think and the way we act. I will then discuss some of the key issues that need to be addressed in responding to the AIDS crisis. These provide the outlines of an agenda for historical and social science research, and for the political and social approaches needed to live with HIV and AIDS.

■ Responses to AIDS

Looking back over the years since 1981, when AIDS first emerged as a new and devastating collection of diseases there is a potential danger that we will see the period as a monolithic whole, characterised by a deepening crisis and geometric spread of the disease. Emotionally, certainly, it sometimes feels like that, and in a sense recent political responses are based on the premise that only a deepening crisis could justify the actions that governments were forced to take in the late 1980s. But it is not ultimately useful to try to understand the history of AIDS in these terms. There have, in fact, been at least three distinct phases in the social responses to AIDS so far. The boundaries between these are neither clear-cut, nor absolute. Many features recur throughout, though with different weightings and emphases. Nevertheless, each period has its own distinct characteristics. Each needs looking at in turn.

☐ The dawning crisis (1981-2)

There is, of course, a prehistory to AIDS stretching back to the mid-1970s or earlier, and by 1980 the dimensions of the potential crisis were already beginning to appear in statistics recording health problems amongst gay men.[5] It was not until the summer of 1981, however, that these developments became an embryonic public issue. It was then that the first stories began to appear in medical journals and in the gay press reporting the emergence of mysterious new illnesses among gay men in the USA. There were three major features of this first phase.

First, there was an awakening sense of anxiety amongst those most immediately affected, mainly gay men in the American cities with large gay populations (New York, San Francisco and Los Angeles), but also members of the Haitian community in America, and haemophiliacs. At the same time, this was accompanied by a certain moral and sexual complacency which suggested that this new illness was either a scare story or a minority problem. This was the period when gay men began debating whether they needed to change their sexual habits, when fears began to emerge about the possible effects of AIDS on the achievements of gay liberation, and when those who advocated sexual abstinence or safer sex[6] were denounced for delivering the lesbian and gay community back into the embrace of the medical discourse from which it had all too recently escaped.[7] Because the cause, or causes, of the syndrome of illnesses were unknown, so the responses were contested and confused.

Second, there were exploratory medical and scientific attempts to define the nature, epidemiology and significance of this new phenomenon. These can be traced in the evolution of the terminology used to describe the syndrome – from "the gay cancer" to GRID (Gay-Related Immune Deficiency), to the eventual acceptance in 1982, of the acronynm AIDS, the Acquired Immune-Deficiency Syndrome – a shift, at least in the scientific world, from the initial identification of the disease with the community that first experienced it to a recognition of a more general danger. The four Hs were rapidly identified as "risk categories": homosexuals, heroin users, haemophiliacs and, most controversially of all, Haitians. Allied to this shift were certain problems. Too narrow a definition of AIDS, relating only to its terminal stages, threatened to encourage the view that the illness was invariably fatal, and resistance to it hopeless. But too broad a definition, to cover all of what became known as AIDS related conditions and the presence of sero-positivity, threatened equally to obscure important distinctions. Alongside these debates, feeding them and confusing them, was the beginning of a highly competitive and personally

poisonous race to identify the cause of AIDS, and find a cure –
a race tainted by the lure of Nobel laureates, high prestige and
profits.[8]

Third, this period saw the development of the characteristic
style of governmental response that was to dominate the next
phase: widespread indifference. There were many factors
influencing this, including the coincidence that in the USA, and
to a lesser extent elsewhere, the onset of AIDS occurred at the
very moment that the Federal Administration was intent on
cutting public expenditure. But over and above this, there was
the overwhelming fact that AIDS was a disease that seemed to
be confined to marginal, and (with the possible exceptions of
haemophiliacs) politically and morally embarrassing, communities. More particularly, it was seen as a gay disease at a
time when the view was being sedulously cultivated that the
gay revolution had already gone too far.[9]

☐ Moral panic (1982-5)

The marginality of people with AIDS, and its identification as a
"gay plague", were central to the second phase which occurred
between 1982-5, that of moral panic. Moral panic occurs in
complex societies when deep rooted and difficult to resolve
social anxieties become focused on symbolic agents which can
be easily targetted. Over the past century sexuality has been a
potent focus of such moral panics – prostitutes have been
blamed for syphilis, homosexuals for the Cold War and
pornography for child abuse and violence. Whilst the concept
of a moral panic does not explain why transfers of anxiety like
these occur – this has to be a matter for a historical analysis – it
nevertheless offers a valuable framework for describing the
course of events.[10]

From about 1982, AIDS (now identified as a distinctive set
of diseases with definable if as yet not precisely known,
causative factors), became the bearer of a number of political,
social and moral anxieties, whose origins lay elsewhere, but
which were condensed into a crisis over AIDS. These included

issues such as "promiscuity", permissive lifestyles and drug taking. In this particular context, Paula Treichler has made the point that whilst safer sex might protect us from the virus, it can not protect us from this expanded meaning of "AIDS", which now becomes a potent symbolic agent in its own right.[11]

This period of moral panic was characterised by a number of features. First, it saw the rapid escalation of media and popular hysteria. This was the golden period of the New Right and Moral Majority onslaught in the USA, with leading lights claiming to see in AIDS God's or nature's judgment on moral decay. This was the period also when the term "gay plague" became the favourite term of tabloid headline-writers.[12] This was the time when people with the syndrome were blamed for it. These were the years which witnessed the widespread appearance of "rituals of decontamination": lesbians and gay men were refused service in restaurants, theatre personnel refused to work with gay actors, the trash cans of people suspected of having AIDS were not emptied, children with the virus were banned from schools, and the dead were left unburied. "AIDS" as a symbolic phenomenon thereby grew out of, and fed into, potent streams of homophobia and racism.

Second, during 1983 and 1984, despite rather than because of the frantic international rivalry, the Human Immuno-deficiency Virus (HIV) was at last identified and given its agreed name. This opened new opportunities for responding to the diseases; but it also, inevitably, signalled the formidable difficulties in producing a vaccine against it, or a cure for it.

Third, this period saw the emergence of a massive self-help response from the communities most affected, and particularly from the lesbian and gay community. Organisations such as Gay Men's Health Crisis in New York or the Terrence Higgins Trust in London emerged as much more than special interest pressure groups. They became, in the absence of a coherent national strategy, the main vehicles of health education and social support. As Robert Padgug[13] has suggested, one of the most striking features of AIDS has been the unusual, perhaps unique degree to which the group that was most affected by it took part in all aspects of its management. This included the provision of social aid and health care to people with AIDS, whether gay or not, the conduct of research, lobbying for funds and other government intervention, the creation of educational programmes, and negotiation with legislators and health insurers.

While governments throughout the West remained largely silent, these self-help groupings achieved remarkable results in safer-sex education. The identification of the virus, and its likely modes of transmission, made it clear that it was wrong to talk of risk categories; there were instead *risk activities*. And risk itself could be reduced by relatively simple measures – by using condoms, by cutting out certain unprotected sexual activities, and by not sharing needles if you were an injecting drug user. What was needed above all was education on prevention. Whilst national governments were as yet reluctant to undertake this, others by necessity picked up the candle, and with notable success too. By 1984, to take one example, 95 per cent of gay men in San Francisco knew how AIDS was transmitted and knew the risk guidelines. To take another, sexually transmitted disease rates amongst gay men began to drop significantly as safer sex guidelines were codified and made readily available.[14] This was almost entirely due to work within the lesbian and gay community itself.

☐ Crisis management (1985 to the present)

1985 was the turning point. Partly this was a result of chance factors, the most important of which was the well publicised illness and death of Rock Hudson which dramatised the impact of the disease, and the inadequacy of American facilities: Hudson went to Paris, where in fact the virus had first been isolated, for treatment. The major reason, however, was the increasing evidence that AIDS was not just a disease of execrated minorities but a health threat on a global scale, and one which in world terms, largely affected heterosexuals. This initiated the period in which we now live, one in which the dominant response has been crisis management.

There are a number of key characteristics of this period. First, governments began to respond on a scale that approximated a little more to the magnitude of the crisis. As Randy Shilts has reminded us, by the time President Reagan had delivered his first speech on AIDS, six years into the crisis, over 36,000 Americans had been diagnosed with the syndrome, and some 20,000 had died.[15] From 1985, however, we can trace a new urgency in governmental response. In Britain there had been virtually no government response until 1984. Only then was there intervention to prevent the further contamination of the blood supply (and by implication, prevent the spread of AIDS to "the innocent"). In 1985, the government took powers compulsorily to detain in hospital people who were perceived as likely to ignore medical advice and were at risk of spreading the disease. Both these measures were dictated by a fear that AIDS might infiltrate the so-called general population. But in 1985 only £135,000 was set aside by the government for education and prevention. By the end of 1986, with the dramatic adoption of a new policy in November of that year, this had leapt a hundredfold.[16]

This change of heart was not the result of a sudden excess of altruism. The key factor was the generalisation of risk, and the key precipitating event came with the publication of the US Surgeon-General's report on AIDS in October 1986. This allowed AIDS to achieve the "critical mass" to become a major issue on the official social agenda.[17]

The new policy was organised around a sustained public campaign aimed at preventing the spread of the virus – this is the second major characteristic of the period. There was a certain historical irony therefore in the fact that the shift in policy was inspired by an arch-conservative Reaganite appointee in the USA (the Surgeon-General, Dr C.E. Koop), and led by the Thatcher government in Britain at a time when its moral agenda reasserting traditional family values, rolling back the tide of "permissiveness", and sharply defining the limits of sex education in schools, was unfolding. For a policy of prevention aimed not only to warn the general population about the risks, but to work with, and to take advantage of experience generated within the very lesbian and gay community it elsewhere sought to challenge.[18]

A third characteristic flowed from this shift in policy, accentuating trends already in existence: the period witnessed a significant "professionalisation" of organised responses to AIDS. In part, this involved a professionalisation of the self-help groupings themselves, as public funds flowed into them, and demands upon their services increased. A new alliance, not without its problems, between the medical profession and the communities at risk began to be forged. At the same time, a different sort of professionalism began to emerge which actively distanced itself from the lesbian and gay community as AIDS became seen as a universal problem. Moreover, as Silverman points out, as a consequence of HIV, genito-urinary medicine and allied medical practice moved from being Cinderella specialisms to well-funded, high status work.[19]

As if by a necessary reflex, this period also saw the rapid growth of alternative health care and therapies, as people with AIDS and HIV infection have sought to retain responsibility for the condition of their own bodies.[20]

Finally, the period has seen a deepening of the health crisis itself, as the dimensions of AIDS and HIV infection have become clearer and its costs to individuals and society were widely understood. Today we live in a situation where there is widespread understanding of the nature of AIDS and its mode of transmission; where some of the early fear and loathing has perhaps diminished; but where prejudice and discrimination against people with AIDS and HIV is widespread; where the disease has been defined as a major public issue deserving of public funding, though still not to the degree necessary; and where the very term AIDS still carries with it a symbolic weight it should not have to bear.

■ Issues

I now want to turn to a number of key issues raised by this attempt at a typology of the AIDS crisis so far, because these provide the agenda which must be addressed if we want to move beyond crisis management towards a more rational and long-term strategy. As Cindy Patton has remarked: to those outside AIDS organising, AIDS continues to be viewed primarily as a single issue. To those inside, the range and complexity of issues tapped seems almost impossible to combat.[21]

It is the complexity of these issues which most needs discussion because it will help us grasp why AIDS carries such a burden of meaning. I want to isolate a number of critical themes which illustrate this complexity.

☐ Historical and social science issues

The key problem here is: why did this disease, at this particular time, become the symbolic carrier of such a weight of meaning. Other new diseases have emerged in the recent past – Legionnaire's Disease is the best known – and there have been epidemics of others. Some, such as genital herpes and hepatitis B, have caused major bouts of anxiety and much social philosophising, in ways that prefigure the reaction to AIDS. But it was AIDS that became the disease of the 1980s, and it was AIDS that came to public consciousness as the twentieth-century plague.

One of the most important factors behind this was the association of AIDS with marginal populations. As a disease that appeared to disproportionately affect black people and gay men, anxiety about AIDS was thereby able to draw on pre-existing tensions concerning race and sexual diversity, ones which were already coming to the fore in the early 1980s in the contemporary political discourse of the New Right.[22] But this only pushes the question a little way back. These factors themselves clearly relate to wider anxieties. At the heart of these, I would argue, are deeply rooted fears about the unprecedented rate of change in sexual behaviour and social mores in the past two generations.

It is now quite well established that sexuality has been at the heart of public discourse since at least the early nineteenth century, as a barometer of social anxiety and a conductor of social tensions. Sexuality has become both central to personal identity and a key element in social policy.[23]

The response to AIDS was able to draw on a variety of beliefs and concepts which often reach back into the mists of time, or at least the sexual debates of the last century. The definition of AIDS as a medico-moral problem echoes the debates in the 1830s and 1840s in England about the environmental factors associated with the spread of cholera and typhoid.[24] The categorisation of gay men as a risk category replays the definition of prostitutes as the reservoir of venereal disease in the mid-nineteenth century. Even the suggestion that those at risk should be segregated and quarantined has a precedent in the Contagious Diseases Acts of the 1860s which sought compulsorily to test women suspected of being prostitutes in various English garrison towns.[25] There is little new, it seems, in the field of sexual regulation.

But what is new, however, is the fluidity of sexual identities and the emergence of new sexual communities since the 1960s. These have provided opportunities for many, but anxiety for others whose own sense of self, and perception of the normal order of things, has been severely threatened by the speed of social change. Such change has provided a fertile recruitment ground for the moral politics of the New Right and has helped to create those constituencies most frightened by the emergence of AIDS.[26] For such people, AIDS comes to represent all the changes that have occurred over recent decades, as well as their fearful consequences. Culturally, the ground for the social reaction to AIDS was prepared before any one noticed the range of illnesses afflicting gay men and others. In a sense therefore there was already an imminent problem awaiting a symbolic resolution. To this extent, AIDS was a crisis waiting to happen.

☐ Political issues

AIDS is a cultural phenomenon, but in an age when culture and politics are more inextricably mingled than ever before, and when the politicisation of everyday life continuousy expands, it is inevitable that it should also become a political issue. AIDS first appeared in a period of profound political re-formation in most Western countries, represented most clearly by the rise of the New Right inflected administrations of Reagan in the USA and Thatcher in Britain.

The significance of this political shift for AIDS was two-fold. First, these governments were ideologically committed to cutting government expenditure at a time when the emergence of a major health crisis clearly demanded a substantial increase in governmental spending on health services. After 1985, resources were indeed put into AIDS support services and AIDS-related research, but more often than not the sums involved were much less than was demanded by those in the front line. They were also often provided as part of a redistribution of resources within an already determined budget.[27]

A clear example of this occurred in March 1988 when the British government decided it could allocate no extra cash to implement a series of measures designed to stop the spread of HIV infection through injecting drug use, despite the advice received from its own statutory body, the Advisory Council on Misuse of Drugs. A newspaper report summarised the government's position thus:

> The government acknowledges the importance of the preventative measures which have been recommended by the council but has only agreed to continue a £1m allocation first made a year ago. New services need to be created for addicts and existing services expanded, the Department of Health says in a circular to health authorities and local authorities, but no additional means will be provided to achieve these aims.[28]

Governments always have to prioritise expenditure decisions, and no-one could realistically expect that in a world of finite resources all that is demanded can be readily provided. But clearly, also, decisions about AIDS funding have been shaped by wider political considerations. In the case just cited, it was politically difficult for a government committed to a moral crusade against drugs simultaneously to fund syringe exchange schemes – an action likely to be seen by its more avid supporters as condoning drug abuse. From the beginning of the crisis, there has therefore been an ultimately irresolvable contradiction between the needs of people with AIDS and the political imperatives of New Right regimes.

This brings me to the second political factor relevant to AIDS, the importance of symbolic issues in New Right politics in the 1980s. In both the USA and Britain, high priority has been given to restoring national pride and economic strength. This has produced material effects (strengthened defence, a more nationalistic foreign policy, economic well-being), but also a number of less tangible outcomes: a desire to "walk tall" in the world, a desire to restore old values and so on.

At the centre of New Right discourse has been a symbolic crusade against what were seen as the moral excesses of the 1960s and 1970s, what in Britain has been called "permissive-ness", and an effort to reaffirm traditional family and sexual values. In practical terms, the effects have been limited. President Reagan found it virtually impossible to carry through any of his family policy, and Mrs Thatcher's direct ventures into moral politics were on the whole (with some important exceptions) rhetorical rather than legislative. But New Right propagandists have been more successful in setting the terms of the debate on sexuality, and AIDS has provided a convenient marker for their case.

Thus within New Right rhetoric we can find many examples of explicit links being made between permissiveness and AIDS. To quote one example from a former government minister, Sir Rhodes Boyson:

> . . . .It is wrong Biblically, is homosexuality. It is unnatural. AIDS is, to me, a part of the fruits of the permissive society. The regular one-man, one-woman marriage would not put us at risk with this in any way. . . .[29]

Arguments such as this, however incoherent, help create an environment in which it becomes permissable for people to be openly hostile towards non-traditional sexual life-styles. The effects of this may be incalculable. It has been argued that in fact the anti-gay backlash stimulated by AIDS has been much exaggerated,[30] and certainly there has as yet been no wholesale abrogation of gay rights in the wake of AIDS. On the other hand, there are signs of a substantial drop of support for lesbian and gay rights in Britain. It is difficult to find any other reason for this shift, in a climate that still remained relatively liberal on sexual matters, except for anxiety over AIDS.

Similarly, there were many factors behind the Thatcher government's introduction of measures to limit the "promotion" of homosexuality by local authorities via Section 28 of the 1988 Local Government Act, not least the wish to wrong-foot the opposition Labour Party over its ambivalent support for gay rights. On the other hand, it is at least open to question whether the government would have intervened here were it not for the climate generated by AIDS. The introduction of Section 28 coincided with a new readiness in the tabloid (and government supporting) press to use explicit terms of abuse against lesbians and gay men, and at least part of the rationale for this new statutory limitations on gay rights suggested that they were a political response to a changing political climate on homosexuality – a climate increasingly receptive to, as well as shaped by, a wider moral-political agenda.[31]

It would be wrong, however, to believe that this political agenda has been easily accepted, or uncontested. One of the interesting features of the political response to AIDS has been the divisions it has revealed within the dominant political movements and agencies of government. In recent years both America and Britain have witnessed sharp, if often covert, conflicts within government about how to respond to AIDS: conflicts of priorities and of interest between politicians and civil servants, medical and scientific advisors and pressure groups.[32] As a sensitive political issue, not susceptible to easy solution, AIDS has therefore provided important insights into the complexities of policy formation in pluralist societies.

☐ Social policy/social welfare issues

These complexities help explain the difficulties associated with the development of a coherent social policy towards HIV and AIDS. In many Western countries, AIDS has erupted in a period when the Welfare State policies forged as part of the post-war social settlement have reached a period of acute crisis. Partly this is a consequence of the fiscal crisis of Welfarism, as most Western countries have found it impossible, first politically and then ideologically, to increase expenditure on welfare services to the degree necessary to sustain their quality. This has led inevitably to the search for new policies of selectivity, targeting and privatisation in order to reduce expenditure. AIDS, on the other hand, clearly demands more resources and by implication a co-ordinated national, and international, strategy.

There are interesting tensions at play here, for the challenge to Welfarism in the 1960s and 1970s came as much from the New Left as the New Right, though the rationale and logic were different in each case. Both however were concerned to redefine what might be an appropriate balance of public obligations and private rights.

Put at its crudest, the New Right has been essentially concerned with as far as possible diminishing the role of the state in the provision of social care, and encouraging the devolution of this responsibility to the "private sphere". This logically implies reliance on those community support networks that already exist, many of which have their origins within the lesbian and gay communities. This of course conflicts with a different ideological strand in the New Right agenda, that which is familialist and anti-gay. In fact, as I have argued elsewhere, there has always been an uneasy contradiction in the New Right social agenda between the economic liberal and the social authoritarian.[33] The latter strand comes to the fore in proposals for the segregation of people with AIDS, for compulsory testing, and for stringent immigration control. But such proposals scarcely augur well for trust in the community and the diminution of state involvement that the other component of this agenda advocates.

The New Left position, on the other hand, is not without equivalent contradictions. A progressive approach to social policy assumes two things: that it is possible to develop a spirit of altruism, social responsibility and solidarity in the population at large; and that this will be accompanied by the democratisation and social accountability of the services provided by and for the community and its constituent parts. With regard to AIDS, this has led to some problems within self-help groupings about the proper relationship they should have with the local and national state.

This situation is complicated by questions of whether self-help organisations should act as pressure groups or campaigning organisations for better governmental involvement in the fight against AIDS, or the vehicles for the delivery of services,[34] which in turn raises fundamental issues about both accountability and professionalisation. Cindy Patton has raised these problems in her attack on what she calls the "AIDS industry". She argues that in the US there was a major shift in the fight against AIDS between mid-1985 and mid-1986 away from gay-movement inspired organisational forms and resistance to a hostile government and the medical establishment, and towards a mode of professionalisation which separated the new industry from its original roots. The politics of gay liberation lost out to what Patton calls the "new altruism", an outcome complicit with the privatising zeal of the New Right.[35]

Often, therefore, the self-help organisations become service agencies, increasingly reliant on state funding. At the same time, more militant groupings emerge to reaffirm the original radicalism, as for example in the direct action ACT-UP. This is an important analysis, and pinpoints key shifts. The problem with this argument, however, is that it is in danger of ignoring the fact that AIDS is much more than a gay issue, and that many of the groups worst affected by AIDS do not have the organisational traditions to be able to sustain a fight against AIDS without the support of other, better organised groups. Ironically, in view of the ways in which the health crisis has developed, gay-led groups, now "professionalised", can provide the essential support.

These debates raise a number of fundamental issues about social policy: about the balance between the needs of individuals and communities of choice, about the conflict between the demands of governments for appropriate accountability and standards of professionalism, and the fear of politicians that they may be seen to be acting on behalf of unpopular special interests. A few examples do exist of a close relationship between community groups and other voluntary and government agencies serving the needs of individuals and groups at risk.[36] It is important to recognise though that these represent attempts to work out new ways of relating need to service provision under the pressure of a health crisis. They are thus new models for social policy rather than traditional ones.

☐ Medico-moral issues

All these debates are framed by what we can term "medico-moral" issues. It has long been clear that medicine is far from being the neutral force that its own history would generally have us believe. Medicine is deeply involved in the relations of power – and hence the morals – of the culture in which it is embedded. One has only to think of the different medical cultures in the US and Britain, the first rooted in a private-enterprise culture where medical services are sold, and the second in a welfarist and altruistic tradition where medicine is a service to be provided, to realise the profoundly different outcomes that are likely to emerge. To take a simple example, which had a bearing on the early history of the AIDS crisis: blood is still often sold in the USA; in Britain it is contributed voluntarily, as part of the "gift relationship" which underpinned the formation of the National Health Service. This difference can have profound effects.[37]

Medicine is an essential element in the fight against AIDS, but it has also been a constituent agent in the formation of "AIDS" as a social issue. The medical profession, for example, played a major role in defining homosexuality as a disease during the course of the past century.[38] The easy slippage that took place in the early stages of the present health crisis which encouraged AIDS to be seen as a disease of diseased people owed a great deal to that tradition, challenged during the years of gay liberation, but continuing nevertheless as an unconscious element in medical discourse. A recent example of this in Britain is provided by a group of "Christian doctors" who proposed to halt the epidemic by segregating and isolating tens of thousands of people carrying the virus.[39]

These are minority views, yet this history has powerfully structured the relations between the communities most affected by AIDS and the medical profession itself. There can be no doubt that the response of many gay activists to AIDS in the early years of the crisis was shaped by a deeply rooted fear of the "re-medicalisation" of homosexuality. More recently, Silverman[40] has compared the "culturally-shared moral forms" of the people with HIV that he observed in a medical situation to the clinical approach of the doctors. Part of this is a necessary balance; part of it reflects a cultural divide.

At the same time, as Silverman goes on to argue, the publicity given to HIV infection and AIDS, and the structures of the community most affected by AIDS in the West, mean that patients are more knowledgeable than usual about official, as opposed to folk or lay, health knowledge.[41] In turn, many of the medical personnel involved in caring for people with AIDS are themselves from the community itself. This makes for major challenges to the traditional clientillistic relationship between doctor and patient. Here too, *new* models of social interaction and care may emerge in response to the health crisis.

☐ International issues

So far, I have concentrated on a limited range of national and Western responses. But AIDS is of course an international crisis. This poses questions about the necessity, and difficulty, of international co-operation to deal with AIDS in a world riven by political, economic and ideological divisions. It is surely significant that even as countries come together to find ways of co-operating, the way in which AIDS is understood is highly culturally specific. Western countries have debated whether students or long-term residents from Third World countries should be compulsorily tested. At the same time, others from the developing world bitterly resent suggestions that the disease originated and spread from Africa and see this as a typical piece of neo-colonial and racist propaganda.[42] At an international meeting of health ministers early in 1988, the Princess Royal suggested that AIDS was an "own goal" for mankind (the *Guardian*, 27 January 1988), as if blame could be collectively attributed to particular groups of people. Suggestions like these inevitably lead to the assumption that there are "innocent" and "guilty" victims of the disease. Apart from the ethics of so differentiating between those infected, there is an underlying philosophical dilemma; whom you regard as innocent and whom guilty is ultimately a matter of where you live and whom you stand with. The truth is that while AIDS as a syndrome of diseases has common features in all parts of the world, the social meanings it gives rise to can be profoundly different. If this is the case, it has implications for the ways in which AIDS is likely to be coped with in each culture. In the years ahead we will therefore need to adjust the treatment of AIDS to local customs and traditions, and to specific social and ethical values.

Nevertheless, AIDS is potentially a crisis of global proportions. It has implications for population growth and for the structure of family and sexual relations. It has troubling financial and economic consequences for a world economy already dangerously unbalanced, and incapable of finding commonly agreed solutions to already identified problems, let alone new, and politically fraught, health issues. Above all, it pinpoints both the challenge, and hazardous nature, of international cooperation.

☐ Personal and community issues

Finally, I want to return to the personal, to people with HIV infection and/or AIDS, and to the communities to which they belong. James Baldwin once remarked, "That isolation and death are certain and universal clarifies our responsibility".[43] As members of the community most affected, lesbians and gay men have had to learn this lesson very rapidly. In a world where the dying have conventionally "been removed so hygienically behind the scenes of social life",[44] people have suddenly needed to come to terms with illness, bereavement and loss on a massive scale. Yet the evidence is overwhelming that far from buckling under the strain, ties of community in the lesbian and gay world have been strengthened during these years. As Shilts remarks, at the end of a book which is otherwise partisan and critical of many aspects of gay life during the 1980s, "there was a new community emerging. . .of people who had learned to take responsibility for themselves and for each other".[45] There is a paradox here worth pondering on: suffering and bereavement appear to bring people together in a way that health and prosperity do not.

■ Conclusion

It will not have escaped anyone's attention that none of the issues discussed above are peculiar to HIV and AIDS. This echoes my conviction that the only way to understand the political and ethical implications of AIDS is to see it in a wider social context: of rapid social change and the anxieties attendant upon this, especially those changes which have affected sexual behaviour and values, race and social non-conformity; of political and moral struggles in which old certainties have collapsed and new and competing ones emerged; of new personal identities, many of them now fashioned in the furnace of personal suffering.

I began by describing three phases within the AIDS crisis so far, and suggested that we are currently living through a period of crisis management. This by definition means that we are addressing symptoms rather than fundamental causes. The subsequent discussion of key issues suggests that latent in the current situation is a more developed and rational response based on a realistic assessment of risk, a balanced understanding of the nature of AIDS and HIV infection, an awareness of the resources needed to deal with this, and the political and moral will necessary to find and use those resources. The challenge to society and governments in the next few years lies in harnessing this potential in order to move toward a more rational and progressive solution.

In many ways AIDS is like many other illnesses which devastate individual lives. What is remarkable about AIDS, however, is not simply its virulence, but the weight of symbolic meaning that it carries. Because of this, it throws into sharp focus the murkier preoccupations of our age. It carries a burden which those who experience it most personally should not have to bear. Perhaps the real signal that a new period is upon us will come when AIDS does become just another disease demanding the same care, attention and social resources as any other.

8 Pretended family relationships

■ Preface

We live in a culture which is suffused with familial values, and where the language of alternatives is feeble and etiolated[1]. Yet, of course, large numbers of people live in unconventional families or in no families at all. Alternatives exist. The real problem lies not in discovering them, but in evaluating and validating them.

Most of the time the various unorthodox patterns of intimate relationships and domesticity develop quietly under the surface of social life, leading an often subterranean existence. Occasionally, a particular way of life breaks surface and becomes a *locus classicus* of moral anxiety. It could be the alleged dysfunction of single-parent black families as a factor in the deprivation of inner cities. Or there might be a flurry about young girls getting pregnant in order to obtain social welfare benefits. Or it might be outrage at the alleged "promiscuity" of gay lifestyles as the harbinger of plague. At such moments, the borders of the private and the public become blurred, and the contours of the social are redefined – often, perhaps usually, at the expense of what is unconventional and different.

[This essay was written for a volume of essays in honour of the sociologist Jacqueline Burgoyne, who died tragically young in 1988. It is dedicated to her memory.]

134

In this essay I want to explore the place of the unconventional or the alternative in the debates on the family. It is an exploration of the limits of otherness in a moral and political climate which gives powerful obeisance to "the family" even as social trends and political decisions made or not made contribute to its continual transformation. The argument begins with an incident which while ostensibly about homosexuality is extremely revealing about the standing of the family. Then I explore the somewhat inconclusive discussions about "alternatives to the family" and "alternative families" which have punctuated the wider debate about the family over the past few decades. Finally I shall return to the "subterranean social order" where diverse patterns of life are shaped, and new moral communities develop. It is here, and not in the heads of theorists, that genuine "alternatives" are created.

■ Clause 28

Certain social events become, in Jacqueline Rose's useful phrase, "flashpoints of the social".[2] In a heightened moral climate underlying social shifts and the sense of anxiety to which they give rise are crystallized in what one can only call an ideological seizure, a symbolic moment which casts light not only on a murky past but illumines the present in a new way.

One such moment occurred towards the end of 1987 with the introduction of a backbench amendment to the local government bill, then trundling quietly, if not entirely innocently, through the House of Commons. The declared aim of this new clause was to prevent the "promotion" of homosexuality by local authorities, and although its introduction, and subsequent acceptance by the government, was unexpected it was the culmination of a sustained campaign by a group of Conservative MPs over the previous year. Eventually passed into law as section 2a of the Local Government Act 1986, Clause 28, as it became know during the sharp campaign preceeding its enactment, offered a revealing snapshot of the balance of political and moral power in the Britain of the late 1980s.

The terms of this amendment were important in themselves and for what they revealed about current attitudes
towards homosexuality. But even more significant was the
light that this episode cast on prevailing attitudes to the family
and sexuality, and to the new social identities that were an
increasingly visible part of the social and political geography
of the industrial nations.

Like all such symbolic moments, this one was heavily
overdetermined. The moral enthusiasts of the New Right had
long been concerned with "the family", and in particular with
the threats posed to its stability by "permissiveness", the
weakening of traditional gender demarcations posed by
feminism, and the threat of sexual diversity posed by the
modern lesbian and gay movement. These anxieties had
focussed on the issue of "sex education": its tendency towards
explaining the choices that might actually confront the child,
rather than the adumbration of firm moral positions, seen as a
critical element in the weakening of traditional values.

In the previous year Conservative MPs had already
secured significant concessions with the placing of responsibility for sex education in the hands of school governors,
with the assumption that these would be parent-dominated
(and with the implication that this would mean a more
"traditional" curriculum). As it turned out, this early victory
was in the end to vitiate the effectiveness of Clause 28. Local
authorities had very little power to promote any alternative
way of life.

But that lay in the future. What gave a particular saliency
to the issue in 1987 were the controversies generated by the
efforts of several Labour-controlled local authorities to
encourage the development of "positive images" of homosexuality. In the run-up to the 1987 general election this issue
had been particularly effective in marking out the "loony-left
councils", and almost certainly in further helping to detach
working-class support from its traditional Labour allegiance.
The confused reaction of the Labour opposition in the
immediate aftermath of the introduction of the new Clause
provided graphic testimony to the success of this ideological
mobilisation.[3] Despite formal endorsement by the Labour
Party of support for the rights of lesbians and gay men, the

uncertain response of some of its leading members following the introduction of the clause suggested that this policy was far from being instinct on the part of the main party of opposition.

In fact, the government was almost certainly taken aback by the eventual opposition that Clause 28 did produce. There was an unprecedented mobilisation of lesbian and gay political energies, supported in the end by important sections of liberal opinion. Although this did not prevent the amendment becoming law, significant concessions were extracted during the course of its passage through parliament, and even before it was safely on the statute book, it became clear that its effects were likely to be less draconian than first anticipated, or intended.[4] Yet more significant was its impact on the main target: far from diminishing the public presence of lesbians and gay men, it greatly contributed to an enhanced sense of identity and community. After many years of fissiparous divisions, lesbians and gay men of various social and political positions found it possible to work together in a common cause. Like many such moral eruptions in the past, the unintended consequences of this episode were as important as the intended.

Nevertheless, the whole *demarche* was extremely revealing, as a closer examination of the terms of Clause 28 illustrate. As finally passed, the Clause stated that:

A local authority shall not –
(a) intentionally promote homosexuality or publish material with the intention of promoting homosexuality;
(b) promote the teaching in any maintained school of the acceptability of homosexuality as a pretended family relationship.

The two key phrases, "promoting homosexuality" and "pretended family relationship", are clearly closely related. The first is a direct reference to the attempts of several local authorities to support "positive images" of homosexuality, which by implication advanced the argument that homosexuality should be regarded as of equal validity with heterosexuality. The belief that "heterosexism", that is

compulsive heterosexuality, was at the heart of the denigra-
tion of homosexuality was central to the positive images
campaigns.[5] Whether or not positive images could in any real
sense "promote" the practice of homosexuality was a highly
debated issue during the passage of Clause 28, and subsequently.[6] It was undoubtedly the case that the diminution of
hostility towards homosexuality would inevitably encourage a
climate where homosexuality could indeed be seen as a valid
sexual choice.

But as the phrase "pretended family relationship" suggested, it was more than simply sexual preference that was at
stake. Much more threatening, apparently, was the affirmation
of alternative patterns of relationships that this implied. As
David Wilshire, the Conservative MP who originally introduced the amendment, put it:

> Homosexuality is being promoted at the ratepayers' expense,
> and the traditional family as we know it is under attack.
> (Letter to the *Guardian*, 12 December 1987.)

This is the key to the whole episode.

It may well be true that "homosexuality is much less anti-
family than families are anti-homosexual" as Muller has
suggested.[7] Nevertheless, it is also undoubtedly the case that
the significant growth in the lesbian and gay community over
the previous two decades had posed an implicit challenge to
the hegemony of family values, or at least family values as
endorsed by leading exponents of the New Right, the strongest
advocates of Clause 28.[8] There is no reason to doubt the
statements of those supporters of the clause who argued that
they were not actually in favour of re-criminalising homosexuality; their stated objective was to restore the "compromum-
ise" embodied in the 1967 Sexual Offences Act, whereby
(male) homosexuality had been decriminalised under certain
limited circumstances.

As a number of judicial statements made clear following
reform this did not mean that homosexuality was either fully
legal, morally acceptable, or to be regarded as on a par with
heterosexuality.[9]

The problem was that in the succeeding twenty years, as a

result of the impact of the lesbian and gay movement and the associated massive expansion of the gay community, homosexuals had acted as if their full social rights were there for the asking, as if homosexuality could legitimately be regarded as on a par with heterosexuality, as if lesbian and gay relationships were as valid as traditional family relationships. Clause 28, in this light, can be seen as a great halt sign: thus far, and no further.

In adopting this position, the supporters of Clause 28 appeared to be swimming with the tide of public opinion. The British Social Attitudes Survey for 1987[10] found that the British public had apparently become marginally less discriminatory in attitudes towards homosexuality since 1983, with a greater reluctance to see homosexuals banned from certain professions, such as teaching, simply on the basis of a person's sexual preference. (This was markedly the case with social classes iv and v). At the same time, when asked if they approved of "homosexual relationships", there was evidence of a sharp increase of hostility over 1983: in 1983, 62 per cent had censured such relationships; in 1985, 69 per cent; and in 1987, 74 per cent.

The drift of public opinion was even clearer when people were asked their opinions about recognising the rights of homosexuals to adopt children on the same grounds as heterosexuals. In 1987, 86 per cent would forbid lesbians adopting children, while an overwhelming 93 per cent would prevent gay men.

This survey suggests that while the slowly developing liberalisation of attitudes towards sex was continuing, and still influencing attitudes to the rights of individual homosexuals, when confronted by homosexuality as the focus for alternative forms of relationships, the public drew back. The British Social Attitudes Survey findings were confirmed by a subsequent Gallup poll (*Sunday Telegraph*, 5 June 1988) which found that 60 per cent thought that homosexuality should not be considered an accepted lifestyle, compared to 34 per cent who did (though interestingly, 50 per cent of those under 25 were accepting).

Many factors can be adduced to explain this situation, not least the impact of AIDS in generating hostility towards homosexuality.[11] But perhaps there is a more deep-seated reason, hinted at by other statistics in the British Social Attitudes Survey. These indicated that public hostility to extra-marital sex of any sort had increased significantly during the decade, from 83 per cent in 1983 to 88 per cent in 1987, and this was at a time when acceptance of pre-marital sex had become widespread. Such evidence suggests that while the long term growth of more liberal values was continuing, it was very much in the context of the general acceptance of monogamous heterosexual coupledom as the basis for in-timate relationships and domestic life. Alternative patterns, whether heterosexual or homosexual, might receive more tolerance than they did in, say, the 1960s, despite that decade's much reviled leaning towards "permissiveness".[12] But there could be no doubt about the strength of the norm, which appeared to be increasing rather than diminishing as the 1980s wore on. If this is the case, however, it makes all the more interesting and revealing that it was at this particular time that there there was a political intervention against homosexuality.

■ Family values

To understand this we must look at the wider context of political concern about the family. Clause 28 can be seen as a crystallization of anxieties about the stability of the family which had been growing over the previous decades, not only in Britain but throughout the advanced industrial countries. In the late 1970s, Demos[13] observed a "diffuse sense of 'crisis'" about domestic arrangements generally, reflected in a flowering of commissions, task forces, conferences and publications on various aspects of family life. The family became increasingly defined as a problem area in social arrangements, and this was the prelude to the emergence of "the family" as a charged political talisman, engaging the energies of politicians on left and right.[14]

On the surface this new preoccupation with the family was paradoxical, for despite all the usual indices usually cited for "decline" – increasing divorce rates, growing cohabitation, the number of one-parent families, the impact of feminism – familial values remained sturdily entrenched. The number of marriages in Britain, which had dipped in the late 1970s, increased again in the 1980s, rising to 400,000 by 1986 (compared with a peak of 480,000 in 1972). Some 21 per cent of live births were outside marriage, but half of these were registered by both parents, suggesting the growth of stable non-married relationships. Even the high divorce rates, with a third of marriages likely to end in divorce courts, could be seen in an optimistic light, for the majority re-married, seeking presumably the fulfilments of family life not found in the first attempt.[15]

This has led commentators to talk of the rise of the "neo-conventional" family.[16] As Fletcher, an ardent defender of the family has put it:

> . . .there is no doubt whatever that *the family* is not only what
> the great majority of the people of Britain *want*, it is also what,
> in fact, they actually *have*.[17]

But to state this is not to resolve the issue, for apparent continuity can obscure crucial changes taking place under the patina of stability, and an emphasis on normative affirmation may hide a genuine crisis of subjective meanings. As the liberal journalist Melanie Phillips has suggested, the family "is now suffering from a chronic crisis of identity and self-confidence".[18] This was underlined by the wave of moral anxiety induced by the Cleveland child abuse crisis in 1988.[19] Here was a situation where two apparently stable and complementary discourses (about the needs of children and the rights of parents) became entangled and apparently contradictory as medical evidence suggested that child sex-abuse within families was widespread.

In the resulting moral panic contradictory messages about family life emerged from the miasma of rumour, suspicion and political ambition. Many of those who had previously been most vociferous in the search for child sex-abuse found themselves unable to believe that so many (middle- as well as working-class) respectable parents (that is, fathers) might be involved. Whilst those who had long disputed any medical hegemony over sexual issues found themselves supporting the controversial evidence of doctors using largely unproven methods of detecting abuse. But what it revealed above all was that the family could not be seen as unproblematic haven of harmony. As the director of Newcastle's social services said, "Belief in the sanctity of the family must not blind us to the fact that the family is a hotbed of violence".[20] Whether or not this generalisation is true, the very fact that it could be made is suggestive.

I want to argue that a widespread anxiety about the family has three inter-related focuses. The first concerns the contradictory demands made upon the family in a period of rapid social change. As Deakin and Wicks[21] point out, these demands bear particularly strongly on women: a greater reliance in social policy on care in the community places an ever-increasing burden on women. Simultaneously, demographic changes and the changing patterns of employment increasingly pull women into the workforce. Such contradictory pulls not only impose growing burdens on women; they also, inevitably, underline the potentially contradictory interests of women and men in domestic life.

These pressures are being experienced – and this is the second potential focus – at the same time as other forces are working to emphasise the value of family life. Barbara Laslett has argued that:

> . . .changes in household composition, in the demography of kinship, and in the relationship between the family and other institutions have contributed to the increased emotional significance of the family.[22]

But the very intensity of emotions that the family generates and which are in turn re-invested in the family is potentially both unsettling and dangerous. It can offer the possiblity of support and a sense of belonging. It can also act as the fulcrum for the generation of violence, against women and against children.

Problems occur within families; but there are many types of families, and this is a third potential focus of anxiety. As Rayner Rapp put it, "People are recruited and kept in households by families in all classes, yet the families they have (or don't have) are not the same".[23]

The existence of a diversity of family and household forms is, as these quotations suggest, perhaps the most challenging issue of all, because it poses in an acute fashion the question of value: not only the empirically verifiable issue of what is changing in the family, or families, but the more critical question of what ought to change, and what are the most appropriate means of satisfying individual and collective needs.

It is in this context that we must try to understand the ways in which the family has entered political discourse. It is an issue which cuts across traditional political boundaries, but it is nevertheless the case that over the past decade, in the USA and Britain, it has become an issue *par excellence* of the political right.[24] A re-assertion of what were conceived of as traditional family and sexual values was at the moral centre of the New Right's agenda from the 1970s onwards. In practice, the political regimes associated with the New Right, such as those of Reagan in the USA and Thatcher in Britain, were much less energetic or successful in pursuing this cultural reversion than in achieving other strategic goals. Despite Mrs Thatcher's espousal of "Victorian values" there was no sustained effort to turn back the clock in Britain, even beyond the much attacked 1960s. Nevertheless, just as the "permissive" reforms of the 1960s were shaped by the brief emergence of the "liberal moment", so the new moralism of the 1980s, represented by Clause 28, depended upon the initiative being seized by the New Right.

The attraction of the re-assertion of traditional values concerning family and sexual life is that it offers a symbolic focus for the resolution of personal and social problems that might otherwise seem intractable. The reality might actually be quite different as affluence, social dislocation and social policy continue to undermine those values. But "the family", with its powerful myth of harmony and personal integration and fulfilment, retains a powerful appeal.

This is all the more significant because of the absence of any alternative patterns of relating that had widespread acceptance. The language of non-family life remains feeble compared to the power of the familial, despite the heat and fury generated by earlier debates. An examination of these attempts to define alternatives to the family will help to reveal why.

◼ Alternatives to the family

There is a long history of critiques of the family, and of the offering of alternatives to it. But for both practical and ideological reasons we must start with the 1960s. This is the period which has been most starkly pin-pointed as the source and origin of attacks on the family, the period, in Margaret Thatcher's graphic phrase, which taught the citizenry to never say "No".[25]

Fletcher, within a more academic if scarcely less polemical mode, has identified the 1960s as the period of a new, and much sharper assault on the family than ever before. He has described five types of attack:

(a) that associated with the anthropologist Edmund Leach, which identifies the family as the "source of all our discontents";
(b) the critiques of psychologists such as Laing, Cooper and Esterson which see the family as the "destroyer" of its members' sanity;
(c) revived Marxist interest in the family which identifies it as a material and ideological prop of capitalism, and an "ideological state apparatus";
(d) the developing feminist critique, which sees the family as a "prison", a site of oppressive socialisation, gender stereotyping and sexual exploitation; and
(e) the commune movement, with its proferred, if somewhat amorphous, alternative to the family.[26]

Despite Fletcher's pulling of all these together under the label of "abolitionists", clearly these critiques have different theoretical origins and are attached to differing and sometimes conflicting political agenda. Leach in his famous Reith lectures of 1967 might lament the dominance of the family, "with its narrow privacy and tawdry secrets",[27] but it was difficult to see what the programmatic implications of this were. Feminist critiques of women's subordination within the family do not necessarily involve a radical call for abolition, as later writings made clear.[28] Nor did the Marxist interventions against the family inevitably imply a radical challenge to existing gender and sexual relations.

Nevertheless, it is possible to link these critiques together in a loose but vital way. In the first place they were able to draw on a long, if often buried tradition of critical explorations of family life and the search for alternatives going back at least to the earliest days of industrialisation. The commune movement, in particular, could look back to a real history of attempts to build alternative communities as the basis of new ways of life, either within the hostile environment of capitalist society or as far away from its heartlands as possible.[29]

Second, despite their disparate origins and implications, the critics of the family in the 1960s were reflecting a widespread feeling, echoing the critical findings of sociologists, anthropologists and psychologists that the family as it existed was becoming increasingly dysfunctional.[30] It was not surprising that these findings were readily incorporated into the more amorphous aspirations of what became known as the "counter-culture". At the heart of the 1960s challenge to the family was a strong libertarian belief that the traditional family was a bulwark of hierarchical, class society.[31] It followed that it was necessary to build freer alternatives: hence the revived interest in communal ways of living.

As Abrams and McCulloch noted, "the positive qualities of communes are perceived with overwhelming frequency in contra-distinction to the negative qualities of the nuclear family".[32] Hostility to the nuclear family was the strongest element in giving a sense of common purpose to the commune movement.

The sociological research on communes confirms this. Rigby developed a six-fold typology to consider the communes:

(1) self-actualising communes, seen by its members as contributing to a new social order;
(2) communes for mutual support, whose member sought individual self realisation in a supportive framework;
(3) activist communes, providing a base for "outside" social and political activities;
(4) practical communes, defined primarily in terms of the economic and practical material advantages to be obtained;
(5) therapeutic communes, having the prime purpose of therapy; and
(6) religious communes, where the goals are defined primarily in religious terms.[33]

Despite his great enthusiasm for the movement Rigby was able to find little common ground either within or across these, whether in forms of leadership, attitudes to relationships, patterns of money distribution or work, decision making and types of accommodation. What most of them did have in common, however, was a desire to challenge the taken-for-granted naturalness of family life.[34] As the movement's newsletter observed, "we have no uniting ethic apart from a belief in communal life as a possibly happier alternative to the normal family unit".[35]

The real limits of this challenge can be observed if we look a little more closely at the heart of Rigby's case. The following quotation is representative:

> If our aim is not merely to change the system of ownership and control of wealth and property in society, but to transform all areas of life and in the process create a world where everyone is his own master, where we care for each other in a spirit of love and fraternity. . .then it can only be achieved through means which embody these ideals in the here and now, through people in all walks of life working to put these ideals into practice in their daily living. This is the message of the communes.[36]

Two points are striking: the aspiration towards (and expectation of?) total transformation ("Not merely to change. . ."), which provided the sharp counter-cultural energy; and the frankly masculinist terms in which these are expressed (". . .his own master", "spirit of love and fraternity"). No doubt such verbal lapses are typical of the period, but they reveal a more fundamental hesitation. In spite of the commitment to total change, and the genuflection to the then-new feminist and gay movements, there is no real integration of their critiques into the analysis of communes. As Abrams and McCulloch comment, in their noticeably more jaded examination of the commune movement, there is an impression of "the virtual irrelevance of communes as a solution to the problem of sexual inequality".[37]

Both the women's liberation movement and the gay movement, in their heroic period of the early 1970s, flirted with the idea of collective living, embracing much of the ideology of the commune movement whilst attempting to go beyond it in relation to gender and sexual relations. But sexual enlightenment did not necessarily prevent other problems in collective living. Birch for example describes life in the gay commune in which he lived in the early 1970s as one of constant meetings, incessant self-questioning, and a commitment to openness to such an extent that "to be honest, perhaps we were never honest":

> At times the tension was so great, especially around the formal
> sessions themselves, that everyone dreaded the house meetings.
> The commitment to the ideal prevented us from asking whether
> we really liked or understood one another.[38]

Nava, while examining feminist attitudes to collective living in the early 1970s, has pin-pointed more fundamental problems: the domination of a moralism and voluntarism concerning alternative living styles that limited their appeal to very narrow circles, and led to the censure of those who did not share the vision. This was accompanied by an optimistic failure to recognise the power structures in the outside world that shaped the relations of men and women with regard to domestic responsibilities, child-care and paid employment.[39]

By the mid 1970s the commune movement had lost its *elan*, at precisely the time when the first sociological surveys were appearing (though the movement still claimed fifty functioning communes in Britain in 1989).[40] Even at its height the movement was relatively small (it is noticeable how commentators like Rigby and Abrams and McCulloch tend to home in on the same examples). Neither its rise nor demise had a major effect on the way most people lived.

Yet it is worthy of an extended note precisely because it did represent an "alternative to the family", on paper at least, of the most uncompromising sort. Like others that have been mooted over this century, such as the kibbutz,[41] the hopes proved more extensive than the realities. Nevertheless, its theory, if not its practice, did offer a different type of model for organising domestic life from that offered in the traditional nuclear family of the movement's mythology. As such its traces can be found both in the personalism of the "lifestyle politics" that were to develop in the later 1970s and early 1980s, and in the revived critiques of the family that were to re-emerge during the 1980s. Which is why, no doubt, the shadow of its myth continues to dog that of the family.

■ Alternative families

The demise of the radical critique of the family permitted the emergence of a more pluralist perspective. Its hallmark was a concentration on the variety of family forms, and an attempt to recognise and do justice to "alternative families". More than the commune movement, its starting point was an awareness of social diversity. The problem, as ever, was what to do with it.

The spirit of this new emphasis is captured in this statement in the first annual report of the Australian Institute of Family Studies:

> The family is the most basic unit. . . ."The family", however, is
> not and never has been, of one uniform type or structure. . . .
> Moreover, the family changes both its function and composition
> over the life cycle. Thus any arbitrary definition of "the family"
> is unhelpful and misleading in that it defines out of existence
> many family forms that are a reality, and which social policy and
> social arrangements must take into account.[42]

This new emphasis during the late 1970s and early 1980s, was interestingly signalled at the highest official level by President

Carter's convening of a White House conference on *families* in 1980.[43] Underlying it is a clear attempt to affirm the values of family life whilst attempting to come to terms with the fact of change and variety.

The dual aim is reflected in the book sponsored by the "British Family Research Committee" in 1982, with the significant title, *Families in Britain*.[44] In his introduction, the distinguished family historian, Peter Laslett, denied the existence of a single British family.[45] In the book itself five types of diversity are postulated:

(1) organisational, dependent on the internal division of labour and relations to the external world;
(2) cultural, as a result of different ethnic, religious, class, political and child-rearing traditions;
(3) class, as a result of differential resources and social access;
(4) life course, resulting from change over time;
(5) cohort, resulting from historical changes, in patterns of work, marriage, divorce, the ratio of young to old people, etc.[46]

These are variations within something which can still recognisably be defined as "a family". The problem becomes more difficult if you attempt to broaden your definition. Macklin lists a range of what she calls "non-traditional" families. These include: never-married singlehood, non-marital singlehood, voluntary childlessness, the "bi-nuclear family", involving joint custody and co-parenting, the step-family, open-marriages/ open-families, extra-marital sexual relations, same-sex intimate relations, and multi-adult households.[47]

Such "non-traditional" forms have been seen as essentially alternative lifestyles, "relational patterns around which individuals organize their living arrangements", a "smogarsbord" from which individuals must select the options they prefer, with all the opportunities and risks that suggests.[48] The assumption is, however, that they offer, in their different ways, viable ways of organising personal life, both at the level of domestic living arrangements and in intimate relations.

According to Zinn and Eitzen, "These alternatives exist together with traditional family forms and in this way contribute to the diversity and flexibility of the family".[49] It is, however, difficult to see what, apart from their assumed viability, all these forms have in common. Some are the result of contingent factors (such as changing patterns of divorce and re-marriage); others are clearly a matter of personal choice, and perhaps favourable circumstances or social possibilities. Some are obvious variations on traditional patterns, such as the "commuter marriages", heterosexual co-habitation or "singlehood" described by Zinn and Eitzen. Such patterns can involve quite large numbers of people. "Commuter marriages", where the partners live in different parts of the country and commute to be together at weekends or holidays, are estimated to involve a million people in the USA.[50]

Other relationships, however, while they may have a long historical lineage, have not hitherto been seen as family forms at all. Lesbian and gay relationships fall most clearly into this category. Can or should they all be easily assimilated under the rubric of the family?

To deploy the term "families" instead of family is still, as Morgan argues,[51] "to maintain some, perhaps changed or expanded, notion of what 'family' is, of what all the different varieties have in common". If the key elements of the family are seen in classic terms as socialisation of the young and reproduction (in the broad sense of social reproduction as well as biological); intensity of interaction between members and continuity over time; domestic arrangements with a sustained degree of co-habitation; and the ordering of gender and sexual relations, then clearly not all "non-traditional" patterns or life-styles fit in. Lesbian and gay relationships might when they involve parenting, but not when they involve complex patterns of "non-exclusive" relationships.[52]

The broadening of the term "family" to embrace a variety of both domestic arrangements and types of relationships (and it is important to stress that these are not necessarily the same) must be seen as a political response to diversity rather than a useful sociological categorisation. In effect it takes for granted the discourse of family life, and simply incorporates every other form of workable life-style into it. Against this, it is important to stress that not all household patterns can be called families, whatever their "family-like" qualities. On the contrary there exist a plurality of relational forms which are regarded by many as both legitimate and desirable and which are different from any recognisably familial pattern.

For some, this diversity is a welcome sign of the growth of personal choice and freedom; for others, it is a sign of potential societal breakdown. Fletcher for example, wonders whether conditions in the modern world are leading to a "de-moralization" of society as a result of a disturbance of the "natural-social" sequence of socialisation, rearing and caring. Lasch attacks the advocates of "choice" and an easy pluralism as a surrender to the culture of consumerism. Berger and Berger fear for the breakdown of stable identity formation through the unthinking acceptance of diverse patterns. They in particular deplore the way in which the empirical fact of diversity is quietly turned into a norm of diversity, where "demography is translated into a new morality".[53]

These challenges can not be answered simply by reiterating the merits of choice. If diversity is to become a new norm then its contours need to be more clearly defined. This is the challenge facing those who want to continue to offer critiques of the family.

■ The subterranean social order

Social diversity is a fundamental given of modern life, a product of ever increasing social complexity.[54] The patterns of life and domestic organisation that currently exist are therefore the result of a complex play of determination and contingency, historical legacy and rapid social change. In such a situation it is tempting to search for the security of what we know, or believe, to be secure and stable, a haven, in Lasch's famous diatribe, where those who feel beseiged may find find protection.[55]

This has always been the classic attraction of the family as myth, certainly since the early nineteenth century and is a powerful element in the rhetoric of today's defenders of the family. But more significantly, perhaps, as we have seen, the family is a potent trope even in the hands of those whose adherence to a traditional model is dubious. The language of the family pervades our thinking about private life.

That is another way of saying that there is a poverty of thought, and of language, concerning non-family forms. A classic example of this can be found in the rhetoric of fraternity (and to a lesser extent sorority) which echoes through the language of the movements of the left over the past one hundred years, and was replicated in the conventional terms of the feminist and gay movements of the 1970s at the very time when their critiques of the family were most pointed.[56] It seems that we can only find the terms to describe even our most passionate loyalties within the language of family relationships.

This is only symptomatic of a wider inability to forge a generally recognisable and acceptable language of belonging which can describe at both the intimate and the public level the complex patterns of relationships that actually bind people to one another.

Yet there is much evidence of the richness and depth of other, non-family relations, some forged across the boundaries of family life, some entirely outside the field of family relations altogether. Recent historical work has powerfully challenged the belief that the family is a natural, unitary organism, subversive of all states, hierarchies, churches and ideologies as the conservative polemicist Ferdinand Mount would have it.[57] On the contrary the family can most usefully be seen as a variable set of relationships, between men and women, adults and children, shaped and structured by uneven power relations, whose unity is historical and ideological rather than natural.

Taking this rather abstract formulation as a starting point, it becomes possible to explore the strength of other loyalties that strain against family ties. Some are loyalties that affirm the existing hierarchies of power, ensuring male dominance and female subordination, such as the affiliations of clubs and pubs, business and trade union cultures, senior common rooms and working-class subcultures, that work to preserve and assert the bonds between men. Others, on the contrary, are cultures of obligation, support and resistance, such as the bonds of kin, neighbourhood and friendship forged by women within and across their broad family commitments. Still others are transparently outside the cultures of families altogether, such as those of all female institutions and of the subcultures of lesbians and gay men that have become increasingly apparent over the past one hundred years.

These are just examples of what Peter Willmott has described as a "subterranean social order" which incorporates relationships with friends, relations, neighbours and work colleagues.[58] Such relationships are mediating structures which connect the public and the private, provide sociable human contact, value systems and socialisation, and act as major sources of support and practical help.

Relationships like these have no necessary essential meaning, any more than being a member of a family magically conveys the promise of happiness or fulfilment. They have a different weight in the lives of people at different times and places. The meanings of neighbourhood are different for a white, middle-class family in a leafy suburb from those of black youth in the embattled inner city, where the temples, churches, clubs and cafes can provide the focus of powerful cultural and political identities. Similarly, the neighbourhoods organised around sexual preferences (such as San Francisco's gay Castro district) or religious enthusiasm may provide the continuity over time and the "generalized reciprocity", in which people give gifts and perform services for each other unconditionally in the general expectation that similar gifts and services will be at some time be returned, normally associated with family and kin relationships.[59]

It is potentially misleading, therefore, always to see sharp breaks between family or kin relations and other patterns (which is not to deny the unique weight given to kin relationships). This becomes clearer if we look at the deployment of two other key terms, friendship and community. Peter Willmott, following Abrams, has argued that family relationships are entirely different from friendships, and generally weaker than ties of kin or neighbourhood for primary social support.[60]

But for many, whether organised into households or not, non-family relationships do act as the primary source of social belonging. Parker Rossman, for example, has described the growth of "network families", groups of people ("friends") bonded together for mutual support. These have been a marked characteristic of the new urban gay communities of the past twenty years. The language used is still unavoidably familial, but the social relationships are different: based on choice rather than ascription, although carrying many of the characteristics of family type obligations.[61]

The situation is yet more complex with regard to the idea of community. Willmott has distinguished three types of community: of territory, of interest, and of attachment. All can give rise to intense loyalties, and clearly the categories can overlap to a considerable degree.[62] But it is the last category, the "community of attachment" that is most interesting. It is equivalent to the "expressive cultures" identified by Gilroy in relationship to the experience of black people in Britain, or the "community of affect" described by Hebdige around inter-racial music and efforts of international solidarity such as Band Aid,[63] or the communities of identity so characteristic of the lesbian and gay networks of the 1980s.

Such attachments give rise to what can best be termed "moral communities", in which solidarities of mutual support and need give rise to value systems in which the community itself becomes the focus of attachment and the location for the growth of intimate relationships. One powerful example of this derives from the experience of HIV disease or AIDS. Here is a disease and illness where both the people with AIDS and the syndrome itself are highly stigmatised because of the linkage of the disease with socially unpopular or execrated groups (drug users, male homosexuals). Yet the experience of stigma and pain and death has given rise to a sophisticated culture of survival, particularly among gay men in which "buddying" (the informal but carefully structured system of individual support for the sick or dying) has become symbolic of new ties of solidarity.[64]

Attachments such as these are, like kin-relationships, often dispersed communities, and provide the context of relationships rather than the primary focus. But their role in the formation and sustenance of personal and social identities can be crucial. If, as Berger and Berger[65] lament, the family as the source of strong social identities is now under challenge, it is in these moral communities that alternative sources of identification and value are emerging.

Communities like these affirm simultaneously identity and difference: what we have in common and what divides us. In the contemporary world, the differences can often be antagonistic, as different world views contest. The attempt to re-assert the values of traditional family relations in embattled

Asian communities in Britain against the forces of assimilation and secularisation sit uneasily side by side with the frankly sexual-political ties that bind homosexual people in the gay community. At the same time, it would be wrong to believe that even within the self-designated communities of identity there are universal patterns of domestic life. The point is that these communities reflect the increasing complexity and diversity of the modern world and in their very existence challenge the idea that there can possibly be a single pattern of relationships universally applicable to all. In practice, there never has been in the past; there is highly unlikely to be such a pattern in the future.

This suggests that the real challenge lies not in attempting to find alternatives to the family, nor in attempting to make the term family so elastic that it embraces everything, and comes to mean nothing. On the contrary, the more dangerous and difficult task lies in the attempt to forge a moral language which is able to come to terms in a reasoned way with the variety of social possibilities that exist in the modern world, to shape a pluralistic set of values which is able to respect difference.

An ethical pluralism need not mean an easy acceptance of everything that exists. On the contrary, it should challenge us to work through the principles that make a pluralistic society possible: a common acceptance of the value of diversity and choice; a sensitivity to the power relations that hinder and inhibit the fulfilment of individual needs; and above all, an avoidance of the proselytising zeal of those who believe that they have the key to the good life. It does not mean that "the family" is redundant or that it can contribute nothing to individual or social well-being. But a true pluralism must begin with the assumption that happiness and personal fulfilment are not the privileged prerogative of family life.

■ Conclusion

We have moved a little way from the political manouevrings of 1987, but not perhaps so far from the underlying issues. At stake in the debate about Clause 28 was the degree to which the state through parliamentary fiat had the right to intervene in the dense world of civil society to declare what was right or wrong, appropriate or inappropriate in personal moral and sexual choices. This is not an easy issue to deal with, because it raises profound questions about the desirable balance between individual rights and social needs. There can be no single boundary drawn, saying this far and no further.

But that is precisely what the British parliament and government sought to do at the end of 1987 in introducing Clause 28. In their actions both were in effect insisting that one way of life was preferable to another. This essay has attempted to adopt a less imperialistic stance, by offering a modest defence of those much maligned "pretended family relationships".

9 Uses and abuses of Michel Foucault

I write as a historian whose work has been very much influenced by a reading of Michel Foucault. But I speak also as someone whose preoccupations, whilst superficially similar in many ways to those of the later Foucault, in fact pre-date any serious encounter with his work. For something like twelve years I have been researching and writing about the history and sociology of sexuality, and have been particularly preoccupied with three key aspects. In the first place, I have tried to explore the complexities of sexual identities, and in particular the historical emergence of a modern homosexual identity. In my book *Coming Out* and in various articles I have tried to show how the contemporary lesbian and gay identities are products not of nature or the imperatives of desire but of social categorisation and self-definition, in a complex, shifting history. Second, and obviously closely related to this, I have tried to understand the relationship between the social and the sexual, and the changing focus of the social regulation of sexuality and endeavour which culminated in my next book, *Sex, Politics and Society*. Third, I have for a long time been interested in the dubious origins of sexology, the would-be science of sex and of the truth of our nature. Almost the first thing I wrote on sex was an essay on Havelock Ellis, and in my most recent books I have tried to show how little Nature has to do with our contemporary sexual beliefs and behaviours.[1]

The point I want to emphasise is that all these preoccupations, and two of the books, were conceived and largely written before I had read Foucault. I say this not to claim any special prescience, but to underline why I, like many other radical historians and sociologists, have been drawn to his work: because his corpus of work seemed highly relevant to what appeared as intractable theoretical and political problems in work that was already creatively going on.

Foucault's writings offer no alternative theory or politics, though inevitably they have theoretical and political implications. Their impulse is analytical and critical, deconstructionist rather than positive. Like his friend Gilles Deleuze, he insists on treating theory as a "box of tools" to be taken up and used as we need them. We are not under any obligation to accept all his positions. There is, indeed, much that is ambiguous in his work; some of his history can be, and should be, disputed as history; his political friends have sometimes been dubious, and his political positions muted. His work can and should be contested. But as he said of Nietzsche's work,

> I prefer to utilise the writers I like. The only valid tribute to thought such as Nietzsche's is precisely to use it, to deform it, to make it groan and protest.[2]

In the same way we must use Foucault – not to arm ourselves with a new orthodoxy but to ask old questions in new ways, and new questions of old problems.

In the rest of this paper I want to pick out three areas where it seems to me his influence has been wholly beneficial in contributing to reassessments of critical issues: in thinking through the relationship between history and politics; in developing a critique of sexual essentialism; and in the analysis of new social antagonisms and political subjectivities.

■ History and politics

It has become a commonplace on the Left that many of the most important contributions to radical political analysis in recent years have been in the forms of historical investigation. But there is no easy or straightforward way of marrying "history" and "politics".[3] Two approaches have been particularly common. The first is "history as a lesson". Here the stress is on learning from the past in order to understand the present and find guidelines for the future. History has a heuristic function which sensitises us to the complexities of our contemporary world. If history repeats itself, we are given to understand, it is less likely to repeat itself as farce if we already know of the tragedy. Unfortunately, this assumes a transparent past whose warnings are clear, and alas, history never moves along a single tramline: its discontinuities are as evident as its continuities. More crucially, how do we really know that we know the past? If the past is a foreign country its languages can baffle the most agile translator. "The horrid spectacle is seen", Nietzsche wrote, "of the mad collector raking over all the dust heaps of the past"[4] – and still coming up with the wrong answer.

A second characteristic approach offers us "history as exhortation". The chief note here is the advice to the class, or nation, or gender, or oppressed minority to listen to its past, to find in its buried glories the moral example and histories of resistance to give us strength in present difficulties, to rescue, as E.P. Thomson powerfully put it, the downtrodden from the "enormous condescension" of posterity, and of historians. At its best this strategy can evoke lost worlds of struggle, investigate hidden byways, reassess the way we see the development to the present. It recovers from the victors the pain, work and aspirations of the vanquished. It challenges us to challenge their defeat and looks to their triumph. But at its worst it can provide only a consoling myth, a false hope, an unrealistic reading of the present based on a false image of the past and an unrealisable hope for the future. In such an approach there is a real danger that the dead might well end up burying the living.[5]

A third approach seems to me more appropriate today for the investigation of our current discontents: to see history and politics as inextricably combined, to attempt to understand the ways in which the past has a hold on, organises and defines the contemporary perception. The aim is to understand "the present" as a particular constellation of historical forces, to find out how our current political dilemmas have arisen, to see, in a word, the present as historical. What is needed is a history of the historical present as a site of definition, regulation and resistance. History and politics in this reading are not uneasy bedfellows: they are essential partners.

Hence the appeal of Foucault's advocacy of a "history of the present". He is not so much concerned with analysis of the past as with the uncovering of what he describes as traces of the present. There is a rich diversity in his writings: from his early studies of psychology and madness, through the birth of modern medicine and the sciences of man, to the analysis of modern disciplinary forms and the three volumes of the *History of Sexuality*. Beneath this variety there have been two, closely related concerns: to expose the conditions for the emergence of modern forms of rationality, especially as expressed in the "human sciences"; and to construct a history of the different modes, by which, in our culture, human beings are made subjects.

Clearly this is a specific sort of history – what Cousins and Hussain call "case history"[6] – concerned not with an exhaustive searching out of the truth of the past but with the intelligibility of the present. He has located an area of interest which has hitherto been little investigated, the history of the discursive realm, and has set out to investigate a precise intellectual problem: the nature of the relationship between the discursive and the non-discursive as it structures those grids of meaning which organise the present. He does not deny the validity of other types of history, but his concern is elsewhere: in understanding the mechanisms of thought and action which delimit our modernity.

The scandal (for some), and the attraction for others is that he does this without recourse to any master scheme of history or ultimate theory of causation. In Foucault the task of historical investigation is not to seek a "real history" that slides inexorably under the surface of events or works invisibly behind humanity's back, but to address itself to these surfaces, the grids of meaning and language, which are "the real" in the way we live social relations. He compares what he calls a general history with total history[7]. Total history attempts to draw all phenomena round a single causative centre or spirit of a society or civilisation. The same form of historical influence is then seen to be operating on all levels, the economic, the social, the political, the religious, with the same type of transformation and influences playing on all these levels. General history, on the other hand, is concerned with "series, segmentations, limits, differences of level, time lags, anachronistic survivals, possible types of relation". The aim is not, however, to offer a jumble of different histories, nor the investigation of analogies or coincidences between them. Nor is it a simple revival of crude positivism, of "one damn thing after another". The task proposed by general history is precisely to determine what forms of relation may legitimately be made between the various constituents of "the present". This present is not a homogeneous product of a unified history. It is more a promiscuous amalgam of specific histories, whose relationship it is the task of analysis to uncover. So what he calls – after Nietzsche – his genealogical method, is not concerned with the origin of the present, but with beginnings; not with causes but with emergences and effects.

The ultimate aim of all this, as Foucault puts it, is a diagnosis of the present, for history is a "curative science". And "the purpose of history, guided by genealogy, is not to discover the roots of our identity but to commit ourselves to its dissipation",[8] to refuse those categorisations that are imposed upon us as truth. Clearly an approach such as this radically challenges any general theory of history and of society. There is no trans-historical economy which provides the substratum for a social superstructure, no society whose laws silently shape the imperatives of daily life. The "economic", like "the social" and "the sexual", are themselves discursive unities whose histories, and temporal coexistence, must be traced. With such a radical scepticism about the fixity of social phenomena and their relationship one to the other, no rational theory of the world seems possible.

But if we look at the implications of Foucault's work from another angle, then something more constructive appears. He does not deny that complex relationships between say, the economic, the social, the familial and the sexual exist. He challenges us to investigate them in their singular emergence. We are encouraged to move away from an unthinking reliance on abstract determinism and a deterministic functionalism and urged to probe the actual relationship between one social form and another, the actual mechanics of power. The explanations are not written before the investigation nor deduced from first principles, and this must surely be a healthy emphasis in our efforts to understand the historic present.

■ The history of sexuality

At the heart of our present is the continent of sexuality and its claim to hold the key to the truth of our individuality. Throughout the 1970s a large number of people, chiefly products of modern feminism and gay politics, battled with theoretical and political questions about sex: about the historical forces that shaped sexuality, about the relationship between capitalism and the construction of sexual difference and sex oppression, about the relevance of sexual liberation to socialist politics. These were not new questions on the Left. They have been consistently asked both in the libertarian and Marxist traditions of socialism since the mid-nineteenth century. What is striking, however is the dearth of useful responses to these problems from the traditional Left. Perry Anderson recently confessed that there were blind spots in the Marxist tradition – with regard to war and peace, the meaning of nature, women's oppression and the possibilities of a "socialist morality".[9] But in this elegant re-statement of classical Marxism there seems to be no room for rethinking the meaning of sexuality. Certain questions are never asked, perhaps because they cannot be asked within the inherited framework of socialist thought. Its priorities have been elsewhere: in class relations, the state, political organisation. For those of us who were interested in questions of sexual politics as well, there was no useful echo in the Marxist tradition. It was at this point of deadlock that Foucault's work appeared as relevant.

Foucault's *History of Sexuality* is not, of course, a history of behaviours or beliefs or of the highways and byways of desire.[10] True to his general approach it is a study of the emergence, development and effects of a specific configuration

of discourses and practices. This has become clearer still with
the publication of volumes two and three of the *History* where
the conditions for the emergence of the whole apparatus in pre-
Christian Hellenic and Roman culture are slowly and majesti-
cally being delineated. Foucault no more offers a total theory of
sexuality than he does of history or politics. But in asking
certain key questions, in challenging various received ideas, in
analysing crucial connections he has contributed to a rethinking of the whole relationship between the social and the sexual.

A central feature of the work is a critique of sexual
essentialism – and this is in line with his wider project.
Madness, the ostensible subject of Foucault's first major text[11]
and sex, the apparent theme of his most recent, seem eminently
"natural" objects to study. There are commonsensical definitions of their nature, and untold texts detailing their abundant
manifestations. A history of these phenomena, therefore, it
might be supposed, could only be a history of attitudes toward
them. But it is Foucault's main task precisely to question the
naturalness and inevitability of these historical objects. Their
pre-existence as natural unchanging objects is not to be taken
for granted. All his work is based on this assumption but it
becomes increasingly explicit as his work develops. In *Madness
and Civilisation* he does not, of course, claim that phenomena
to which the term madness can refer never existed. On the
contrary, in this work there is a strong romantic naturalism,
which gives the impression that Foucault is posing the truth of
madness against the falsity of reason. But even here the main
concern is with the way reason was conceptually separated
from unreason, to provide the conditions for the emergence of
modern psychiatric medicine. It is the social categorisation
which unifies the disparate phenomena known collectively as
"madness".

By the time he comes to write the first volume of *The
History of Sexuality* the lingering naturalism has all but
disappeared. In this book, sex, far from being the object to
which sexual discourse refers, is a phenomenon constructed
within the discourse itself. He does not deny the existence of
the material body, with its desires, aptitudes, potentialities,
physical functions and so on, but he argues that the historian's
task is to re-read the discursive practices which make them

meaningful and which change radically from one period to another. Why is it, he asked in the mischievously iconoclastic first volume of the *History*, that the Christian West has been so obsessed with sex, has given it such a central symbolic significance, that we can claim to know ourselves by knowing our sex? Is it possible, he wondered, that far from being repressed, sexuality has been encouraged and produced as a central element in the operation of power? Could it be that in the very belief that through our sexuality we can be free, we are most truly enslaved?

It has to be said that few of Foucault's speculations were original or new in themselves.[12] Post-Kinsey sex research had convincingly demonstrated that sexuality was socially constructed, and Foucault's work is saturated with its findings. Feminists had begun investigating what Foucault was to call "technologies of power" around sexuality long before his work appeared, especially with regard to the regulation of prostitution. Gay historians had already demonstrated the historical peculiarity of a "homosexual species" and identity. Freudo-Marxists such as Marcuse had already vividly painted the shape of that gilded cage that paraded under the name of the sexual revolution. What Foucault offered was something more than all these: a powerful image of a great domain of sexuality which had a history – beginnings in the Christian preoccupations with sin and salvation; a middle in various strategies of regulation and control, of women, of children, of procreative behaviour and of sexual perversity; and a possible point of resistance in the evocation of the "body and its pleasures".

It was also, of course, a partial picture. Foucault's emphasis on the imprisoning nature of the categories of thought which organise how and what we can think seemed to leave little room for resistance and change. The challenge to the fixity of sexual identity seemed to undermine the need for any coherent sense of identity at all. Could he really be advocating what he once described as "the happy limbo of a non-identity",[13] with its implied abnegation of any organising ego? And if sexuality was simply a ruse of power, were rational choices about sexual relations in any way possible? Was Foucault really denying the need for sexual politics or simply subverting their more bloated pretentions?

Foucault has tackled many of these issues in interviews and lectures since 1976, and indirectly responds to his critics in the two new volumes of the History, *L'Usage des Plaisirs* and *Le Souci de Soi*. He has shifted from analysing how people are defined, categorised and subjected to the tyrannies of sex, to how people, in a culture antecedent to our own, were defining themselves as subjects of ethical choice around the erotic. In place of describing the modes of modern sexuality as once promised, he now seeks to throw the whole edifice into historical relief by looking at its predecessors. And in place of our current Western belief that in sex lies truth, we are shown how the erotic, whilst still an object of moral concern, can take its part not at the centre of existence but as one aspect of an aesthetics of existence. We are nudged quietly into thinking what such a concept could mean for us today.

I do not particularly want to endorse all of this. The whole work on sexuality as it has now emerged can be challenged in historic detail, and no doubt that will be done by professionals for years to come. But whatever our detailed criticisms, this is a very important body of work and it poses three major questions. The first is historical. What is the relationship between the apparatus of sexuality and the diverse workings of power? Why, and by what processes, has sexuality come to the heart of our contemporary discourses? What is the relationship between the regulation of sexuality and other relations of exploitation and oppression? Foucault's answers are necessarily tentative, indirect, oblique. But these are vital questions and are posed more clearly than ever before.

Second, the work as a whole asks testing theoretical questions, about the relationship between desire and social categorisation, between social regulation and subjectification, between definition and self-definition, power and resistance. I believe there is an important role here for psycho-analysis for the theory of the dynamic unconscious, a topic Foucault himself is notoriously sceptical about. But again, in failing to offer positive guidelines, Foucault challenges us to rethink what we mean by subjectivity and its historically changing forms.

Third, important political questions flow from Foucault's deconstruction of sexuality. One response to Foucault's challenge has been to deny the existence of any general categories of women, of homosexuals, and to suggest that, in Stephen Heath's phrase, sexuality does not really exist, and therefore, by implication we can more or less slough off its pretentions.[14] This seems to me to be misguided. "Sexuality" may be an historical invention but we are ensnared in its circle of meaning. We cannot escape it by act of will. This does not mean that we must simply accept the hegemonic definitions of our true sex handed down to us by theologians and sexologists. It does mean we need to rethink the criteria by which we can choose our sexualities. Foucault's work moves in the direction of a celebration of sexual diversity and choice, and his later interviews interestingly illustrate the degree to which he was working through some of the challenges this poses. He suggests the need to distinguish between freedom of sexual acts and freedom of relationships. The first must be questioned because it might lead to a toleration of rape and violence. The second should be embraced because it points to a new right to construct different forms of relations, breaks away from the sterile arguments about which forms of activity are natural or unnatural, normal or abnormal, and asks instead searching questions about context and meaning and alternative forms of friendship. Far from denying the possibility of sexual change, Foucault beckons us to think about it in different ways: not as a point of transcendence to power, not as a mythic moment of liberation, but as a possibility for inflecting the dominant codes, undermining the truth claims of the arbiters of desire, and making new relationships. As he put it in a late interview:

> We have to understand that with our desires, through our desires, go new forms of relationships, new forms of love, new forms of creation. Sex is not a fatality; it's a possibility for creative life.[15]

■ Politics

This leads us finally to the political implications of Foucault's work. He distinguishes in his paper on "The Subject and Power" between three types of struggles:[16] against forms of domination, whether ethnic, social or religious; against forms of exploitation that separate individuals from what they produce; and "against that which ties the individual to himself and submits him to others – that is, struggles against subjection, forms of subjectivity and submission. The first, Foucault suggests, was dominant in the Middle Ages, the second in the nineteenth century, the third is increasingly important today. This does not mean that the first two have been superseded:

> It is certain that the mechanisms of subjection cannot be studied outside their relation to the mechanisms of exploitation and domination. But they do not merely constitute the "terminal" of more fundamental mechanisms. They entertain complex and circular relations with other forms.[17]

This is fully in accord with Foucault's general reluctance to see the present as constructed upon a single contradiction, whether between capital and labour as the Marxist tradition would prefer or between men and women as some feminists might argue. The present is a mobile ensemble of specific histories, and manifests a host of social antagonisms. As Mouffe puts it:

> The emergence of new political subjects women, national, racial and sexual minorities, anti-nuclear and anti-institutional movements, etc., are the expression of antagonisms that cannot be reduced to the relations of production.[18]

The failure of the orthodox socialist tradition to address all, or any, of these new antagonisms and subjectivities, in an appealing way, has opened the door to alternative modes of analysis, either in the form of alternative universalisms, as in feminist theories of patriarchy, or in the microscopic investigation of specific modalities of power and domination, which has been the specific contribution of Foucault.

Again, therefore, we see that Foucault's approach fits in with a tendency amongst many on the Left to try to rethink the nature of contemporary struggles and to accord full recognition to the diversity of conflicts that fracture contemporary society: for Foucault power is constructed and functions on the basis of particular powers, myriad issues, myriad effects of power.[19] It is a complex domain that must be analysed and combatted in the mechanisms and social practices through which power is actually exercised. This implies a multiplicity of struggles around specific configurations of power. It is, on the other hand, radically abstentionist about the possibility of forging links between the diverse struggles.

Foucault is deeply sceptical about the effectivity of "programmes" for change. Programmes, in a sense, always fail, and we have to live with their unintended consequences. The programme of reforming the prisons in the early nineteenth century produced greater surveillance – and created criminals. The sexological programme of replacing moralistic definitions by scientific ones led to new forms of control over sexual diversity, and the imposition of new forms of correct behaviour. The revolutionary programme can lead as easily to the Gulag as to human liberation. We find in Foucault, therefore, no programme for social advance, no strategy for a new society.

But why should we seek it? Why should we look in the writings of a single intellectual for guidelines that others should follow in the future? For Foucault, the role of the intellectual in modern society is not to offer prescriptive analysis but to lay bare the mechanisms of power.

> The intellectual no longer has to play the role of an adviser. The project, tactics and goals to be adopted are a matter for those who do the fighting. What the intellectual can do is to provide instruments of analysis and at present this is the historian's essential role. . . .In other words, a topological and geological survey of the battlefield – that is the intellectual's role.[20]

Political conclusions are left to us, who are involved in the disparate conflicts of social life.

Foucault's rejection of the role of radical guru does not mean that links cannot be drawn between different struggles, that we cannot understand hierarchies of power, that political strategies are unnecessary or impossible – simply that we should not seek them in the body of work that Foucault himself produced. That strikes me as a wholly admirable modesty.

At the same time there is a more positive message we can learn from Foucault and especially from his later work. "Maybe the target nowadays," he suggests, "is not to discover what we are, but to refuse what we are." Against the insidious impact of modern power structures which simultaneously totalise and individualise we need to imagine what we could be:

> We have to promote new forms of subjectivity through the refusal of the kind of individuality which has been imposed on us for several centuries.[21]

The new political subjects that have emerged over the past twenty years illustrate a similar refusal of imposed definition. We ignore their challenge at our peril.

10 The Fabians and Utopia

There is a long, though frequently buried, tradition of seeing socialism as a "new way of life", of emphasising in the compendious socialist agenda those elements that project an alternative reality and an empowering hope. One of the many functions of a Utopia, as Raymond Williams has reminded us, is the "education of desire", the imaginative construction of a different way of being as a yardstick by which to judge the present and measure the winning of the future.[1] In the 1880s, the decade that marked Fabianism's obscure birth, the quick of desire flared brightly and socialist Utopianism was an enlivening current. If socialists failed to educate desire, socialism's contemporary giant, William Morris, warned in the early years of the Fabian Society's life, "to sustain steadily their due claim to that fullness and completeness of life which no class system can give them", then they would fall victim to the "humbug of a kind of utilitarian sham socialism".[2] Many saw the Fabians as mundane representatives of such cosmic hypocrisy.

If solid policy proposals and planning are the necessary mediations between possibility and hope, the aspiration for a different way of being is the energy which keeps the political will from wilting. A concentration on the Utopian wish at the expense of realistic tactics and bold strategy for socialist change renders the dream truly Utopian in another (classically Marxist) sense: unattainable, out of kilter with the real, "objective", possibilities of the age. But a concentration on the means, at the expense of cultivating some vision of at least the staging

170

post to the "city upon the hill", desiccates the socialist project, making it not only unappealing but positively undesired. It is all very well to celebrate the journey, refreshing to question the idea that history has any ultimate end, but it is surely deadening to have no concept of the liberating effects of achievable change, what we are transforming things for.

The Fabians of the 1880s had some appreciation of this. Although the Society had been founded in a conscious break from the romantically Utopian Fellowship of the New Life (based, as its constitution put it, upon the "subordination of material things to spiritual" and aiming at "the cultivation of a perfect character in each and all") there was no absolute divide between the people involved in each, or movement to the sectarian barricades. Edward Pease, ostensibly the very model of the colourless Fabian bureaucrat, wrote of the second edition of Edward Carpenter's long Whitmanesque poem, *Towards Democracy*, that "no sane person expects that the millennium will be inaugurated in the House of Commons, or that the chosen of caucuses will discover the results of universal happiness".[3] For Pease, as for many other socialists of the period, Carpenter's work was a necessary "poetry for grown-up people". Unfortunately, it seemed to many critics, including other Fabians, that much of the poetry left the "Old Gang" of the Society (though some had never revealed much of it) as the hopes of the nineteenth century were hostaged to the realisable political and social possibilities of the twentieth. To Crosland, revising the Fabian tradition in the 1950s, the Webb ethos, which had dominated it for so long, seemed bleak, non-conformist and forbidding.[4] There is, indeed, something chilling in the Webbs' deterministic elaboration of their credo in 1913:

> it is from the actual facts and coldly impassive arguments that socialism draws its irresistible cogency.[5]

As G.D.H. Cole remarked of the society at about the same time:

> In endeavouring to persuade the world that socialism was a "business proposition", it forgot that it must be a "human"

proposition also: it found definiteness and collectivism and lost idealism, which is essential for real Socialism.[6]

The dedication to socialism of such leading Fabians as the Webbs and Shaw, and the moral earnestness with which they pursued their goals, was never in doubt, and it is fair to say that the self-sacrificing commitment of the early Fabians to their cause was usually greater than that revealed by many of their putative successors whose "socialism" proved to be a rather movable feast. But the very dryness of the Fabian vision, designed to maximise its appeal to the respectable classes as the common sense of the age, seemed to many of even its own enthusiasts to represent a catastrophic abandonment of inspiration. As S.G. Hobson saw it:

> Practicability, efficiency, organisation, statistical proof – these are the Fabian passwords. In such an atmosphere faith and hope and strivings of the spirit speedily droop and die.[7]

Or as Crosland put it much later:

> Total abstinence and a good filing-system are not now the right sign-posts to the socialist Utopia.[8]

Many of course thought that they never had been the appropriate signposts.

Sue Cartledge has written of a conflict between duty and desire at the heart of the modern women's movement.[9] Perhaps any great progressive cause will manifest a similar and necessary tension. The difficulty with the Webbs and their closest associates in the early Fabian Society was that duty seemed to suppress desire altogether, imagination was enslaved to obligation and reason floated free from passion. Mrs Webb characteristically confessed in her Diary on the eve of the First World War that she was a "benevolent bureaucrat" objected to by all the "A's, the artist, the anarchist, and the aristocrat".[10] But what many other socialists really objected to was what they saw as the basic pessimism implicit in this benevolence. It was, Cole suggested:

The "doubting Thomas" of the socialist faith; there is but a veneer
of humanitarianism over its belief in the mid-Victorian heresy of
original sin. Upon such a gloomy gospel of despair no great
society can be built.[11]

There were and are legitimate alternative perceptions of what
might constitute this "Great Society". For many socialists
emerging contemporaneously with the Fabians in the 1880s a
"new life" implied a transformation of all relationships, not
only economic, social and political, but also of gender and sex.
Engels had noted a "curious fact", a "phenomenon common to
all times of great agitation, that the traditional bonds of sexual
relations, like all other fetters, are shaken off".[12] Inscribed in
the politics of many socialist pioneers of the 1880s, like Edward
Carpenter, was a belief inherited from the early "Utopian
socialists", and prefigured in the Owenite experiments of the
1820s and 1830s, that it was the duty of socialism to help
loosen the fetters, and that changes in sexual relations were a
measure by which the progress of socialism in general could be
gauged.[13]

This was, however, a controversial and contested claim,
with the arguments taking place both over means (overtly) and
over ends (covertly). At the heart of the debate over means was
the anxiety that espousal of too outrageous a programme would
jeopardise the support necessary even to begin its implementation. The "advanced programme" might well be "desirable" in
the abstract but it was likely to be too radical for the masses
and the classes whose winning over was regarded as
indispensable for necessary social advance. This had already
been an issue in the Owenite circles of the 1820s and 1830s
when experiments, often contradictory, in new forms of
marriage and sexual freedom had been common.[14] It became
acute in the 1880s and 1890s as gender relations and questions
of sexuality emerged as more centrally political issues on a
wider stage. In the last decades of the nineteenth century a new
"social purity" consensus was achieving a precarious hegemony, expressed in new legislation on sexual matters, energetic
moral vigilance campaigns and a respectable reaction to a
notable series of sex related scandals.[15] This suggested a

necessary caution or the risk of public obloquy. By the late 1890s the sexologist Havelock Ellis, an early luminary of the Fellowship of the New Life, had gained some notoriety as the result of a scandal surrounding the publication of his study of homosexuality, *Sexual Inversion*.[16] Edward Carpenter, who had been drawn to socialism in the 1880s because of the conflicts between respectability and desire signalled by his growing awareness of his (homo)sexual nature, was also by the mid-1890s beginning to reveal his sexual as well as political radicalism in a series of books, beginning with *Love's Coming-of-Age*.[17] In this work, essays on the sex passion and marriage lay side by side with espousal of women's freedom and (in a later edition) a panegyric to the "intermediate sex", with the ultimate radicalism tempered only by a cautious obscurity.

But as Carpenter himself observed, the subject of sex was difficult to deal with: "There is no doubt a natural reticence connected with it. There is also a great deal of prudery."[18] Much of it, he could have added, came from his fellow socialists. While the German Social Democracy saw in the trial and conviction of Oscar Wilde in 1895 a prime example of bourgeois hypocrisy and took the opportunity to attempt to marry advanced sexological thinking and socialist principles ("It is necessary", as the proto-Fabian Eduard Bernstein felt, "to discard judgments based on more or less arbitrary moral concepts in favour of a point of view deriving from scientific experience"[19]), in Britain there was a discreet silence. George Bernard Shaw privately sympathised with Carpenter's efforts to make people understand the "curious reversal" of homo-sexuality as a "natural accident" but was appalled at the prospect of any propaganda for it: "No movement could survive association with such propaganda."[20] This was then, as it is today, the crux. Robert Blatchford's warning to Carpenter that open advocacy of sex radicalism would make impossible the achievement of socialism, the only long-term guarantee of sex reform, has had a long after echo.[21] Shaw went further and dismissed this "sex nonsense" as a question that should be outside issues of political organisation.[22] In his essay in *Forecasts of the Coming Century*, edited by Carpenter, Shaw had warned (almost certainly against his own editor) that "Socialism, if it is to gain serious attention nowadays, must come into the field as political science and not as sentimental dogma."[23] At stake here, of course, were two distinct views of how socialism could be brought about. For Carpenter it meant the making of socialists, and that involved appealing to the sexually discontented as much as the economically deprived, the spiritual aspiration as much as the material need. Shaw, on the other hand, in authentically Webbian tones, argued for the making of socialism, which could only come "by prosaic instalments of public regulation and public administration enacted by ordinary parliaments, vestries, municipalities, parish councils, school boards, and the like".[24]

Concealed in this argument over means were different perceptions of ends. When Carpenter spoke to the Fabian Society in the New Year lecture of 1889 he scandalised his audience by likening "civilisation" to a malignant "disease", causing a loss of unity in men and women, and by criticising the cult of intellect whilst celebrating feeling and urging the recognition of the "savagery within". Communism, for Edward Carpenter, represented the moment of reunification and reconciliation between nature and society. In response, Hubert Bland hastened to defend "civilisation" and feared that Carpenter's tone might mislead "the ignorant Philistine" as to the aims of the Society. Shaw was even sharper, fearing that such lectures "could only bring contempt on the socialist cause".[25] What it really revealed was a fundamental emotional divide. There could only be a frustrated marriage between Carpenter's belief in the destructive force of commercialism, on the one hand, and Sidney Webb's dithyramb in *Fabian Essays* to the potency of the Zeitgeist and the triumph of "unconscious socialism" through municipalisation, monopolisation and bureaucratic devotion, on the other.[26]

"We are not dealing with Socialism as a religion, nor as concerned with questions of sex or family", Sydney Olivier noted in his contribution to *Fabian Essays*:

> we treat it throughout as primarily a property form, as the scheme of an industrial system for the supply of the material requisites of human social existence.[27]

So, as he carefully stated, the essay was concerned with the

"Moral Aspects of the Basis of Socialism" not with "The Socialist View of the Basis of Morals". The Fabians offered a social morality rather than a socialist morality, stressing the elimination of want through the ending of competitive chaos rather than the development of new patterns of relationships (about which, in any case, they adopted a self-denying ordinance). They were concerned with quantity of provision rather than quality of relations. These were not ignoble ambitions; but to socialists like Edward Carpenter they were scarcely enough.

The early Fabians were not immune from the complex processes and cross-currents that were transforming social relations at the end of the nineteenth century, but the personal and political positions the leading Fabians adopted had the curious effect of suppressing the inevitable contradictions rather than providing means of living them. Jane Lewis has pointed out that Beatrice Webb's *Diary* is a powerfully representative record of the struggles of a middle class woman in the 1870s and 1880s.[28] She experienced at first hand (not least in her agonising relationship with Joseph Chamberlain) the devastating conflicts encountered by an educated, autonomous woman, between desire and independence, intellectual strength and emotional dependence, and passionately recognised the painful effect on women of the moral code of sexual restraint. "God knows celibacy is as painful to a woman as it is to a man",[29] she wrote in 1899, the year she signed the "Appeal Against Female Suffrage". But as her support for that Appeal underlines, she was simultaneously unsympathetic to what she saw as the particularist claims of feminism; and she resolved her personal crisis of identity by a partnership to a man whose basic view of the sexual division of labour was no less conventional than Chamberlain's, and by adherence to a socialism where feminist aspirations were clearly subordinated to socialist reorganisation.

The "Appeal Against Female Suffrage" which had appeared in *The Nineteenth Century* in June 1899, had argued that:

> the emancipating process has now reached the limits fixed by the physical constitution of women, and by the fundamental

differences which must always exist between their main
occupation and those of men.[30]

When in 1906, Beatrice publicly changed her mind over the
suffrage question, she did not abandon this fundamental
position, only her judgment about the effectiveness of the
political arena in allowing women's sex determined character
to flourish. The demand for suffrage, Beatrice remarked, was
not a "claim to rights or an abandonment of women's
particular obligations but a desire more effectively to fulfil their
functions by sharing the control of State action in those
directions".[31] As the Webbs reaffirmed in their last major
public production, on Soviet civilisation, the emancipation of
women would come from the "conscious will of the community", with the feminist issues "as part of the great social
question".[32]

It is no surprise that the Webbs adhered to a "separate
spheres" ideology for this was the common discourse of the
times. It would have been especially strange if Beatrice, as an
intellectual foster child of Herbert Spencer, had fundamentally
broken with Spencer's view of sexual difference, or his belief
that there was an early arrest in women's evolution to permit
the conservation of energies necessary in the interests of
maternity.[33] But the nature of the relationship between men
and women was still negotiable. According to the most
advanced theories of the time, nature might inhibit but it did
not necessarily dictate a given pattern of behaviour. Beatrice,
however, had no doubt that women had a special duty to fulfil
their natural instincts for motherhood, and if this were
impossible, as she believed it was for herself, then social
motherhood or a contribution to social good was the necessary
adjunct. She spoke of the "holiness of motherhood" and its
infinite superiority over any other occupation that a woman
could take to. As she wrote in her letter to Mrs Fawcett, the
raising of children, the advancement of learning and promotion
of the spiritual were the particular obligations of women, and
the appropriate discharge of their duties were becoming more
and more an appropriate preoccupation for the community as a
whole.[34] Such interests of the community clearly overrode the
rights of the individual or the special claims of women. There

could be no endorsement of a "right to choose" when confronted by the social obligation of motherhood.

But the flame of desire was always too unpredictable to be easily organised and controlled, and the early Fabians displayed the usual contradictions between values and life-styles. A streak of bohemianism sat uneasily with conventional partnerships or the hard core of fundamental conservatism. Hubert Bland's own marriage to the novelist Edith Nesbitt was certainly unconventional and his own promiscuity famous, but he reacted with rage when his daughter Rosamund formed a liaison with the equally priapic H.G. Wells.[35] At the other extreme of behaviour, G.B. Shaw's exotic appearance and erratic flirtatiousness went with a sexual passivity that surprised even his friends. As Ellen Terry noted:

> Aren't you funny, preaching against marriage and marrying?
> Against other things, and doing 'em.[36]

Or, she might have added, promising other things and not doing them. Only those on the fringes of Fabianism, or exiled from it, like Wells, risked scandal by advocating "free love" and group marriage in such works as *A Modern Utopia*, *In the Days of the Comet*, *New Worlds for Old*, and *Ann Veronica*. As Beatrice remarked in response to the disastrous impact of one of Wells's affairs:

> we none of us know what exactly is the sexual code we believe in
> – approving of many things on paper which we violently object
> to when they are practised by those we care about.[37]

The truth was, of course, that most of the leading "Old Gang" had lives of unimpeachable rectitude. Looking back at the five partnerships at the heart of early Fabianism (the Peases, the Oliviers, the Shaws, the Wallases, and the Webbs) Beatrice wryly observed that they were "the utter essence of British bourgeois morality, comfort and enlightenment".[38] Such paragons were likely to display little aptitude for disruptive scandal.

The emergence of the Fabians as would-be scientists of society, constructing a historic justification for their beliefs on an understanding of the laws of social development, coincided with the emergence of sexology, a new "continent of knowledge" with privileged access to what Havelock Ellis enthusiastically endorsed as "the laws of nature".[39] At the centre of these early sexological excursions was a hypothesised conflict – Krafft-Ebing called it an "ever-lasting duel"[40] – between the elemental forces of "sex" and the constraints of "society", between nature and culture. But there were two ways of conceiving of this conflict. For a sexual radical like Carpenter or a liberal sexologist like Havelock Ellis, "nature" was essentially benign; it was society which was malignant and damaging. Carpenter believed that "the glory of sex pervades and suffuses all Nature", while Ellis argued that "It must be among our chief ethical rules to see that we build the lofty structures of human society on the sure and simple foundations of man's organism."[41] But there was another tradition – of which Krafft-Ebing was the chief exemplar – which saw sex as a domain of danger, which if unbridled "is a volcano that burns down and lays waste all around it; it is an abyss that devours all honour, substance and health",[42] and which demanded regulation and control. With a touch of poetic licence we may understand the Webbs and Shaw as the Krafft-Ebings of socialism, seeing in the "average sensual man" (Beatrice's famous dismissive phrase) or the "animal in men" a threat rather than an opportunity. The Webbs noted with approval in the 1930s that in the Soviet Union "sexual promiscuity", like all forms of self-indulgence, was seen as definitely contrary to community ethics:

> it is a frequent cause of disease; it impairs the productivity of labour; it is disturbing to accurate judgement and inimical to intellectual acquisition and scientific discovery.[43]

Not surprisingly, the leading Fabians believed in the superiority of "reason" to "instinct", and looked forward, in Shaw's phrase, to "the elimination of the mere voluptuary from the evolutionary process".[44]

This was the background to the strange flirtation of many leading Fabians with eugenics, the planned breeding of the best and the elimination of the "unfit". H.G. Wells's *Socialism and the Family* (1906) was explicitly a systematic Utopia which looked forward to the "replacement of a disorder by order" in reproduction.[45] A eugenicist rhetoric became pervasive in the decade before the First World War, covering a political range from far right to far left. It is not totally clear even now to what degree leading Fabians like the Webbs and Shaw actually believed in eugenics as opposed to using its vogue. Searle points to what seems an almost wilful obscurity in the arguments of the Fabians when confronting the issue, and in particular their refusal to differentiate clearly between environmental and hereditarian positions.[46] Beatrice believed that "the breeding of the right sort of man" was the most important of all questions, and was delighted at Shaw's mischievous vision of a "State Department of Evolution" and even a "joint stock human stud farm".[47] Here was a scientistic Utopia with a vengeance! But (apart from the fact that even leading eugenicists were shocked by Shaw's breezy iconoclasm in recommending "an extensive use of the lethal chamber"[48]), there were clear differences of emphasis between the Fabians and eugenicists proper. Eugenics had been born out of a belief that environmental reform had failed to produce the necessary changes in the human stock to eliminate the unfit and inadequate. The only resort, therefore, was to purify the stream of life at the source, to eliminate not so much the social causes of evil but the core biological defects by selective breeding.

The Fabians, on the other hand, who shared the eugenicists' fear of "race deterioration", if not "race suicide", were fundamentally concerned that social factors had encouraged over-breeding on the part of the poor and under-breeding on the part of the thrifty. The Fabian tract on *The Decline of the Birth Rate* written by Sidney Webb in 1907 argued that the State should adopt some policies (such as "Endowment of Motherhood") which would induce the right sort of people to assume parenthood.[49] Eugenics might be relevant in eliminating the biologically feeble, but only social policies could help the socially disadvantaged to improve their lot. It was social engineering not biological engineering that chiefly interested the Webbs.

Hence their enthusiasm for the greatest experiment of all in social engineering, the Soviet Union of the 1930s. Amidst its harsh realities they found at last their model. Beatrice reported that they had "fallen in love with Soviet Communism", and perhaps not the least of its attractions was the fact that "there is no spooning in the Parks of Recreation and Rest".[50] The Webbs's visits to the Soviet Union were undertaken in the midst of its headlong retreat from the radical experiments in social relations that had followed the 1917 revolution. Marriage laws were tightened up, abortion limited, homosexuality once again made illegal. Necessity, it seemed, dictated such "drastic action", and the Webbs concluded the second edition of their book on *Soviet Communism* with a well-formed sneer at those who ignorantly criticised the resurrection of puritanism in the Soviet Union.[51] Indeed, the dispassionate writing away of the abrogation of genuine sex reforms betrays a certain lack of basic humanity when confronting the purposes of a socialist policy. The Webbs had found a Utopia; but it was unfortunately lacking in most of the attributes of desire.

It is perhaps wrong to see in the sublime moral certainties of the Webbs the quintessence of Fabianism. Their intellectual weight in the Society before the First World War did not preclude heated debates, or diversity of views or behaviour. But what Crosland pointed to as the Webb ethos undoubtedly did survive, if only as a gestural presence, into the post Second World War period and offered the neatest of targets for Fabian revisionism. In the blood of socialists, Crosland famously suggested in *The Future of Socialism*, "there should always run a trace of the anarchist and the libertarian, and not too much of the prig and the prude".[52] He looked forward, as "society becomes more social-democratic" to "the cultivation of leisure, beauty, grace, gaiety, excitement, and of all the proper pursuits, whether elevated, vulgar, or eccentric, which contribute to the varied fabric of full private and family life".[53] If the Webbs belonged to the Krafft-Ebing generation here was an apparent representative of the generation of Alfred Kinsey, celebrating choice rather than restriction, diversity rather than uniformity, pleasure rather than restraint.

And yet, if we look more closely, we can find definite continuities. Beatrice Webb, after all, had expressed her belief in "the maximum of personal intervention and individual divergence alike in ends and means from the common mean",[54] and while the tone may have been less eloquent than Crosland's, the meaning was similar. Surely, too, there are echoes of Sidney's "inevitability of gradualness" in Crosland's confidence in social progress: "as our traditional objectives are gradually fulfilled".[55] But more fundamentally, there are continuities in the logic of the two phases. For the founding members, questions of morality were legitimately outside the socialist project, though State policies might well nudge individuals towards more socially responsible behaviour. For the Crosland generation there was a recognition that society impinged on private life in a restrictive and puritanical manner, but this did not lead (despite that touch of anarchism and libertarianism) to an abandonment of social regulation. In both periods the paramount difficulty lay in the balance between social intervention and private choice.

The dilemma of the Crosland generation was more acute because it was faced with a task of actual implementation. Amongst the socially imposed restrictions that needed relaxing Crosland listed:

> The divorce laws, licensing laws, pre-historic (and flagrantly
> unfair) abortion laws, obsolete penalties for sexual abnormality,
> the illiterate censorship of books and plays, and the remaining
> restrictions on the equal rights of women.[56]

This was the agenda for the so called "permissive reforms" that were actually implemented during the 1960s. But more interesting in retrospect is not the way in which the reforms removed restraints but the modest shift that actually took place in the modes of regulation of social (and especially sexual) behaviour. The "Wolfenden strategy" that lay behind most of the reforms relied on a distinction between private behaviour (which was regarded as a domain of choice between consenting adults) and public behaviour which was the legitimate realm of regulation and control.[57]

The actual reforms set out to demarcate this divide more clearly than ever before. Partial decriminalisation of male homosexual behaviour in private was balanced by more effective policing of public behaviour; the legalisation of abortion in certain circumstances was accompanied by a shift in the locus of regulation from the law to medicine.

But the point that needs underlining is that none of the reforms relied on a qualitative reassessment of the practices concerned. There was no positive affirmation of homosexuality in the Sexual Offences Act, no espousal of a woman's right to choose in the Abortion Act, no explicit adoption of divorce by consent in the Divorce Act. All the reforms, as Greenwood and Young have indicated, were concerned with "drawing the lines between freedom and licence".[58] The ultimate definition of the content of that freedom was suspended in social democratic Britain as it had been in the first Fabian formulations in late Victorian Britain. Crosland's "piece-meal moral engineering" was not ultimately dissimilar to the Webbs' more aggressive social engineering.

There is a real dilemma here. To endorse particular patterns of behaviour as appropriate or correct for the new socialist man or woman runs obvious risks of absolutism and authoritarianism, and most socialist traditions have rightly rejected such a move. But to make no statements at all about the sort of life that is desirable opens up a political and moral vacuum which could dangerously weaken the socialist aspiration. The revived interest in recent years in the writings and practices of the "Utopian socialists" testifies to the existence of a need that Fabianism, with all its worthy ambitions, has not been able to satisfy: for some perception of what socialism can offer in terms of an alternative way of life. The socialist project demands ideals as well as realism, ends as well as means, and it is here that the Fabian tradition has been most lacking.

11 The value of difference

■ A question of values

Identity is about belonging, about what you have in common with some people and what differentiates you from others. At its most basic it gives you a sense of personal location, the stable core to your individuality. But it is also about your social relationships, your complex involvement with others, and in the modern world these have become ever more complex and confusing. Each of us live with a variety of potentially contradictory identities, which battle within us for allegiance: as men or women, black or white, straight or gay, able-bodied or disabled, "British" or "European". . . .The list is potentially infinite, and so therefore are our possible belongings. Which of them we focus on, bring to the fore, "identify" with, depends on a host of factors. At the centre, however, are the values we share or wish to share with others.

"Identity-politics" were initially defined by and for the new social movements that came to public consciousness from the late 1960s: the black movement, feminism, lesbian and gay liberation and so on. The question of integrating these creative but diffuse and potentially divisive forces into the political mainstream has been part of the agony of the left during the last decade. Issues of identity are now, however, at the centre of modern politics. When Mrs Thatcher utters anathemas against Brussels and all its works, or interfers in the details of the history curriculum, she is engaged in an exercise in delineating

184

a cultural and political identity, in this case of "Britishness", which she wants us to share. When President Gorbachev discourses on "our common European home" he is striving to re-form our perception of the Soviet identity, and to re-fashion our idea of Europe. When the Bradford mullahs organise against *Satanic Verses* and follow the Ayatollah's *fatwa* they are simultaneously affirming and fashioning an identity: as Muslims, but also as black British entitled to the protection of the blasphemy laws like Anglicans and Catholics and evangelicals. When we mourn with students in Beijing, or express solidarity with black South Africans, or run (or sing, or joke) "for the world", we are striving to realise our identities as members of the global village, as citizens of the world.

Identities are not neutral. Behind the quest for identity are different, and often conflicting values. By saying who we are, we are also striving to express what we are, what we believe and what we desire. The problem is that these beliefs, needs and desires are often patently in conflict, not only between different communities but within individuals themselves.

All this makes value debates particularly fraught and delicate. They are not simply speculations about the world and our place in it. They touch on fundamental, and deeply felt, issues about who we are and what we want to be and become. They also pose major political questions: how to achieve a reconciliation between our collective needs as human beings and our specific needs as individuals and members of diverse communities, how to balance the universal and the particular. These are not new questions. They are likely, nevertheless, to loom ever-larger as we engage with the certainty of uncertainty that characterises "new times".

■ The return of values

This is the background to a new concern with values in mainstream politics. Most notoriously, Mrs Thatcher has invoked "Victorian values" and has discoursed about everything from soccer hooliganism, to religion, to litter. But even the Labour Party, in an uncharacteristic burst of philosophising, have produced a statement on *Democratic Socialist Aims and Values*. And these are but the tips of an iceberg.

Such flurries have not been entirely absent in the past from British political and cultural history. But on the whole, from the Second World War until recently, the political class eschewed too searching a discussion of values, preferring, in Harold Macmillan's world-weary remark, to leave that to the bishops. During the years of the social-democratic consensus, welfarism, with its commitment to altruism and caring, provided a framework for social policy, but offered little guidance on the purposes of the good society.

Similarly, in the sphere of private life, the most coherent framework of moral regulation, that enshrined in the "permissive reforms" of the 1960s of the laws relating to homosexuality, abortion, censorship, etc., is based on a deliberate suspension of any querying of what is "right" or "wrong". It relies instead on subtle distinctions between what the law may accept for public behaviour in upholding "public decency", and what can be tolerated in private when the curtains are closed. Most of us are probably quietly grateful for such small mercies.

As the post-war consensus has crumbled, however, the search for more or less coherent value systems has become rather more fevered. On a personal level some people have moved promiscuously through drugs and alternative life-styles to health fads and religion. A number seek to be "born again". Perhaps most of us just share a vague feeling that things are not quite right. On the level of politics, various fundamentalisms (on left and right) have burst forth, each articulating their own truth, whether it be about the perils of pornography, the wrongs done to animals, the rights and wrongs of this or that religion, or the marvels of the market economy. There is a new climate where values matter, and politicians, willy-nilly, are being drawn into the debate.

"Speaking of values", as the philosopher Paul Feyerabend has said, "is a roundabout way of describing the kind of life one wants to lead or thinks one wants to lead"[1]. Mrs Thatcher has been clearer about the sort of life she wants us to lead than any other recent political leader. She does not trust her bishops.

So the values of the cornershop and the cautious housewife have expanded inexorably into the culture of enterprise and the spiritual significance of capitalism. From her paean to "Victorian values" in the run-up to the 1983 general election to her address to the General Assembly of the Church of Scotland in May 1988, Mrs Thatcher's moral outlook has had, in Jonathan Raban's phrase, a peculiar "integrity".[2]

Questions of value have traditionally been more central to socialist debates than to conservatism but during the 1970s and early 1980s the nervous collapse of the left allowed little room for such niceties. Recently, there have been welcome signs of a revival of concern with basic values. The Labour Party's 1988 statement, *Democratic Socialist Aims and Values*, intended to frame the party's policy review, may have been too bland for many people's taste ("The true purpose of democratic socialism. . .is the creation of a genuinely free society.."[3]) but it was the first time since 1917 that the party had attempted to define its purposes, and in a recognisable philosophical tradition (essentially the rights based liberalism of the American philosopher, John Rawls).

At the same time the party seems to be attempting to resurrect the half-buried collectivist traditions of the British population. The lyrical Kinnock election broadcast in 1987 subliminally told us of the importance of rootedness and belonging as the basis for political advance. The Labour Party's poster campaign early in 1989 – "The Labour Party. Our party" – similarly articulated a sense of shared values, of communal spirit, lying latent in the collective unconscious.

In part, of course, these Labour Party innovations illustrate the wizardry of ad-men skills. But it is not too fanciful to see them as a reflection of broader tendencies towards re-asserting universal humanistic values, which transcend conventional political divisions. In their different ways, President Gorbachev and green politics have made an impact because of their expression of a human solidarity underlying the divisions of the world. Gorbachev's address to the United Nations in 1988 turned on a call to respect "universal human values", and looked forward to an ending of the arbitary divisions between peoples. Green philosophy calls on the same sense of our common destiny and interdependence, as human beings, and as fellow inhabitants of spaceship earth, and in doing so claims to displace traditional divisions between left and right.

It is impossible to underestimate the power of these various (and perhaps sometimes contradictory) appeals to human solidarity after a decade dominated by an ethic of human selfishness. We are reminded that what we have in common as human beings is more important than what divides us as individuals or members of other collectivities.

■ Difference

Nevertheless there are difficulties for the left in an all-embracing humanism. As a philosophical position it may be a good starting point. It does not, however, readily tell us how to deal with difference. As President Gorbachev could bitterly affirm, it is difference – economic, national, linguistic, ethnic, religious – and the conflicting identities and demands that diversity gives rise to, that poses a major threat to perestroika, and to human solidarity. If ever-growing social complexity, cultural diversity and a proliferation of identities is indeed a mark of the post-modern world, then all the appeals to our common interest as humans will be as naught unless we can at the same time learn to live with difference. This should be the crux of modern debates over values.

In confronting the challenge of social and moral diversity, the responses of left and right are significantly different. The right has a coherent, if in the long run untenable, view of the moral economy. At its most extreme, expressed in Mrs Thatcher's dictum that there is no such thing as society, only individuals and their families, difference becomes merely a matter of individual quirks or pathologies. Social goods are products of individual wills or desires, mediated by family responsibilities. In the economic sphere, this leads to a privileging of individual choice, "the essence" as Mrs Thatcher put it during the 1987 election campaign, of morality. But moral choice in turn, particularly with regard to issues such as sexuality, is limited by the commitment to a traditional concept of domestic obligation, in and through the family.

The left, on the other hand, is heir to a strong sense of

collective identities, of powerful inherited solidarities derived from class and work communities, and of different social constituencies, however inadequately in the past it has been able to deal with them. Multi-culturalism, as it was articulated from the 1960s in the legislation on racial equality, embodied a notion of different communities evolving gradually into a harmonious society where difference was both acknowledged and irrelevant. In rather less hopeful times, the commitment to the co-existence of different value systems is implied in the statement in *Democratic Socialist Aims and Values* that: "Socialists rejoice in human diversity"[4].

But the left has been less confident and sure footed when faced by the reality of difference.

When the Livingstone-led Greater London Council attempted to let one hundred flowers bloom at County Hall in pursuit of a new majority of minorities, the response of the Labour Party establishment varied from the sceptical to the horrified. Nor should we be entirely surprised at that. Despite its political daring, and commendable commitment to those hitherto excluded from the political mainstream, it was difficult to detect behind the GLC policy anything more coherent than the belief that grass roots activity and difference in itself were prime goods. "Empowerment", yes; but whom should the left empower?

The Salman Rushdie crisis has dramatised the absence of any clear-cut philosophy on the left. The Rushdie affair is important for socialists not simply because it concerns the fate of an individual (and an individual of the left at that) but because it underscores in the most painful way the dilemmas of diversity. At its simplest we have an apparent conflict of absolutes: the right of an author to freedom of speech, to challenge whomsoever he wishes in a democratic society, set against the claims of a distinctive moral community not to have its fundamental religious beliefs attacked and undermined. But of course the real divisions are more complex, and profound.

The left has not on the whole been willing to endorse an absolute right of free speech. On the contrary it has supported campaigns against racist and sexist literature, whilst a strong minority has supported the banning of pornography. And on the other side, the Muslim communities at the centre of the crisis are themselves not monolithic, bisected as they inevitably are by class, gender and political conflicts. At the same time the issues raised do not exist only in a meta-realm of principle: they work their way through the murky world of politics, in this case the complexities of international politics as well as the ward by ward, constituency by constituency problems of Labour politicians.

Nevertheless, there is a central question at the heart of the Rushdie affair, and it concerns the possibilities and limits of pluralism in a complex society. Let's take as an example the question of religious education in schools. The government, by insisting under the 1988 Education Reform Act that there should be a daily act of Christian worship in maintained schools, is in effect asserting the centrality of the Christian tradition to, in Mrs Thatcher's words, "our national heritage": "For centuries it has been our very life-blood". People with other faiths and culture are always, of course, welcome in "our land". But their beliefs can only, by implication, ever hope to have a secondary position in relation to "ours"[5].

Labour, however, accepts a less monolithic view of our religious past and present. As a result it seems prepared to support the principle of state-funding of separate fundamentalist Muslim schools. There is a certain multi-cultural rationale in this. If Anglican, Jewish and Roman Catholic schools are supported by the state, there seems no logic in not supporting the schools of other faiths as well. But schools transmit cultural values, some of which in the case of fundamentalists run counter to oft-declared values of the left. In this case, the schools will be based on a principle of sex-segregation which elsewhere Labour opposes. As a letter to the *Guardian* from Southall Black Sisters put it,

> The Labour Party is prepared to abandon the principle of equality where black women are concerned. Instead, they deliver us into the hands of male, conservative and religious forces within our communities, who deny us our right to live as we please.[6]

This underlines the danger of seeing communities as unified wholes, rather than as the locus of debate and divisions.

Not surprisingly, the "multi-culturalist" values of the Labour Party seem as likely to cause confusion, conflict and distrust as the explicitly uni-culturalist views of the right.

It is perhaps appropriate that these dilemmas should have been brought to the surface by the publication of, and reaction to Rushdie's *Satanic Verses*. Not only was the book written by an "immigrant" and about "immigrants". The book itself, as Malise Ruthven argued on its publication, is about "changing identities", about the transformations of identities that affect the migrant who leaves the familiar reference points of his homeland and finds himself in a place where the rules are different, and all the markers have been changed.[7] But this is not simply the experience of the migrant. The sense of dislocation and disorientation, of the rules of the game subtly changing, of the co-existence within us of conflicting needs, desires and identities, is becoming a major cultural experience for us all.

■ Choice

The basic issue can be stated quite simply: by what criteria can we choose between the conflicting claims of different loyalties? To ask the question immediately underlines the poverty of our thinking about this. Can the "rights" of a group obliterate the "rights" of an individual? Should the morality of one sector of the population be allowed to limit the freedom of other citizens? To what extent should one particular definition of the good and justice prevail over others? These are ancient questions, but the alarming fact is that the left lacks a common language for addressing them, let alone resolving them.

There have been two characteristic approaches on the left in confronting these dilemmas. First, there is the "discourse of rights", probably still the most potent mobilising force in the worlds of politics and morality. In the United States the protection of individual rights is enshrined in the constitution, and the claim to group rights has become the basis of many of the transforming currents of recent American politics, from the civil rights and black power movements to the women's movement and lesbian and gay liberation. Elswhere in the

West, a rights-based politics is similarly enshrined in written constitutions, bills of rights, constitutional courts, and so on.

In Britain, the tradition is enfeebled. Individual rights, though much bandied around in the political rough and tumble, are not entrenched in a constitutional settlement, and the concept of group rights barely exists. Rights are, however, clearly back on the agenda of the left. The response to the launch of Charter 88, with its appeal for a new constitutional settlement, with government subordinate to the law, and basic rights entrenched, suggests there is a strongly felt need for a codification and protection of fundamental rights.

Unfortunately, the claim to right, however well established at a constitutional level, does not help when rights are seen to be in conflict. Take the issue of abortion, yet again the focus of moral debate in America and Britain. Here the conflict is between two violently conflicting claims to right: the rights of the "unborn child" against the rights of a woman to control her own body. In these stark terms the conflict is unresolvable, because two value systems tug in quite different directions. The problem is that rights do not spring fully armed from nature. They cannot find a justification simply because they are claimed. Rights are products of human association, social organisation, traditions of struggle, and historical definitions of needs and obligations: whatever their claims to universality, they are limited by the philosophical system to which they belong, and the social and political context in which they are asserted.

This is not to deny the importance of rights-based arguments. But if we are to take rights seriously we must begin to articulate the sort of rights and the type of political culture we want.[8]

This is the starting point for the second major approach to the dilemma of choice, the politics of emancipation. In his essay "On the Jewish Question" in the 1840s Marx counterposed to the "morality of Rights" a "morality of emancipation", and even more powerfully than the claim to rights this has proved a potent mobilising force.[9] It offers a vision of a totally free society, where everyone's potentiality is fully realised, and a powerful analysis of the constraints on the realisation of human emancipation. At its heart is a denial that want, division, selfishness and conflict are essential parts of human nature. True human nature, it claims, can flourish in a truly emancipated society.

Most of us who are socialist must have been inspired by this vision. As a politics of liberation it shaped the rhetoric of the social movements that emerged in the 1960s. It is still latent in the hunger for Utopia and for the transendence of difference that shades our politics. The difficulty is that the practice has rarely kept up up with the vision, particularly in the history of Marxism. The Marxist tradition has been reluctant to define the nature of the emancipated society, and has been noticeably blind to questions of nationalism, ethnicity, gender and sexuality. Nor do the experiences of the *soi disant* socialist countries offer much confidence in the attainability of emancipation in the terms offered by the tradition so far.

We must not confuse a noble goal with the sordid practices of particular regimes. But we need to ponder whether the very project of human emancipation as conventionally set forth is not itself the fundamental problem. The glorious goal has all too often justified dubious means, whilst the absence of any detailed exposition of the meaning of emancipation has left us floundering when faced by the reality of conflicting claims to right and justice.

■ Radical pluralism

The Rushdie affair has underlined the inadequacy of the existing languages of rights and emancipation for dealing with real conflicts. Rights-based arguments leave us staring blankly at conflicting claims, while an emancipatory rhetoric leaves Rushdie trapped in his safe-house. In practice, in the absence of anything better we seem to be faced by two stark alternatives. On the one hand we have a call to respect absolutely the rights of a specific community to organise its own way of life, regardless of the traditions of the wider community as a whole. This has been put most clearly by Keith Vaz MP: "To goad and mock the new religions is to rob them of their roots and sensitivities. They must be left to develop in their own way".[10] This in effect is an appeal to give full play to cultural difference, whatever the implications, simply because enough people are willing and able to affirm the importance of what is different.

On the other hand, there is a sort of despair of the challenge of diversity. The novelist Fay Weldon has put it sharply: "Our attempt at multi-culturalism has failed. . . .The uniculturalist policy of the United States *worked*, welding its new peoples, from every race, every belief, into a whole".[11] Pluralism is in fact institutionalised rather than obliterated in the US, and inter-communal strife is not exactly unknown. But the philsophy of assimilation, where differences dissolve in the great "melting pot" of America, obviously still has a powerful appeal.

Neither position really deals with the fundamental issues. One in effect insists that it is impossible to evaluate different traditions. The other hopes that the claims of other traditions may dissolve into a greater whole. These opposed positions are effectively mirror-images of each other, both assuming that differences must be absolute. The reality is much more contradictory.

Different identities, and the social solidarities that sustain them, reflect the variety of individual and social needs in the modern world. Such needs are in constant flux, and change over time. They cannot be frozen by any moral system; indeed, the fervour and anger of fundamentalism can be seen as a reflex against the rapidity of change, where everything that was fixed begins to seem radically uncertain. To be able to deal with the world as it is, and to change it, we need a language of politics that is able to speak to difference and uncertainty within a framework of common principles.

There is no ready made blueprint for this. But, as a first step we could usefully learn the value of what Feyerabend calls a "democratic relativism",[12] which recognises that there are many different ways of being, and many truths, in the world; people should have a right to live in the ways that satisfy their needs.

In the Rushdie case, this implies respect for the traditions and aspirations of the Muslim community, and the creation of protected spaces where their voices may be heard. But radical relativism can only work if arguments over needs can be

conducted freely and democratically in each community, and
between different communities. Communities of identity are
never monolithic; they embody traditions of arguments and
debate, as the feminist interventions within the Muslim
community illustrate. We need a democratic framework which
allows debate to flourish.

So the recognition of a plurality of truths is a starting point
only. It in turn must be governed by what David Held has
called the principle of democratic autonomy.[13] This argues that
citizens should be free and equal in the determination of the
conditions of their own lives, sharing equal rights and
obligations, so long as they do not use their freedoms to negate
the rights and claims of others. Democratic autonomy implies a
respect and tolerance for other people's needs as the guarantee
of your own freedom to choose. Groups and communities
become potentially undemocratic, as fundamentalists of whatever flavour do, when they begin to proclaim the universal
truth of their particular experiences. The freedom to live your
own life in the way you choose must imply an acceptance of
other ways of life. Rushdie has found to his cost that this
principle as yet has very little leverage in the fundamentalist
community he was addressing.

Such principles, simple to write, painful to live, imply the
existence of a wider political community based on acceptance
of diversity and democracy. We may not be able to find,
indeed we should not seek, a single way of life that would
satisfy us all. That does not mean we cannot agree on common
political ends: the construction of what can best be described
as "a community of communities", to achieve a maximum
political unity without denying difference.

Such a political community will necessarily embody a
notion of the common good and of justice, in order to regulate
the variety of rights and demands. We can list, as socialists
have always done, the goals of a just society: the ending of
economic exploitation, social inequality, racism, gender and
sexual oppression and all the other relations of domination and
subordination that inhibit human potentials. But if the desirable
ends are not to be undermined, we must pay more attention
than many socialists have been willing to do in the past to the
means: the development of a polity where differences can be

aired and negotiated, and unavoidable conflicts mediated, in a democratic fashion.

These principles are not new. In essence they can be traced back to the earliest discussions of democracy in ancient Greece, and to the ideals of localised democracies of the early American republic. They represent a revitalisation of the communitarian tradition of politics and of a "civic republicanism".[14] At the same time they build on those elements of the British socialist tradition which have always stressed the importance of grass-roots activity and democratic control of social and economic life, supported feminist struggles and advocated sexual freedom. "Radical pluralism" as outlined here is congruent with the best in the democratic and socialist traditions.

This approach to socialist values is at best a framework within which we can begin to rethink the question of difference at both the individual and collective level. Rather more effectively than a simple claim to right, such a position offers a set of criteria for assessing conflicting claims. More modestly than a morality of emancipation it avoids declarations about a final resolution of all conflict in a magical escape from oppression and exploitation. The aim instead is to offer a concept of politics as a process of continuous debate and mutual education, and to broaden the democratic imagination through the acceptance of human variety and difference.

Reference notes

1. Introduction: writing about sex

1. Roland Barthes, *Writing Degree Zero*, London, Cape Editions, 1967, p.7.
2. George Orwell, "Why I write", in *Decline of the English Murder, and Other Essays*, Harmondsworth, Penguin, 1968, p.188.
3. Barthes, op.cit., p.25.
4. Orwell, op.cit.
5. London, Quartet Books, 1977; 2nd, revised edition, 1990; for a list of my other relevant publications, see the Select Bibliography.
6. Published in English as Michel Foucault, *The History of Sexuality, Volume 1, An Introduction*, London, Allen Lane, 1979.
7. Umberto Eco, *Reflections on the Name of the Rose*, London, Secker and Warburg, 1985, p.7.

2. Discourse, desire and sexual deviance: some problems in a history of homosexuality

1. A.P. Bell, and M.S. Weinberg, *Homosexualities: A Study of Diversity Among Men and Women*, London, Mitchell Beazley, 1978.
2. Guy Hocquenghem, *Homosexual Desire*, London, Allison & Busby, 1978.
3. Randolph Trumbach, "London's sodomites: homosexual behaviour and western culture in the 18th century", *Journal of Social History*, Fall, 1977, p.1.
4. Richard Burton, *A Plain and Literal Translation of the Arabian Nights Entertainment with Terminal Essay*, Benares, Kamashastra Society, 1885-8; Edward Westermarck, *The Origin and Development of the Moral Ideas*, London, Macmillan, 1906; C.S. Ford and F. Beach, *Patterns of Sexual Behaviour*, London, Methuen, 1952.

5. Edward Carpenter, "The intermediate sex", in E. Carpenter, *Love's Coming of Age*, London, Allen & Unwin, 1952.

6. Henry Havelock Ellis, *Studies in the Psychology of Sex*, vol.2, *Sexual Inversion*, 3rd edn. Pennsylvania, F.A. Davis, 1920; Iwan Bloch, *Sexual Life in England, Past and Present*, London, Francis Alder, 1938.

7. A.L. Rowse, *Homosexuals in History: A Study of Ambivalence in Society, Literature and the Arts*, London, Weidenfeld & Nicolson, 1977.

8. H. Montgomery Hyde, *The Other Love: An Historical and Contemporary Survey of Homosexuality in Britain*, London, Heinemann, 1970.

9. D.S. Bailey, *Homosexuality and the Western Christian Tradition*, London, 1955.

10. F. Lafitte, "Homosexuality and the law", *British Journal of Delinquency*, vol.9, 1958-9, pp.8-19.

11. D.W. Cory, *The Homosexual Outlook: A Subjective Approach*, New York, Nevill, 1953.

12. J. Lauritsen, and D. Thorstad, *The Early Homosexual Rights Movement (1864-1935)*, New York, Times Change Press, 1974; Ford and Beach, op.cit.; Jonathan Katz, *Gay American History: Lesbians and Gay Men in the USA*, New York, Thomas & Crowell, 1976; J.D. Steakley, *The Homosexual Emancipation Movement in Germany*, New York, Arno Press, 1975.

13. Katz, op.cit., pp.6-7.

14. A.D. Harvey, "Prosecutions for sodomy in England at the beginning of the nineteenth century", *The Historical Journal*, vol.21, no.47, 1978, p.944.

15. *See*, for example, Public Record Office HO 79/1 66: Lord Hawkesbury to Lord Sydney, 8 November 1808.

16. Trumbach, op.cit., p.9.

17. K.G. Dover (1978), *Greek Homosexuality*, London, Duckworth, 1978.

18. Mary McIntosh, "The homosexual role", *Social Problems*, vol.16, no.2, 1968, pp.182-92.

19. Jeffrey Weeks, *Coming Out: Homosexual Politics in Britain from the 19th Century to the Present*, London, Quartet, 1977.

20. L. Radzinowicz, *A History of English Criminal Law (vol.4): Grappling for Control*, London, Stevens & Sons, 1968; A.N. Gilbert, "The Africaine court martial", *Journal of Homosexuality*, vol.1, 1974, pp.111-22, A.N. Gilbert, "Buggery and the British Navy 1700-1861", *Journal of Social History*, vol.10, 1976; A.N. Gilbert, "Social deviance and disaster during the Napoleonic wars", Albion, vol.9, 1977.

21. *Journal of Mental Science*, October 1884.

22. Michel Foucault, *The History of Sexuality*, vol.1, London, Allen Lane, 1979.

23. McIntosh, op.cit.; Trumbach, op.cit.

24. Lawrence Stone, *The Family, Sex and Marriage*, London, Weidenfeld & Nicolson, 1977; Carroll Smith-Rosenberg, "The female world of love and ritual: relations between women in nineteenth century America", Signs, vol.1, 1975.

25. Edward Carpenter, *The Intermediate Sex*, London, Allen & Unwin, 1908, p.9.

26. Jeffrey Weeks, *Coming Out*, p.2; F.B. Smith, "Labouchère's Amendment to the Criminal Law Amendment Act", *Historical Studies*, vol.17, 1976; E.J. Bristow, *Vice and Vigilance: Purity Movements in Britain Since 1700*, Dublin: Gill and Macmillan, 1977.
27. Henry Havelock Ellis, Studies in the Psychology of Sex, vol.2, *Sexual Inversion*, New York: Random House, 1936.
28. Weeks, op.cit., p.107.
29. Arno Karlen, *Sexuality and Homosexuality: The Complete Account of Male and Female Sexual Behaviour and Deviation with Case Histories*, London, MacDonald, 1971, p.185.
30. J.A. Symonds, *Studies in Sexual Inversion, Embodying "A Study of Greek Ethics" and "A Study in Modern Ethics"*, New York, Medical Press, 1964.
31. V.L. Bullough and M. Voght, "Homosexuality and its confusion with the 'secret sin' in pre-Freudian America", *Journal of the History of Medicine*, vol.27, no.2, 1973; H. Ellis, *Studies in the Psychology of Sex*, op.cit.; M. Hirschfeld *Sexual Anomalies and Perversions*, New York, Encyclopaedia Press, 1938 and 1946; R. von Krafft-Ebing, *Psychopathia Sexualis: A Medico-Forensic Study*, New York, G.P. Putnam's & Sons, 1965.
32. On youth, *see* J. Gillis *Youth and History*, New York, Academic Press, 1974; D. Gorham "The 'maiden tribute of modern Babylon' re-examined: child prostitution and the idea of childhood in late Victorian England", *Victorian Studies*, vol.21; and on housework and motherhood, *see* A. Oakley, *Housewife*, Harmondsworth, Penguin, 1976, and A. Davin, "Imperialism and motherhood", *History Workshop*, vol.5, 1978, pp.9-65.
33. Weeks, *Coming Out*, p.17.
34. M. Brake, "I may be queer but at least I'm a man: male hegemony and ascribed 'v' achieved gender" in D.L. Barker and S. Allen, *Sexual Divisions and Society*, London, Tavistock, 1976, p.178.
35. Ibid., p.176.
36. M. McIntosh, "The homosexual role", p.184.
37. M. Poster, *Critical Theory of the Family*, London, Pluto Press, 1978, p.xvii.
38. Krafft-Ebing, op.cit., p.1.
39. J.H. Gagnon, and W.S. Simon, *Sexual Conduct: The Social Sources of Human Sexuality*, Chicago, Aldine, 1973.
40. Gordon Rattray Taylor, *Sex in History*, London, Panther, 1964.
41. Gagnon, and Simon, op.cit., p.11.
42. Herbert Marcuse, *Eros and Civilization*, London, Sphere, 1969. For Wilhelm Reich's comments on homosexuality *see* Wilhelm Reich, *The Sexual Revolution*, New York, Farrar Strauss & Giroux, 1970. "It can be reduced only by establishing all necessary prerequisites for a natural love life among the masses". For a useful comment on the historical context of Reich's views, see Juliet Mitchell, *Psychoanalysis and Feminism*, London, Allen Lane, 1974, p.141. A similar leftist view that homosexuality was "a symptom of arrested or distorted development" can be seen in A. Craig, *Sex and Revolution*, London, Allen & Unwin, 1934, p.129. Herbert Marcuse's views are to be found in *Eros and Civilization*, London, Sphere, 1969. Reich, *The Sexual Revolution*, expresses a viewpoint that homosexuality is a product of capitalist distortion of the libido.

43. Gagnon and Simon, op.cit., p.26.
44. Foucault, op.cit., pp.105-6.
45. Mitchell, op.cit., M. Campioni and L. Gross "Little Hans: The production of Oedipus", in P. Foss and M. Morris (eds), *Language, Sexualitiy and Subversion*, Darlington, Australia, Ferral Publications, 1978, pp.99-122, propose a useful critique of Mitchell.
46. Foucault, op.cit., p.153.
47. Gagnon and Simon, op.cit., p.17.
48. Kenneth Plummer, *Sexual Stigma: An International Account*, London, Routledge & Kegan Paul, 1975.
49. Mitchell, op.cit.
50. Hocquenghemn, op.cit.
51. G. Deleuze and F. Guattari, *Anti-Oedipus: Capitalism and Schizophrenia*, New York, Viking Press, 1977.
52. G. Weinberg, *Society and the Healthy Homosexual*, New York, Anchor, 1973.
53. Foucault, op.cit., pp.92-3.
54. Rosalind Coward, "Sexual liberation and the family", *M/F*, vol.1, 1978, p.20.
55. Michel Foucault, "Politics and the study of discourse", *Ideology and Consciousness*, no.3, Spring, 1978, p.14.
56. M. Foucault, *The History of Sexuality*, p.107.
57. Michel Foucault, *Discipline and Punish: The Birth of the Prison*, London, Allen Lane, 1977.
58. M. Foucault, *The History of Sexuality*, pp.139-40.
59. M. Foucault, *I, Pierre Riviere*, Brighton, Harvester, 1978.
60. Foucault, *The History of Sexuality*, p.141.
61. Ibid., p.146.
62. Ibid., p.95.
63. Ibid., p.101
64. Michel Foucault, "Power and Sex: an interview with Michel Foucault", *Telos*, no.32, Summer, 1977, p.155.
65. Foucault, *The History of Sexuality*, p.149.
66. Earnesto Laclau, *Politics and Ideology in Marxist Theory*, London, New Left Books, 1977.
67. Plummer, *Sexual Stigma*, p.210.
68. *See* for example, the anonymous author, usually known as Walter, of the nineteenth-century sexual chronicle, *My Secret Life*, 1877.
69. Gagnon and Simon, op.cit., p.180.
70. S. Hall, C. Chritcher, T. Jefferson, J. Clarke, and B. Roberts, Policing the Crisis: Mugging, *The State, and Law and Order*, London, Macmillan, 1978; R. Gray, "Bourgeois hegemony in Victorian Britain", in J. Bloomfield (ed.), *Class, Hegemony and Party*, London, Lawrence & Wishart, 1977.
71. E. Lemert, *Human Deviance, Social Problems and Social Control*, New Jersey, Prentice-Hall, 1967, p.40.
72. Campioni and Gross, "Little Hans", pp.99-122.
73. Ibid., p.103.

3. Inverts, perverts and mary-annes

1. F. Carlier, *Rapport d'un Officier de la Police Municipale de Paris*, Paris, 1864 and *Les Deux Prostitutions*, Paris, 1887. For a comment on Carlier's work *see* Vern L. Bullough, *Sexual Variance in Society and History* New York, John Wiley & Sons, 1976, p.638.
2. Xavier Mayne, *The Intersexes, A History of Similisexualism as a Problem in Social Life*, privately printed; 1908; Alfred C. Kinsey, Wardell B. Pomeroy, and Clyde E. Martin, *Sexual Behaviour in the Human Male* Philadelphia and London, W.B. Saunders Co., 1948, p.596; D.J. West, *Homosexuality*, Harmondsworth, Penguin Books, 1968, p.127.
3. For example, see Simon Raven, "Boys will be Boys, The Male Prostitute in London," in N.M. Ruiteenbeek, *The Problem of Homosexuality in Modern Society*, New York, E.P. Dutton & Co., 1963.
4. Michael Craft, "Boy Prostitutes and their Fate," *British Journal of Psychiatry*, 12, 1966, p.111.
5. Iwan Bloch, *The Sexual Life of our Time*, London, William Heinemann, 1909, p.313.
6. *See* chapter 1, "Discourse, desire and sexual deviance", above.
7. A.J. Reiss, "The social integration of queers and peers", in Ruitenbeek,
8. H. Montgomery Hyde, *The Trials of Oscar Wilde*, Harmondsworth, Penguin Books, 1962, p.172.
9. Work is now (1990) beginning to appear on male prostitution, in the context of the HIV/AIDS epidemic.
10. On France see Carlier, op.cit. Abraham Flexner, *Prostitution in Europe*, New York, 1914, p.30, comments on the German situation. Mayne, op.cit., has a survey of the European legal situation relating to homosexuality.
11. *See*, for example, Carlier, op.cit., p.454; Jacobus X, *Crossways of Sex, A Study in Eroto-Pathology*, 2 vols, Paris, Charles Carrington, 1904, vol.2, p.195; Werner Picton, "Male Prostitution in Berlin", *Howard Journal* vol.3, no.2, 1931.
12. The transcripts of the trial in 1871 are preserved in London in the Public Record Office, DPP 4/6. This section is based on these transcripts.
13. Public Record Office, DPP 4/6, transcript for Day 1, p.193.
14. Ibid., transcript for Day 2, p.256.
15. Alfred Swaine Taylor, *Medical jurisprudence* London, 1861, p.657.
16. Public Record Office, OPP 4/6, transcript for Day 1, p.21.
17. Ibid., transcript for Day 2, p.276. The work of A. Tardieu is referred to in Arno Karlen, *Sexuality and Homosexuality*, London, Macdonald, 1971, pp.185, 217.
18. DPP 4/6, transcript for Day 1, p.82.
19. Ibid., transcript for Day 3, p.299.
20. *See* Henry Labouchère parliamentary statement, quoted in *The Times*, 1 March 1890. For discussion of Labouchère's motives *see* F.B. Smith, "Labouchère's Amendment to the criminal Law Amendment Bill", *Historical Studies*, vol.17, no.67, October 1976.

21. Shaw is quoted in Ian Gibson, *The English Vice, Beating, Sex and Shame in Victorian England and After*, London, Duckworth, 1978, p.164; see also p.160. George C. Ives, *The Continued Extension of the Criminal Law* London, privately published, 1922, gives a useful description of the legal developments.

22. Report of the Royal Commission on the Duties of the Metropolitan Police, Cmnd. 4156, 1908, 1, p.119. For a comment on the 1928 recommendation *see Howard Journal*, vol.2, no.4, 1929, p.334.

23. Abraham A. Sion, *Prostitution and the Law*, London, Faber & Faber, 1977, p.33; Bristow, op.cit., p.54.

24. *Report of the Committee on Homosexual Offences and Prostitution*, Cmnd. 247, London, HMSO, 1957, p.39.

25. cf. Havelock Ellis, *The Task of Social Hygiene*, London, Constable, 1912, p.272.

26. Director of Public Prosecutions to Metropolitan Police Commissioner, 20 July 1889; Director of Public Prosecutions to Attorney General, 14 September 1889: Public Record Office, DPP 1/95/1.

27. Michael Schofield, *Sociological Aspects of Homosexuality*, London, Longman, Green & Co., 1965, p.200.

28. Casement Diaries, 17 April 1903. Public Record Office, HO 161/2.

29. cf. H. Montgomery Hyde, *The Trial of Sir Roger Casement*, London, William Hodge, 1964, p.clv.

30. "Walter", *My Secret Life*, 11 vols, Amsterdam, privately printed, 1877, vol.1, p.14.

31. Evelyn Hooker, "The Homosexual Community" in J.H. Gagnon and W. Simon, *Sexual Deviance*, London, Harper & Row, 1967, p.174.

32. Public Record Office, DPP 4/6, transcript for Day 6, p.243, Hurt to Boulton.

33. cf. J.R. Ackerley, *My Father and Myself*, London, Bodley Head, 1966; Tom Driberg, *Ruling Passions, The Autobiography of Tom Driberg*, London, Jonathan Cape, 1977.

34. As revealed, for instance, in the volumes of *My Secret Life. See also* Leonore Davidoff, "Class and Gender in Victorian England, The Diaries of Arthur J. Munby and Hannah Cullwick", *Feminist Studies*, vol.1, no.5, 1979.

35. As described in Phyllis Grosskurth, *John Addington Symonds, A Biography*, London, Longmans, 1964.

36. This is from one of a series of interviews conducted with homosexual men over sixty, which was part of a Social Science Research Council funded project on the organisation of the homosexual subculture in England. The researchers were Mary McIntosh and Jeffrey Weeks. The research was carried out between April 1978 and July 1979. All unreferenced quotations come from these interviews. Selections of these interviews have been published as Kevin Porter and Jeffrey Weeks (eds), *Between the Acts*, London, Routledge, 1990. The interview quoted here is not included in the book. The next unreferenced quotation can be found on p.38 of the published interview.

37. E.M. Forster, *The Life to Come and Other Stories*, Harmondsworth, Penguin Books, 1975, p.16; Edward Carpenter quoted in Timothy d'Arch Smith, *Love in Earnest*, London, Routledge & Kegan Paul, 1970, p.192; Ackerley, op.cit., p.218; *see also* Anomaly, *The Invert, and His Social Adjustment*, 2nd edn, London, Bailliere, Tindall & Cox, 1948, p.179.

38. H.M. Scheuller and R.L. Peters (eds), *The Letters of John Addington Symonds*, Detroit, Wayne State University Press, 1969, vol.3, p.808.

39. Ackerley, op.cit., p.135.

40. Mayne, op.cit., p.220.

41. On the worship of youth see d'Arch Smith, op.cit.; Brian Taylor, "Motives for Guilt-free Pederasty, Some Literary Considerations", *Sociological Review*, vol.24, no.1, February 1976; George C. Ives, *Obstacles to Human Progress*, London, George Allen & Unwin, 1939, p.200; Michael Davidson, *The World, the Flesh and Myself*, London, Mayflower-Dell, 1966, p.88.

42. cf. Paul Gebhard's comments, quoted in Robin Lloyd, *Playland, A Study of Boy Prostitution*, London, Blond & Briggs, 1977, p.195,

> In female prostitution the prostitute rarely or never reaches orgasm and the client almost invariably does; in male prostitution the prostitute almost invariably reaches orgasm, but the client frequently does not. . . .The homosexual male ideally seeks a masculine-appearing heterosexual male, and the prostitute attempts to fit the image. Consequently the prostitute can do little or nothing for or to a homosexual client lest he betray a homosexual inclination of his own and ruin the illusion.

> This cannot be taken as a general statement of the situation but it does undoubtedly express one type of experience.

43. *See* Edward Carpenter's "Memoir" of George Merrill, Edward Carpenter Collection, Sheffield City Library, Sheffield.

44. Ackerley, op.cit., p.215.

45. Ibid., p.136.

46. Fernando Henriques, *Prostitution and Society*, *A Survey*, *Primitive, Classical and Oriental* London, Macgibbon & Kee, 1962, p.17.

47. M. Brake and K. Plummer, "Rent Boys and Bent Boys", unpublished paper, 1970.

48. L. Thoinot and A. W. Weysse, *Medico Legal Aspects of Moral Offences Philadelphia*, F.A. Davis, 1911, p.346.

49. Quoted in L. Chester, D. Leitch, and C. Simpson, *The Cleveland Street Affair*, London, Weidenfeld & Nicolson, 1977, p.73.

50. H. Montgomery Hyde, *The Cleveland Street Scandal*, London, Weidenfeld & Nicolson, 1976, p.28.

51. *See Reynolds Newspaper*, 12 January 1890 and the *Referee*, 24 November 1889, for comments on the involvement of working-class boys in the Cleveland Street Scandal; and Peter Wild-

blood, *Against the Law*, Harmondsworth, Penguin Books, 1957, p.80, for a similar view in the 1950s.

52. *See*, for examples, the comments of Carlier, *Les Deux Prostitutions*, p.323.
53. Picton, op.cit., p.90.
54. Ibid., p.91.
55. Nanette J. Davis, "The Prostitute, Developing a Deviant Identity", in James M. Henslin, *Studies in the Sociology of Sex*, New York, Appleton-Century-Crofts, 1971, p.297.
56. Public Record Office, DPP1/95/3, File 5.
57. Quoted in Hyde, *The Trials of Oscar Wilde*, p.170.
58. *See* Ackerley, op.cit., p.135; Raven, op.cit., p.280.
59. *The Sins of the Cities of the Plain, or the Recollections of a Mary-Anne*, 2 vols, London, 1881.
60. Saul's deposition, Public Record Office, DPP1/95/4, File 2.
61. *See* the report in the *Star*, 15 January 1890.
62. *Sins of the Cities of the Plain*, vol.2, 109.
63. Quoted in Chester *et al.*, op.cit., pp.46-7.
64. *Truth*, 21 December 1889, p.49.
65. Public Record Office, DPP 1/95/3, File 4, transcript of trial, p.6.
66. Public Record Office, DPP 1/95/4, Saul's deposition.
67. Ibid.
68. Ibid.
69. *Sins of the Cities of the Plain*, vol.2, quoted in Chester et al.
70. F. Carlier, *Les Deux Prostitutions*, p.317.
71. Hyde, *The Trials of Oscar Wilde*, pp.60, 125, 162.
72. Rupert Croft-Cooke, *The Unrecorded Life of Oscar Wilde*, London and New York, W.H. Allen, 1972, p.141.
73. For a colourful example of a male prostitute arrested in female clothes *see* the reference in Mayne, op.cit., p.443. *See also* Quentin Crisp, *The Naked Civil Servant*, Harmondsworth, Penguin Books, 1977, p.26.
74. Picton, op.cit., p.90.
75. Chester et al., op.cit., p.225.
76. Raven, op.cit., p.280.
77. Reiss, op.cit., pp.264-71.

4. Questions of identity

1. Elizabeth Wilson, "I'll Climb the Stairway to Heaven, Lesbianism in the Seventies", in S. Cartledge and J. Ryan (eds) *Sex and Love: New Thoughts on Old Contradictions*, London, The Women's Press, 1983, p.194.
2. Jeffrey Weeks *Sexuality and its Discontents. Meanings, Myths and Modern Sexualities*, London, Routledge & Kegan Paul, 1985.

3. Jane Gallop, *Feminism and Psychoanalysis. The Daughter's Seduction*, London, Macmillan, 1982.
4. H.F. Ellenberger, *The Discovery of the Unconscious. The History and Evolution of Dynamic Psychiatry*, New York, Basic Books, 1970.
5. Ibid.
6. Charles Darwin, *The Descent of Man, and Selection in Relation to Sex*, London, John Murray, 2 vols, 1871.
7. R. von Krafft-Ebing, *Psychopathia Sexualis*, Brooklyn, Physicians and Surgeons Book Co., 1931.
8. S. Freud, *The Standard Edition of the Complete Psychological Works of Sigmund Freud*, ed. James Strachey, London, Hogarth Press, 1953-74, vol.7.
9. Weeks, op.cit., ch.4.
10. Henry Havelock Ellis, *Man and Woman*. London, Walter Scott, 1984.
11. Krafft-Ebing, op.cit, p.vii.
12. J. L'Esperance, "Doctors and Women in Nineteenth Century Society, Sexuality and Role", in J. Woodward and D. Richards (eds), *Health Care and Popular Medicine in Nineteenth Century England*, London, Croom Helm, 1977.
13. Jeffrey Weeks *Sex, Politics and Society. The Regulation of Sexuality since 1800*, London, Longman, 1981, 2nd edition, 1989.
14. Michel Foucault, *Herculine Barbin. Being the Recently discovered Memoirs of a Nineteenth Century French Hermaphrodite*, New York, Pantheon, 1980, p.vii.
15. Barry Adam, *The Survival of Domination: Inferiorization and Everyday Life*, New York, Elsevier, 1978, p.12.
16. P. Gleason, "Identifying Identity: A Semantic History", *Journal of American History*, vol.69, no.4, 1983.
17. John D'Emilio, *Sexual Politics, Sexual Communities. The Making of a Homosexual Minority in the United States 1940-76*, Chicago and London, University of Chicago Press, 1903.
18. Kenneth Plummer (ed.), *The Making of the Modern Homosexual*, London, Hutchinson, 1981.
19. Michel Foucault, *The History of Sexuality vol.1: An Introduction*, London, Allen Lane, 1979.
20. Rosalind Coward, *Patriarchal Precedents. Sexuality and Social Relations*, London, Routledge & Kegan Paul, 1983, chapter 7.
21. Freud, op.cit., p.146.
22. *See* C. W. Socarides, *Homosexuality*, New York, Jason Aranson, 1978.
23. J. Mitchell and J. Rose (eds), *Jacques Lacan and the Ecole Freudienne: Feminine Sexuality*, London, Macmillan, 1982.
24. J.H. Gagnon and W. Simon, *Sexual Conduct. The Social Sources of Human Sexuality*, London, Hutchinson, 1973.
25. Weeks, *Sexuality and its Discontents*, ch.5.
26. Foucault, op.cit.; For a radical feminist view see L. Coveney, M. Jackson, S. Jeffreys, L. Kaye and P. Mahony, *The Sexuality Papers: Male Sexuality*

and the Social Control of Women. London, Hutchinson, 1984; L. Faderman, *Surpassing the Love of Men. Romantic Friendship and Love between Women from the Renaissance to the Present,* London, Junction Books, 1981.

27. D'Emilio, op.cit.; Dennis Altman, *The Homosexualization of America, the Americanization of the Homosexual,* New York, St Martin's Press, 1982.
28. Edmund White, *States of Desire,* New York, Dutton, 1980, pp.65-6.
29. Adam, op.cit., p.123.
30. Plummer, *The Making of the Modern Homosexual,* D'Emilio, op.cit.
31. A.C. Kinsey, W.B. Pomeroy and C.E. Martin, *Sexual Behaviour in the Human Male,* Philadelphia and London, W.B. Saunders, 1948.
32. Barry Dank, "Coming Out in the Gay World", in M. Levine (ed.), *Gay Men: The Sociology of Male Homosexuality,* New York, Harper & Row, 1979.
33. Kenneth Plummer, *Sexual Stigma: An interactionist account,* London, Routledge & Kegan Paul, 1975.
34. Guy Hocquenghem, *Homosexual Desire,* London, Allison & Busby, 1978.
35. Faderman, op.cit., p.142.
36. S. Krieger, "Lesbian Identity and Community: Recent Social Science Literature", *Signs,* vol.8, no.1, 1982.
37. Adrienne Rich, "Compulsory Heterosexuality and Lesbian Existence", *Signs* vol.5, no.4, 1980.
38. Ibid., p.647.
39. *See* essays in A. Snitow, C. Stansell and S. Thompson (eds), *Desire, The Politics of Sexuality,* London, Virago, 1984.
40. Cora Kaplan, "Wild Nights: Pleasure/Sexuality/Feminism", *Formations of Pleasure,* London, Routledge & Kegan Paul, 1983, p.31.
41. Pat Califia, *Sapphistry: The Book of Lesbian Sexuality,* New York, Naiad Press 1980.
42. Ann Ferguson, "On Compulsory Heterosexuality and Lesbian Existence", *Signs,* vol.7, no.1, 1981, p.100.
43. Weeks, *Sexuality and its Discontents,* ch.9.
44. J.P. DeCecco and M.G. Shively, "From Sexual Identity to Sexual Relationships", *Journal of Homosexuality,* vol.9, nos 2 and 3, 1984.
45. J. Minson, "The Assertion of Homosexuality", *m/f,* nos.5-6, 1981.
46. *See* for example, the special edition on "Polysexuality"in *Semiotext(e)* vol. IV, no.1, 1981.
47. Antonio Gramsci, *Letters from Prison,* L. Lawner (ed.), London, Lawrence & Wishart, 1975.
48. Michel Foucault, "An Interview: Sex, Power and the Politics of Identity", by B. Gallagher and A. Wilson, *The Advocate,* no.400, 1984.

5. Against nature

1. Oscar Wilde, "The Soul of Man Under Socialism", *Complete Works of Oscar Wilde,* London, Book Club Associates, 1978, p.1100.

2. Ibid.
3. Jeffrey Weeks, *Sexuality and Its Discontents*, London, Routledge & Kegan Paul, 1985.
4. Jonathan Katz, *Gay/Lesbian Almanac*, New York, Harper and Row, 1983.
5. Jean Francois Lyotard, *The post-modern condition. A Report on Knowledge*, Manchester, Manchester University Press, 1986, p.xxv.
6. Michel Foucault, *The History of Sexuality*, vol.1. London, Allen Lane, 1979.
7. Quoted in Elizabeth Wilson, *Adorned in Dreams*, London, Virago, 1985, p.27.
8. Niklas Luhmann, *Love as Passion*, Cambridge, Polity Press, 1986, p.12.
9. See Jeffrey Weeks, *Sex, Politics and Society. The Regulation of Sexuality Since 1800*, Harlow, Longman, 1981, 2nd edition, 1989.
10. Carroll Smith-Rosenberg, *Disorderly Conduct*, London, Oxford University Press, 1985; Lillian Faderman, *Surpassing the Love of Men. Romantic Friendship and Love Between Women from the Renaissance to the Present*, London, Junction Books, 1980.
11. See Randolph Trumbach, "Sodomite Subcultures, Sodomical Roles, and the Gender Revolution of the 18th Century: the Recent Historiography", *Eighteenth Century Life*, vol.9, n.s., no.3, 1985, pp.109-121; reprinted in R.P. Maccubbin (ed.), *'Tis Nature's Fault. Unauthorized Sexuality during the Enlightenment*, Cambridge, CUP, 1987.
12. Alan Bray, *Homosexuality in Renaissance England*, London, GMP, 1982.
13. Michel Foucault, *The History of Sexuality*, vol.2, *The Use of Pleasure*; and vol.3, *The Care of the Self*, New York, Pantheon, 1985, 1986.
14. See Weeks, *Sexuality and its Discontents*, p.120.
15. Ibid., ch.6.
16. Jacqueline Rose, *Sexuality in the Field of Vision*, London, Virago, 1986.
17. Alasdair MacIntyre, *Against Virtue*. London, Duckworth, 1985, p.219.
18. Jeffrey Weeks, *Coming Out. Homosexual Politics in Britain from the 19th Century to the Present*, London, Quartet, 1977, 2nd edition, 1990.
19. James Baldwin, *Evidence of Things Not Seen*, London, Michael Joseph, 1986, p.122.
20. Weeks, op.cit., 1985, Ch. 4; Jeffrey Weeks, *Sexuality*, London, Tavistock, 1986, Ch. 6.
21. See Jeffrey Weeks, Sexuality, ch.6.
22. Michel Foucault, "On the Genealogy of Ethics: an Overview of Work in Progress", in Paul Rabinow (ed.), *The Foucault Reader*, New York, Pantheon, 1984, p.343.
23. Lyotard, op.cit., p.xxv.
24. Weeks, op.cit., Ch.5; Simon Watney, *Policing Desire: Pornography, AIDS and the Media*, London, Comedia/Methuen, 1987.
25. Frank Kermode, *The Sense of an Ending*. London, Oxford University Press, 1967, p.39.
26. Anthony P. Cohen, *The Symbolic Construction of Community*, London, Tavistock, 1985.
27. Umberto Eco, *Reflections on the Name of the Rose*, London, Secker & Warburg, 1985, p.3.

28. Bernard Williams, *Ethics and the Limits of Philosophy*, London, Fontana, 1985, p.118.
29. Wilde, op.cit., p.1103.

6. Male homosexuality in the age of AIDS

1. Jonathan Dollimore, "The dominant and the deviant: a violent dialectic", *Critical Quarterly*, no.28, nos.1 and 2, pp.179-92, 1986.
2. James Baldwin, *Evidence of Things Not Seen*, London, Michael Joseph, 1986, p.xiv.
3. Jeffrey Weeks, *Sexuality and its Discontents. Meanings, Myths and Modern Sexualities*, London and Boston, Routledge and Kegan Paul, 1985.
4. The *Guardian*, 11 August 1986.
5. A. P. Cohen, *The Symbolic Construction of Community*, Chichester and London, Ellis Horwood and Tavistock, 1986, p.108.
6. Ronald Bayer, *Homosexuality and American Psychiatry*, New York, Basic Books, 1981.
7. Weeks, op.cit.
8. Cohen, op.cit., p.114.
9. A.P. Bell, M.S. Weinberg, *Homosexualities. A study of Diversity Among Men and Women*, London, Mitchell Beazley, 1978, p.115.
10. Cohen, op.cit., p.118.
11. *See*, Dennis Altman, *The Homosexualization of America, the Americanisation of the Homosexual*, New York, St. Martin's Press, 1982.
12. A. Kinsey, W. Pomeroy, C. Martin, *Sexual Behaviour in the Human Male*, Philadephia and London, W.B. Saunders, 1948, p.197.
13. Bell, *et al.*, op.cit., p.72.
14. P. Blumstein and P. Schwartz (1983) *American Couples. Money, Work, Sex*. William Morrow, New York, 1983, p.195.
15. G. Talese, *Thy Neighbour's Wife. Sex in the World Today*, London, Collins, 1980.
16. *See*, for example, G. Hocquenghem *Homosexual Desire*, London, Allison and Busby, 1978; Altman, op.cit.
17. W.H. Masters and V.E. Johnson, *Homosexuality in Perspective*, Boston, Little, Brown and Co., 1979, p.219.
18. D.P. McWhirter and A.M. Mattison, *The Male Couple. How Relationships Develop*, Englewood Cliffs, Prentice-Hall, 1984, p.3.
19. R.M. Berger, *Gay and Gray. The Older Homosexual Man*, Boston, Alyson Publications, 1982, p.125.
20. McWhirter and Mattison, op.cit., p.252.
21. Blumstein and Schwartz, op.cit.
22. B. Voellar, "Society and the gay movement", in J. Marmor (ed.), *Homosexual Behavior. A Modern Reappraisal*, New York, Basic Books, 1980, pp.232-52
23. Bell, *et al.*, op.cit., p.175.
24. Berger, op.cit.

7. AIDS: the intellectual agenda

1. Susan Sontag, *Illness as Metaphor*, Harmondsworth, Penguin Books, 1983; Keith Alcorn, "Illness, metaphor and AIDS", in Peter Aggleton and Hilary Homans (eds), *Social Aspects of AIDS*, Lewes, Falmer Press, 1988.
2. Jeffrey Weeks, "Love in a cold climate" in Aggleton and Homans, op.cit.
3. Frank Mort, *Dangerous Sexualities*, London, Routledge & Kegan Paul, 1987.
4. Neil Small, "AIDS and social policy", *Critical Social Policy*, vol.21, 1988, pp.9-29.
5. Randy Shilts, *And the Band Played On. Politics, People and the AIDS Epidemic*, Harmondsworth, Penguin Books, 1988.
6. See R. Berkowitz and M. Callen, *How to Have Sex in an Epidemic*, New York, News from the Front, 1983.
7. Jeffrey Weeks, *Sexuality and its Discontents*, London, Routledge & Kegan Paul, 1985.
8. Robin Mckie, *Panic, The Story of AIDS*, London, Thorsons, 1986.
9. Shilts, op.cit.
10. J. Weeks, *Sexuality and its Discontents*. For a critique of moral panic theory *see* Simon Watney, "AIDS, 'Moral Panic Theory' and homophobia", in Aggleton and Homans, op.cit., and Simon Watney, *Policing Desire*, London, Comedia/Methuen, 1987.
11. Paula Treichler, "AIDS, homophobia and biomedical discourse: An epidemic of signification", *Cultural Studies*, vol.1, no.3, 1987.
12. Kaye Wellings, "Perceptions of risk – Media treatment of AIDS" in Aggleton and Homans, op.cit.
13. Robert Padgug, "AIDS in historical perspcctive", paper presented at the American Historical Association, 28 December, 1986.
14. Small, "AIDS and social policy", op.cit.
15. Shilts, op.cit.
16. Weeks, "Love in a cold climate".
17. Shilts, op.cit.
18. Weeks, "Love in a cold climate".
19. David Silverman, "Making Sense of a precipice: Constituting Identity in an HIV Clinic", in Peter Aggleton, Graham Hart and Peter Davies (eds), *Aids: Social Representations, Social Practices*, Lewes, Falmer Press, 1989.
20. Christopher Spence, *AIDS, Time to Reclaim our Power*, London, Lifestory, 1986; Peter Tatchell, *AIDS, A Guide to Survival*, London, GMP, 1986.
21. Cindy Patton, "The AIDS Industry: Construction of 'Victims', 'Volunteers' and 'Experts'", in Erica Carter and Simon Watney (eds), *Taking Liberties: AIDS and Cultural Politics*, London, Serpent's Tail, 1989.
22. E. Hammonds, "Race, sex, AIDS: The construction of the other", *Radical America*, vol.20, no.6, 1987.
23. Michel Foucault, *The History of Sexuality, Volume 1, An Introduction*, London, Allen Lane, 1979.
24. Mort, *Dangerous Sexualities*.

25. Jeffrey Weeks, *Sex, Politics and Society, The Regulation of Sexuality Since 1800*, Harlow, Longmans, 1981, 2nd edition, 1989.
26. Weeks, *Sexuality and its Discontents*.
27. Small, "Aids and social policy".
28. The *Independent*, 30 March 1988.
29. The *Guardian*, 1 May 1988.
30. Shilts, op.cit.
31. Weeks, *Sex, Politics and Society*, 1989 edition.
32. Shilts, op.cit.
33. Weeks, *Sexuality and its Discontents*.
34. *See* Tony Whitehead, "The Voluntary Sector: Five Years On", in Carter and Watney (eds), op.cit.
35. Patton, op.cit.
36. H. Homans and P. Aggleton, "Health education, HIV infection and AIDS", Aggleton and Homans, op.cit.; Sheffield AIDS Education Project, *Interim Report, May-October 1987*, Sheffield, Sheffield City Polytechnic, 1988.
37. *See* Weeks, *Sexuality and its Discontents*.
38. Jeffrey Weeks, *Coming Out: Homosexual Politics in Britain from the Nineteenth Century to the Present*, London, Quartet Books, 1977, second edition 1990.
39. C. Collier, *The Twentieth Century Plague*, London, Lion, 1987.
40. Silverman, op.cit.
41. Ibid. *See also* R. Fitzpatrick, M. Boulton and G. Hart "Gay Men's Sexual Behaviour in response to AIDS – Insights and Problems" in Aggleton, Davies and Hart (eds), op.cit.
42. Kobena Mercer, "AIDS, racism and homophohia", *New Society*, 5 February 1988 and R. Chirimuuta, and R. Chirimuuta, *AIDS, Africa and Racism*, London, Free Associations Press, 1989.
43. Baldwin, op.cit.
44. Norbert Elias, *The Loneliness of the Dying*, Oxford, Basil Blackwell, 1985.
45. Shilts, op.cit.

8. Pretended family relationships

1. Michèl Barrett and M. McIntosh, *The Anti-social family*, London, Verso, 1982.
2. Jacqueline Rose, "Margaret Thatcher and Ruth Ellis", *New Formations* no.6, 1988, p.20.
3. *See* Jeffrey Weeks, *Sex, politics and society. The regulation of sexuality since 1800*, 2nd edition, Harlow, Longman, 1989.
4. Geoffrey Robinson, "Fear not Clause 28, only the prejudice behind it", *Guardian*, 1 June, 1988.
5. *See* GLC, *Changing the world. A London charter for gay and lesbian rights*, London, Greater London Council, 1985.
6. John Marshall, "Flaunting it: the challenge of the 1990s", *Gay Times*, no.124, January, 1989, pp.12-14.

7. A. Muller, *Parents Matter. Parents' relationships with lesbian daughters and gay sons*, New York, The Naiad Press, 1987, p.140.
8. Jeffrey Weeks, *Sexuality and its discontents. Meanings, myths and modern sexualities*, London and New York, Routledge and Kegan Paul, 1985; Weeks, *Sex, politics and society*, op.cit.
9. Jeffrey Weeks, *Coming Out: Homosexual politics in Britain from the nineteenth century to the present*, London, Quartet, 1977; 2nd edition, 1990.
10. R. Jowell, *et al.* (eds) *British social attitudes. The fifth report*, Aldershot, Gower, 1988.
11. Simon Watney, *Policing desire. Pornography, AIDS and the media*, London, Methuen, 1987.
12. *See* Weeks, *Sex, politics and society*.
13. J. Demos, "Images of the American family, then and now", in V. Tufte and R. Myerhoff (eds), *Changing images of the family*, New Haven and London, Yale University Press, 1979, p.43.
14. Jeffrey Weeks, *Sexuality*, Chichester and London, Ellis Horwood and Tavistock, 1986; J.G. Pankhurst and S.K. Houseknecht, "The family, politics and religion in the 1980s", *Journal of Family Issues*, vol.4, no.1, March, 1983, pp.5-34.
15. David Clark, "Wedlocked Britain", *New Society*, 13 March, 1987.
16. Robert Chester, "The rise of the neo-conventional family", *New Society*, 19 May 1985 and Robert Chester, "The conventional family is alive and living in Britain", in Jeffrey Weeks, *The Family Directory*, London, The British Library, 1986.
17. R. Fletcher, *The shaking of the foundations*, London and New York, Routledge, 1988, p.81.
18. Melanie Phillips, "Pity the battered family", the *Guardian*, 15 July 1988.
19. Beatrix Campbell, *Unofficial secrets: child sexual abuse – the Cleveland Case*, London, Virago, 1988.
20. Quoted in Phillips, op.cit.
21. N. Deakin and M. Wicks, *Families and the state*, London, Family Policy Studies Centre, 1989. *See also*, Janet Finch, "Whose responsibility? Women and the future of family care", in I. Allen, M. Wicks, J. Finch, D. Leat, *Informal care tomorrow*, London, Policy Studies Institute, 1987.
22. Barbara Laslett, "The significance of family membership", in Tufte and Myerhoff (eds), op.cit.
23. Rayner Rapp, "Family and class in contemporary America", in B. Thorne with M. Yalom (eds), *Rethinking the family: some feminist questions*, New York and London, Longman, 1982, p.170.
24. Miriam David, "Moral and maternal: the family in the right", in R. Levitas (ed.), *The ideology of the New Right*, Cambridge, Polity Press, 1986; Weeks, *Sex, politics and society*.
25. Speech reported in the *Guardian*, 20 March 1989.
26. R. Fletcher, *The Abolitionists: family and marriage under attack*, London, Routledge, 1988.
27. Edmund Leach, *A runaway world? The Reith Lectures 1987*, London, BBC Publications, 1968.

28. *See*, for example, Betty Friedan, *The second stage*, London, Abacus, 1983.
29. Barbara Taylor, *Eve and the New Jerusalem*, London, Virago, 1982; R. Muncy, *Sex and marriage in utopian communities*, Baltimore, Penguin, 1974.
30. D.H.J. Morgan, *The family, politics and social theory*, London and Boston, Routledge and Kegan Paul, 1985; D.H.J. Morgan, *Social theory and the family*, London and Boston, Routledge and Kegan Paul, 1975.
31. P. Abrams and A. McCulloch, "Men, women, and communes", in D.L. Barker and S. Allen (eds), *Sexual divisions and society: process and change*, London, Tavistock, 1976; L. Segal, *What is to be done about the family?* Harmondsworth, Penguin, 1983.
32. Abrams and McCulloch, op.cit., p.248.
33. Andrew Rigby, *Alternative realities*, London and Boston, Routledge and Kegan Paul, 1974.
34. Andrew Rigby, *Communes in Britain*, London and Boston, Routledge and Kegan Paul, 1974.
35. Quoted in Abrams and McCulloch, op.cit., p.248.
36. Rigby, *Communes in Britain*, p.148.
37. Abrams and McCulloch, op.cit., p.248.
38. Keith Birch, "A community of interests", in Bob Cant and Susan Hemmings (eds), *Radical records. Thirty years of lesbian and gay history*, London and New York, Routledge, 1988, p.55.
39. Mira Nava, "From utopian to scientific feminism? Early feminist critiques of the family", in Segal (ed.), op.cit.
40. V. Ansell, *et al.*, *Diggers and dreamers. The 1990/1 guide to communal living*, Sheffield, A Communes Network Publication, 1989.
41. E. Irvine, *The family in the kibbutz*, London, Study Commision on the Family, 1980.
42. Institute of Family Studies, *Annual Report 1980-1*, Melbourne, Australian Institute of Family Studies, 1981.
43. B. Berger and P. Berger, *The war over the family. Capturing the middle ground*, London, Hutchinson, 1983, p.63.
44. R.N. Rapoport, *et al.*, *Families in Britain*, London and Boston, Routledge and Kegan Paul, 1982.
45. P. Laslett, "Foreword", in Rapoport *et al.*, op.cit.
46. Rapoport, *et al.*, op.cit., pp.479ff.
47. E.D. Macklin, "Non-traditional family forms: a decade of research", *Journal of Marriage and the Family*, vol.42, no.4, November, 1980, pp.905-22.
48. M.B. Zinn and D.S. Eitzen, *Diversity in American families*, New York, Harper and Row, 1987, p.370; P. Blumstein and P. Schwartz, *American couples: money, work, sex*, New York, William Morrow, 1983, p.46.
49. Zinn and Eitzen, op.cit., p.387.
50. Ibid., p.394.
51. Morgan, *Social theory and the family*, p.274.
52. F.W. Bozett, *Gay and lesbian parents*, New York, Praeger, 1987; and "Male homosexuality in the age of AIDS", in this volume.

53. Fletcher, *The shaking of the foundations*, pp.186-210; Christopher Lasch, *Haven in a heartless world. The family besieged*, New York, Basic Books, 1977; Berger and Berger, op.cit., p.63.

54. S. Lash and J. Urry, *The end of organised capitalism*, Cambridge, Polity Press, 1988.

55. Lasch, op.cit.

56. A. Phillips, "Fraternity", in B. Pimlott (ed.), *Fabian essays in socialist thought*, London, Heinemann, 1984.

57. Ferdinand Mount, *The subversive family: an alternative history of love and marriage*, London, Jonathan Cape, 1982.

58. Peter Willmott, *Social networks, informal care and public policy*, London: Policy Studies Institute, 1986.

59. Paul Gilroy, *There ain't no black in the Union Jack: the cultural politics of race and nation*, London, Hutchinson, 1987; Francis Fitzgerald, *Cities on a hill. A journey through contemporary American culture*, London, Picador, 1987; Bill Jordan, *The common good: citizenship, morality and self interest*, Oxford, Basil Blackwell, 1989, p.43.

60. Willmott, op.cit., p.71.

61. Zinn and Eitzen, op.cit., p.383; Janice Raymond, *A passion for friends. Towards a philosophy of female affection*, London, The Women's Press, 1986, p.170; Bruce Voellar, "Society and the gay movement" in Judd Marmor (ed.), *Homosexual behaviour. A modern reappraisal*, New York, Basic Books, 1980.

62. Willmott, op.cit., p.85.

63. Dick Hebdige, "After the masses", *Marxism Today*, January, 1989, pp.48-53.

64. L.G. Nungesser, *Epidemic of courage. Facing AIDS in America*, New York, St Martin's Press, 1986.

65. Berger and Berger, op.cit.

9. Uses and abuses of Michel Foucault

1. Jeffrey Weeks, *Coming Out: Homosexual Politics in Britain from the nineteenth Century to the Present*, London, Quartet, 1977; *Sex, Politics and Society. The Regulation of Sexuality since 1800*, Harlow, Longman, 1981; Sheila Rowbotham and Jeffrey Weeks, *Socialism and the New Life*, London, Pluto, 1977; *Sexuality and its Discontents. Meanings, Myths and Modern Sexualities*, London, Routledge and Kegan Paul, 1985.

2. Michel Foucault, *Power/Knowledge*, edited by Colin Gordon, Brighton, Harvester, 1980, pp 53-4.

3. I am here loosely following the schema in Bill Schwarz, "'The People' in history: The Communist Party Historians' Group, 1946-56", in Centre for Contemporary Cultural Studies: *Making Histories*, London, Hutchinson, 1983.

4. F. Nietzsche, *The Use and Abuse of History*, Indianapolis, Bobbs-Merrill Educational Publishing, 1979, p.20.

5. Ibid., p.16.
6. Mark Cousins and Athar Hussain, *Michel Foucault*, London, Macmillan, 1984.
7. Michel Foucault, *The Archaeology of Knowledge*, London, Tavistock, 1972, p.3ff.
8. *See* D.F. Bouchard (ed.), *Language, Counter-Memory, Practice. Selected Essays and Interviews*, New York, Pantheon, 1971, pp.156, 162.
9. Perry Anderson, *In the Tracks of Historical Materialism*, London, Verso, 1983.
10. Michel Foucault, *The History of Sexuality* volume 1, *An Introduction*, London, Allen Lane 1979 (first French publication 1976); volume 2, *The Use of Pleasure*, London, Viking, 1987, volume 3, *Care of the Self*, London, Viking, 1988.
11. Michel Foucault, *Madness and Civilisation*, London, Tavistock, 1965.
12. For a full discussion of the sexological debates *see* my *Sexuality and its Discontents*.
13. Michel Foucault (ed.), *Herculine Barbin. Being the Recently Discovered Memoirs of a Nineteenth Century French Hermaphrodite*, Brighton, Harvester, 1980.
14. Stephen Heath, *The Sexual Fix*, London, Macmillan, 1982; see also debates in the journal *M/F*.
15. "Michel Foucault, An Interview: Sex, Power and the Politics of Identity" by Bob Gallagher and Alexander Wilson, *The Advocate*, no. 400, 1984, p.29.
16. Michel Foucault, "The Subject and Power", Afterword in Herbert L. Dreyfus and Paul Rabinow, *Michel Foucault. Beyond Structuralism and Hermeneutics*, Brighton, Harvester, 1982.
17. Ibid., p.213.
18. Chantal Mouffe, "Hegemony and the Integral State in Gramsci: Towards a New Concept of Politics" in George Bridges and Rosalind Brunt (eds), *Silver Linings. Some Strategies for the Eighties*, London, Lawrence and Wishart, 1981, p.167
19. Foucault, *Power/Knowledge*, p.188.
20. Ibid., p.42.
21. Foucault, "The Subject and Power", op.cit., p.216.

10.   The Fabians and Utopia

1. Raymond Williams, *Towards 2000*, London, Chatto and Windus, 1983.
2. E.P. Thompson, *William Morris: Romantic to Revolutionary*, London, Merlin Press, 1977, p.806.
3. Quoted in C. Tsuzuki, *Edward Carpenter 1844-1929. Prophet of Human Fellowship*, Cambridge, Cambridge University Press, 1980, p.60.
4. C.A.R. Crosland, *The Future of Socialism*, London, Jonathan Cape, 1964, p.356.
5. *New Statesman*, 12 April 1913.

6. G.D.H. Cole, *The World of Labour*, London, G. Bell and Sons, 1913, p.347.
7. S.G. Hobson, *National Guilds: An Enquiry into the Wage System and the Way Out*, London, G. Bell and Sons, 1914, p.110.
8. Crosland, op.cit., p.357.
9. Sue Cartledge, "Duty and desire: creating a feminist morality" in S. Cartledge, and J. Ryan, *Sex and Love: New Thoughts on Old Contradictions*, London, The Women's Press, 1983.
10. Beatrice Webb, *Diary*, December 1913, Passfield Papers, BLPES.
11. G.D.H. Cole, *Self-Government in Industry*, G. Bell and Sons, London, 1918, p.232.
12. K. Marx, and F. Engels, *On Religion*, Moscow, Foreign Languages Publishing House, 1957, p.329.
13. On Carpenter see Sheila Rowbotham and Jeffrey Weeks, *Socialism and the New Life*, London, Pluto Press, 1977; and Tsuzuki, op.cit.
14. See Barbara Taylor, *Eve and the New Jerusalem*, London, Virago, 1983.
15. *See* Jeffrey Weeks, *Sex, Politics and Society. The Regulation of Sexuality since 1800*, London, Longman, 1981, 2nd edn, 1989.
16. Rowbotham and Weeks, op.cit.
17. Edward Carpenter, *Love's Coming-of-Age: A Series of Papers on the Relations of the Sexes*, London, George Allen and Unwin, 1948 (1896).
18. Ibid., p.1.
19. *Bernstein on Homosexuality. Articles from "Die NeueZeit" 1895 and 1898*, Belfast, Athol Books, 1977, p.20.
20. G.B. Shaw to Louis Wilkinson, 20 December 1909 in Dan H. Laurence (ed.), *G. B. Shaw, Collected Letters*, Oxford, Oxford University Press, vol.2, 1972, p.890.
21. Robert Blatchford to Edward Carpenter, 11 January 1894, Ms. 386-46, Edward Carpenter Collection, Sheffield City Library.
22. Quoted in Tsuzuki, op.cit., p.143.
23. Ibid., p.118.
24. Ibid., p.119.
25. Ibid., p.79; see Edward Carpenter, *Civilisation: its Cause and Cure, and other essays*, London, 1899.
26. S. Webb, "Historic" in G. B. Shaw, (ed.), *Fabian Essays in Socialism*, London, The Walter Scott Publishing Co., 1908 (1st edn, 1889), p.50.
27. Sydney Olivier, "Moral" in Shaw, op.cit., p.102.
28. Jane Lewis, "Re-reading Beatrice Webb's diary", *History Workshop Journal*, no. 14, Autumn 1982, p.34.
29. Quoted in N. Mackenzie, and J. Mackenzie, *The First Fabians*, London, Quartet Books, 1979, p.134.
30. Quoted in B. Caine, "Beatrice Webb and the 'woman question'", *History Workshop Journal*, no. 14, Autumn 1982, p.34.
31. Ibid., p.35.
32. S. and B. Webb, *Soviet Communism: a New Civilisation*, London, Victor Gollancz, 1937 (2nd edn), p.812.
33. On Spencer *see* Weeks, *Sex, Politics and Society*, p.146.

34. Caine, op.cit., p.37. Compare the claim in M.A., *The Economic Foundation of the Women's Movement*, Fabian Tract, no. 175, p.18.
35. Mackenzie, op.cit., pp.362-3.
36. Ibid.
37. Ibid., p.372.
38. Ibid., p.411.
39. Weeks, op.cit., chapter 8.
40. Richard von Krafft-Ebing, *Psychopathia Sexualis*, New York, Physicians and Surgeons Book Co., 1931, p.5.
41. Carpenter, *Love's Coming-of-Age*, p.14; Havelock Ellis, *The New Spirit*, London, G. Bell and Sons, 1889, p.9.
42. Krafft-Ebing, op.cit., p.2.
43. Webbs, *Soviet Communism*, p.1057.
44. Shaw, *The Revolutionist's Handbook*, quoted in Angus McLaren, *Birth Control in Nineteenth-Century England*, London, Croom Helm, 1978, p.190.
45. Ibid., p.191.
46. G.R. Searle, "Eugenics and class" in Charles Webster (ed.), *Biology, Medicine and Society, 1840-1940*, Cambridge, Cambridge University Press, 1981, pp.230ff. For a different interpretation see D. Mackenzie, "Eugenics in Britain", *Social Studies of Science*, no.VI, 1976.
47. McLaren, op.cit., p.190.
48. Quoted in G.R. Searle, *Eugenics and Politics in Britain 1900-1914*, Leyden, Noordhoff International, 1976, p.92.
49. *The Decline in the Birth Rate*, Fabian Tract, no. 131, 1907.
50. Cited respectively in Mackenzie, *The First Fabians*, p.407; Crosland, op.cit., pp.356-7.
51. Webbs, *Soviet Communism*, p.1146.
52. Crosland, op.cit., p.355.
53. Ibid., p.353.
54. *See* Beatrice Webb, *Diary*, December 1913.
55. Crosland, op.cit., p.353.
56. Ibid., p.355.
57. For a development of this theme see National Deviancy Conference (ed.), *Permissiveness and Control. The fate of the sixties legislation*, London, Macmillan, 1980, especially Stuart Hall "Reformism and the legisation of consent"; and Weeks, op.cit., chapter 13.
58. Victoria Greenwood and Jock Young, "Ghettoes of control" in National Deviancy Conference, op. cit.

The value of difference

1. Paul Feyerabend, *Farewell to Reason*, London, Verso, 1987, p.54.
2. Jonathan Raban, *God, Man and Mrs Thatcher*, London, Chatto, 1989.
3. *Democratic Socialist Aims and Values*, London, The Labour Party, 1988, p.7.

4. Ibid.

5. The quotations are from Mrs Thatcher's speech to the General Assembly of the Church of Scotland, quoted in Raban, *God, Man and Mrs Thatcher*.

6. The *Guardian*, 22 July, 1989.

7. Malise Ruthven, "A question of identity", in Lisa Appignanesi and Sara Maitland (eds), *The Rushdie file*, London, Fourth Estate, 1989, pp.21-2.

8. Steven Lukes, *Marxism and Morality*, Oxford, Oxford University Press, 1985, pp.64-5.

9. Lukes, op.cit., pp.27-8.

10. The *Independent*, 29 July, 1989.

11. Fay Weldon, *Sacred Cows*, London, Chatto, 1989, pp.31-2.

12. Feyerabend, op.cit., p.54.

13. David Held, *Models of Democracy*, Cambridge, Polity Press 1987.

14. *See* Chantal Mouffe, "The civics lesson", *New Statesman and Society*, 7 October, 1988.

Select bibliography

The essays in this book were written over a period of ten years or so. Inevitably, there have been a number of publications since these were written which throw further light on the themes I have attempted to discuss. I have in fact made no attempt to update the references. Instead, in this bibliographical note I want to indicate some of the most important work that has appeared during this period. Fuller bibliographies appear in my other books, listed below.

Against Nature should be seen as complementing a series of books I have published over the past decade and a half which are concerned with the social organisation of sexuality. The first to appear was *Coming Out: Homosexual Politics in Britain from the Nineteenth Century to the Present*, London, Quartet Books, 1977, revised and updated edition 1990. This was followed by *Sex, Politics and Society. The Regulation of Sexuality since 1800*, Harlow, Longman 1981, 2nd edition 1989, which looks at the wider development of sexual identities. These identities were further explored in *Sexuality and its Discontents. Meanings, Myths and Modern Sexualities*, London and Boston, Routledge and Kegan Paul, 1985, which looks at the impact of sexual ideologies, and at contemporary debates. A fourth book, *Sexuality*, Chichester and London, Ellis Horwood/Tavistock, 1986, supplements these.

During 1978-9, whilst doing the research which led to the writing of the first two essays in this current book, I conducted a number of interviews with older gay men as part of an investigation, carried out with Mary McIntosh at Essex University, on the development of the homosexual subculture and identities. A selection of these interviews

218

has now been published: Kevin Porter and Jeffrey Weeks (eds), *Between the Acts: Lives of Homosexual Men 1885 to 1967*, London and New York, Routledge 1990.

The "social constructionist" position I argue for in the essays in this book clearly owes a good deal to the work of Michel Foucault. The second and third volumes of *The History of Sexuality* have now been translated into English: Vol.2, *The Use of Pleasure*, and Vol.3, *The Care of the Self*, London, Allen Lane, 1986 and 1988. The merits of the constructionist position are debated in Theo van der Meer and Anja van Kooten Niekerk (eds), *Homosexuality, Which Homosexuality?*, Amsterdam and London, An Dekker and GMP 1989. See particularly Carole S. Vance, "Social Construction Theory: Problems in the History of Sexuality??". The essays in Martin Bauml Duberman, Martha Vicinus and George Chauncey Jr (eds), *Hidden from History: Reclaiming the Gay and Lesbian Past*, New York, New American Library, 1989 also reflect the range of theoretical debates that have recently taken place in lesbian and gay studies.

David F. Greenberg has provided the most comprehensive survey of the evidence for *The Construction of Homosexuality*, Chicago and London, University of Chicago Press, 1988. Recent historical scholarship is reflected fully in David M. Halperin, *One Hundred Years of Homosexuality, and Other Essays on Greek Love*, London and New York, Routledge, 1990, Kent Gerard and Gert Hekma (eds), *The Pursuit of Sodomy: Male Homosexuality in Renaissance and Enlightenment Europe*, New York, Haworth Press 1989. The outstanding study of homosexuality in early modern Britain is Alan Bray's *Homosexuality in Renaissance England*, London, GMP, 1982, 2nd edition 1989. The work of Randolph Trumbach similarly illuminates the eighteenth century. For examples of his recent work see: "Sodomitical Subcultures, Sodomitical Roles, and the Gender Revolution of the 18th century: the Recent Historiography", in R. P. Maccubbin (ed.), *'Tis Nature's Fault. Unauthorised Sexuality during the Enlightenment*, Cambridge, Cambridge University Press, 1987; and "Gender and the Homosexual Role in Modern Western Culture: The 18th and 19th centuries compared", in van der Meer and van Kooten Niekerk (eds), *Homosexuality, Which Homosexuality?*

Lesbian and gay history was inevitably overshadowed in the 1980s by the spread of HIV and AIDS. The initial American response, which helped shape the hostile moral climate in Britain is analysed and described in Dennis Altman, *AIDS and the New Puritanism*, London, Pluto Press, 1986 (published in the USA as *AIDS and the Mind of America*, New York, Anchor Press/Doubleday, 1986); Cindy Patton, *Sex and Germs: The Politics of AIDS*, Boston, South End Press, 1985; and Randy Shilts, *And the Band Played On: Politics, People and the AIDS Epidemic*, London, Penguin, 1988. The early British response is passionately dissected in Simon Watney, *Policing Desire: Pornography, AIDS and the Media*, London, Commedia/Methuen, 1987. See also his *Practices of Freedom: Selected Writings on HIV Disease, 1985-1990*, London, Rivers Oram 1991; and Erica Carter and Simon Watney (eds),

Taking Liberties: AIDS and Cultural Politics, London, Serpent's Tail, 1989.

The social context of AIDS in Britain is analysed in various essays in Peter Aggleton and Hilary Homans (eds), *Social Aspects of AIDS*, Basingstoke, Falmer Press 1988; and Peter Aggleton, Graham Hart and Peter Davies (eds), *AIDS: Social Representations, Social Practices*, Basingstoke, Falmer Press, 1989. On women and Aids see Diane Richardson, *Women and the AIDS Crisis*, London, Pandora, 1987. See also Sunil Gupta and Tessa Boffin (eds), *Ecstatic Antibodies: Resisting the AIDS Mythology*, London, Rivers Oram Press, 1990. For the international implications of HIV/AIDS see the Panos Institute, *AIDS and the Third World*, London, 1988.

For the cultural and political context of current value debates the most influential works are Stuart Hall, *The Hard Road to Renewal. Thatcherism and the Crisis of the Left*, London and New York, Verso, 1988; Stuart Hall and Martin Jacques (eds), *New Times. The Changing Face of Politics in the 1990s*, London, Lawrence and Wishart, 1989. See also the essays in Jonathan Rutherford (ed.), *Identity*, London, Lawrence and Wishart, 1990.

Index

Words such as history, homosexuality, identity, sexuality are not separately indexed as they recur throughout the book.

abortion, 192
Ackerley, J.R., 56, 57
Adam, Barry, 74, 78
Africa, 133
AIDS, 6, 95, 97, 100–103, 106–7, 111–12, 114–33, 139–40, 154
Althusser, Louis, 29
American Psychiatric Association, 104
Anderson, Perry, 162
Ayatollah, Khomeini, 185

Bailey, D.S., 12
Baldwin, James, 95, 100, 132
Band Aid, 154
Barthes, Roland, 2
bath houses, 106–7
Benkert von Kertbeny, 16
Bernstein, Eduard, 174
Birch, Keith, 147
bisexuality, 69, 73, 83
Bland, Hubert, 175, 178
Blatchford, Robert, 174
Bloch, Iwan, 11, 46, 71
Body Positive, 112

Boulton, Ernest, 49, 55
Boyson, Sir Rhodes, 126
Bray, Alan, 93
Bristol, 49
buggery, 14, 17, 38, 50

Califia, Pat, 82
Campioni, Mia, 43
Carlier, F., 46
Carpenter, Edward, 18, 57, 96, 171, 173, 174, 175, 176, 179
Carter, President Jimmy, 149
Cartledge, Sue, 172
Casement, Roger, 53–4
Casper, J.L., 16, 20, 71
Chamberlain, Joseph, 176
Charter 88, 192
Christianity, 12, 20, 73, 89, 101, 130, 164, 187, 190
class 27, 77, 91, 92
Clause 28, 6, 105, 126–7, 135–40, 143, 155–6
Cleveland Street scandal, 55, 59, 60, 61, 64
Cohen, Anthony, 98, 105

Cold War, 41, 118
Cole, G.D.H., 171, 172
communes, 144, 145–8
Contagious Diseases Acts, 52, 124
Cory, Donald Webster, 12
Crosland, C.A.R., 171, 172, 181, 182, 183

Dank, Barry, 79
Darwin, Charles, Darwinism, 70
Deleuze, Gilles, 30, 31, 32, 43, 158
drugs, 117, 125, 154, 186
Duchèsne, E.A., 47

Eco, Umberto, 8, 98
Ellis, Havelock, 8, 11, 16, 18, 20, 21, 46, 47, 71, 72, 73, 157, 174, 179
Engels, Freidrich, 173
England, 19, 49
Erikson, Erik, 74
essentialism, 6, 20–22, 24, 64–5, 71–2, 86, 94, 158
Essex, University of, 4, 5
ethics, 85, 95, 96, 99, 155, 165
ethnicity, 13, 77, 154–5, 193
eugenics, 179–80
Eulenburg, Albert, 71

Fabian Essays, 175
Fabianism, 7, 170–83
Faderman, Lillian, 80, 93
family, 23, 38, 44, 134–56
Fellowship of the New Life, 171, 174
feminism, 29, 77, 79, 88, 144–5, 172, 176–7, 184, 185, 191
Féré, Charles, 71
Ferguson, Ann, 82
Feyerabend, Paul, 186, 194
Fletcher, Ronald, 141, 144, 151
Forel, Auguste, 71
Forster, E.M., 56
Foucault, Michel, 7, 18, 24, 25, 26, 27, 30, 32–7, 41–2, 74, 75, 90, 94, 96, 157–69
Free University of Amsterdam, 6
Freud, Sigmund, 16, 24, 25, 30, 43, 46, 71, 73, 75–6, 84, 94
Fromm, Erich, 23

Gagnon, John, 24, 25, 26, 27, 40
Gallop, Jane, 69
gay men, 19–20, 40, 52–3, 80, 109, 157

Gay Men's Health Crisis, 112, 119
Gay Movement, 3, 77, 79, 92, 104, 191
gender, 18, 40, 43, 72–3, 77, 136
Germany, 13
Gilroy, Paul, 154
Goffman, Erving, 74
Gorbachev, President M., 185, 187, 188
Greece, Ancient, 15, 93, 163
green politics, 187–8
Gross, Liz, 43
Guards, 39, 55, 60, 61, 63, 66
Guattari, Felix, 30, 31, 32, 43

Hall, Radclyffe, 40
Harvey, A.D., 14
Heath, Stephen, 166
Hebdige, Dick, 154
Held, David, 195
Henriques, Fernando, 58
hepatitis B, 123
heterosexism, 82, 137
Hirschfeld, Magnus, 11, 16, 20, 46, 47, 71, 72, 96
History of Sexuality, The (Foucault), 7, 160–9 *passim*
History Workshop Journal, 3
Hobson, S.G., 172
Hocquenghem, Guy, 29, 30, 31
homophobia, 31
homosexual role, 22–3, 47
Hooker, Evelyn, 12, 55
Hudson, Rock, 120
Human Area Files, 11
Human Immune Deficiency Virus (HIV), 6, 108, 114–33, 154
humanism, 99, 188
Hyde, H. Montgomery, 12

incest, 38
Islam, 185, 189, 194

Jews, 190
Journal of Homosexuality, 5

Kaan, Henricus, 70
Kaplan, Cora, 82
Katz, Jonathan, 13, 88
Kermode, Frank, 98
kibbutz, 148
Kinnock, Neil, 187

Kinsey, Alfred, 12, 46, 79, 107, 164, 181
Kinsey Institute, 10
Koop, Dr C.E., 121
Krafft–Ebing, Richard von, 8, 23, 47, 69, 70, 71, 73, 179

Labouchère Amendment (Criminal Law Amendment Act 1885), 19, 21, 41, 50–1, 59, 62
Labour Party, 136–7, 186, 187, 189, 190
Lacan, Jacques, 24, 25, 29
Lambroso, Cesare, 71
Lasch, Christopher, 151
Legionnaire's Disease, 123
Lesbianism, 14, 19, 31, 40, 69, 80–3, 97, 104, 109, 157
Levi–Strauss, Claude, 29
Lewis, Jane, 176
"Little Hans", 43
Livingstone, Ken, 189
London, 18, 49, 56, 64
London School of Economics, 3
Los Angeles, 117
Lowenfeld, Leopold, 71
Luhmann, Niklas, 92
Lyotard, Jean Francois, 90, 96

McCarthyism, 78
McIntosh, Mary, 4, 16, 28, 45
MacIntyre, Alasdair, 94
Macmillan, Harold, 186
Magnan, Valentin, 71
Marcuse, Herbert, 23, 164
Marx, Karl, Marxism, 23, 24, 34, 90, 94, 144, 162, 167, 192–3
masturbation, 21, 59
Mattachine Society, 96
Mayne, Xavier, 46
Mead, George Herbert, 27, 76
Mead, Margaret, 76
medical model of homosexuality, 19, 73, 102, 107, 114, 130
Merrill, George, 57
Mitchell, Juliet, 26, 29
Moebius, P.J., 71
Moll, Albert, 16, 47, 71
Moral Majority, 108, 119
moral panic, 118–19
Moreau, J–J., 71
Morgan, David, 150
Morris, William, 170

Mort, Frank, 115
Mouffe, Chantal, 167
Mount, Ferdinand, 152
My Secret Life, 54

National Health Service, 130
Nava, Mica, 147
New Right, 73, 92, 97, 103, 106, 119, 123, 124, 125–6, 136, 138, 143
New York, 15, 105, 117
Nietzsche, F., 92, 158, 159, 161

oedipus complex, 25, 29, 43–4
Offences Against the Person Act 1861, 19
Orwell, George, 1, 2

Padgug, Robert, 119
paedophilia, 27, 36, 68, 69, 83, 97
Park, Frederick, 49, 55
patriarchy, 26, 29
Patton, Cindy, 122, 128, 129
Pease, Edward, 171
permissiveness, 78, 136, 140, 143, 182–3, 187
Phillips, Melanie, 141
Picton, Werner, 60, 64
Plato's Retreat, 108
Plummer, Kenneth, 5, 26, 27, 28, 38, 75, 79
Poor Laws, 38
pornography, 96, 189
Poster, Mark, 23
postmodernity, 87
power, 32–3, 162, 166–7, 169
Princess Royal, 131
prostitution, female, 47
prostitution, male, 39, 46–67, 52
psychoanalysis, 7, 24, 25, 26, 29, 43–4, 75–6

Raban, Jonathan, 187
race, racism, 77, 79, 88, 123, 131, 180
Rawls, John, 187
Reagan, President Ronald, 120, 124, 126, 143
Reich, Wilhelm, 23
Rich, Adrienne, 81–2
rights, 191–2
Rose, Jacqueline, 135
Rowse, A.L., 12, 13
Rushdie, Salman, 189, 191, 193
Ruthven, Malise, 191

sado–masochism, 68, 83, 97
San Francisco, 15, 78, 105, 106, 117, 120, 153
Sandstone Sex Commune, 108
Satanic Verses (Rushdie), 185, 191
Saul, Jack, 61–2, 63
Savage, Sir George, 17
Schrenck–Notzing, Albert von, 71
Scotland, 19
Section 28 (Local Government Act 1988) see Clause 28
sexology, 2, 11, 70, 157, 168, 179
sexual colonialism, 39, 55–6
sexual instinct, 70–1, 75
sexual liberation, 36, 78
Sexual Offences Act 1967, 138, 183
Shaw, G.B., 51, 172, 174, 175, 178, 179–80
Shilts, Randy, 120, 132
Simon, William, 24, 25, 26, 27, 40
Sins of the Cities of the Plain, 61
Smith–Rosenberg, Carroll, 18, 93
social constructionism, 4, 6, 86
social purity, 21
sodomy (see buggery)
Sontag, Susan, 114
Soviet Union, 177, 179, 180–1, 185
Spencer, Herbert, 177
Stead, W.T., 51
Stone, Lawrence, 18
subcultures, homosexual, 18, 44, 49, 54–7
symbolic interactionism, 25, 28–9
Symonds, John Addington, 20, 55, 56
syphilis, 114

Tardieu, 16, 20

Tarnowsky, Benjamin, 71
Taylor, Dr Alfred Swaine, 50
Taylor, Gordon Rattray, 24
Terrence Higgins Trust, 112, 119
Thatcher, Margaret, 124, 126, 143, 144, 184, 185, 186, 187, 188
Thompson, E.P., 159
Tissot, Samuel, 70
transvestism, transvestites, 27, 69, 73
Trumbach, Randolph, 14, 15, 93

Ulrichs, Karl Heinrich, 16, 70, 96
United States of America, 12, 78, 92, 104, 118, 127, 143, 191, 194

Vaz, Keith, 193

Wales, 19
Webb, Sidney and Beatrice, 171, 172, 175, 176, 177–82 *passim*
Weldon, Fay, 194
Welfare State, 38, 127–8
Wells, H.G., 178, 179–80
West, D.J., 46
Westermarck, Edward, 11
Westphal, Carl, 16, 70
White, Edmund, 78
Wilde, Oscar, 19, 39, 40, 48, 55, 57, 61, 63, 86, 87, 99, 174
Williams, Bernard, 99
Williams, Raymond, 170
Willmott, Peter, 152, 153, 154
Wilshire, David, 138
Wolfenden Report, 21, 41, 182
Woolf, Virginia, 1
working class, 39, 55–6